TATTOOS & TEQUILA

TATTOOS & TEQUILA

To Hell and Back with One of Rock's Most Notorious Frontmen

GRAND CENTRAL PUBLISHING

NEW YORK BOSTON

Grand Central Publishing
Hachette Book Group
237 Park Avenue
New York, NY 10017

www.HachetteBookGroup.com

Printed in the United States of America

First Edition: September 2010
10 9 8 7 6 5 4 3 2 1

Grand Central Publishing is a division of Hachette Book Group, Inc.
The Grand Central Publishing name and logo is a trademark of Hachette Book Group, Inc.

Library of Congress Cataloging-in-Publication Data
Neil, Vince.
Tattoos & tequila : to hell and back with one of rock's most notorious frontmen / by Vince Neil with Mike Sager.—1st ed.
p. cm.
ISBN 978-0-446-54804-5
1. Neil, Vince. 2. Rock musicians—United States—Biography.
3. Mötley Crüe (Musical group). I. Sager, Mike. II. Title.
ML420.N3824A3 2010
782.42166092—dc22
[B] 2010015237

To my friends, my family, and especially, to my fans.

WRITER'S NOTE

Much of the information gathered for this book comes from unreliable sources who may have been abusing substances or undergoing other duress at the time of many of the events discussed. Like they say about the eighties: If you remember them clearly, you weren't really there.

EGG BURRITOS

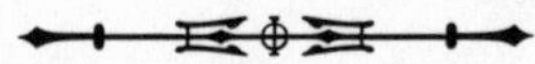

Mike Sager: Is that a true story?

Vince Neil: Absolutely. It was when we'd just had sex with girls in the studio and we didn't want to go home smelling like them. There was a restaurant, called Naugles, it was open twenty-four hours. And we would order egg burritos and wipe our dicks with them. Then if you went home smelling like an egg burrito, you just told your girlfriend, "Oh, I dropped my egg burrito in my lap."

Mike: So did you actually open the burrito and insert? Or did you just, like, use it as a washcloth?

Vince: Used it kind of like a washcloth.

Mike: All right, good. Thanks. I just had to ask. You know, Marlon Brando once fucked a duck in Paris. I wrote about him, too.

CONTENTS

Introduction

THE OPENING ACT

A black-on-black Lamborghini Gallardo Spyder purrs into the parking lot of Feelgoods Rock Bar & Grill, well off the Strip in Las Vegas. The traffic on Sahara Avenue whooshes past with the usual lunchtime urgency; five miles to the southeast, the towers of Sin City can be seen, rising dreamlike from the sprawl. If what they say is true, what happens in Vegas stays in Vegas, then this is most likely where it stays—a nondescript series of suburbs in the western sector of the city where strip malls, housing developments, and schools share a casual proximity with massage parlors, smoke shops, and gambling clubs. Completing the picture is a Crayola blue sky; snow dusts the mountain peaks, which stand aloof and craggy in the distance, glowing in the bright, thin light of the desert winter.

It is December and chilly. Christmas looms. Here and there people have taken the trouble to wrap their palm trees with burlap.

We are already one day behind schedule. The previous day, which was supposed to be our first, was marred by three broken appointments. It was a true rock 'n' roll beginning—an absent star, a frantic dance of enablers, the expense meter spinning, the already-foreshortened deadline ticking away.... The subtext: *We're all trying to make this amazing thing happen. We've talked it to death. All we need is our star.*

Now somebody has pushed the reset button.

It is Tuesday.

Take two.

The star is fifteen minutes *early* for our noon appointment.

"He's notoriously early," I'd been advised the previous day by one of his people at 10th Street Entertainment. (Even as he was pushing back the time of our first meeting.) "You oughtta be early, too. He hates it when people are late."

He's notoriously early...

...when he's decided he's coming.

I guess that's how the sentence should read.

Writing down a man's life will take many such edits, I learn over the coming months. (Not that I expected differently.) We all have our roles. It is best to know which is yours.

The sleek Italian two-seater—512 horsepower; vanity license plate: TATUUD; with yellow stitching on the black leather seats to match the yellow brake calipers, and the single cup holder requested by his fourth wife ("You'd think for a quarter million bucks you could get *one* cup holder," is how she'd put it)—comes to a stop at a rakish angle in a pin-striped lane marked: "Motorcycles Only."

After an interval, the driver's door opens. Out thrusts one battered calfskin UGG boot, followed by a fashionably ripped denim leg. A well-muscled thigh strains the fabric where the tearing is most prominent—in his day, nobody could fill a pair of spandex leopard-skin tights the way he could. A left hand reaches up for purchase—the car is quite low to the ground. Occupying the wrist is a 40-karat diamond and platinum Dunamis watch with a skull design floating inside the overlarge see-through face. A $300,000 bauble, one of five in the world, he will later say. It is a difficult factoid to verify.

With some effort he limbos into an upright position and I see him in person for the first time, unmistakable after thirty years in the limelight:

Vince Neil Wharton—he of the towering platinum Aqua Net hairdo and ultrasonic banshee voice, the ultimate face boy of 1980s glam cock rock, frontman for Mötley Crüe.

Today Vince Neil is forty-eight, a man in his third act; a little thicker than imagined, and smaller, too—five foot nine, 170. He has a stubbly goatee, sparse and gray in spots, and an easy smile, which he displays most often when people are paying attention to him. There is a diamond embedded in his right upper incisor, part of a set of pearly caps, uppers and lowers; at night in a club it sparkles.

Remembered for his epic drug-and-alcohol-fueled debauchery—and for the high heels, full makeup, and glittered tube tops that made him an androgynous sex symbol during the early years of the gender-bending eighties—Vince Neil is now a comfortable, middle-aged man. He spends part of his year in Las Vegas, part in Northern California, from where his wife hails. He has "money but not *fuck you* money," he likes to say. He is quick to point out that group acts make a lot less than solo. (And that 30 percent goes to agent, lawyer, manager, and accountant off the top.) Besides being a rock 'n' roll headliner, Vince is a businessman, with thriving interests on several fronts. There is Tres Rios Tequila, a line of premium tequilas made at his operation in Guadalajara, Mexico. Vince Neil Aviation charters rocked-out jets—think leopard-skin and purple velvet appointments. Vince Neil Ink, a high-end tattoo parlor and apparel shop, has two locations on the Strip in Las Vegas. His tastes run to exotic cars and watches; he has a garage full of old posters and costumes, some of which he has sold to the Hard Rock restaurant chain...and a shit-load of guitars that companies keep sending him, even though he only plays guitar on two songs in his entire repertoire, including both Mötley Crüe and Vince Neil solo. He still collects the lion's share of his income from his one-quarter share in Mötley Crüe, which has sold 80 million albums over three decades. (Mötley continues to sell, even though they haven't written any new songs since 2008's *Saints of Los Angeles*, a sort of aural autobiography of the band members' history, their best—and only original—work in years.)

Instead of spandex he sports a T-shirt from Vince Neil Ink; the neck band is ripped; in our time together I will see him wearing it four times in two different cities, so I assume that's the way it's supposed to look. A fur-lined hooded sweatshirt rides up over a slight paunch as he stretches to work out the kinks. His once–teased and towering hair is regularly seen to at a favorite salon on the Strip. Colored a boy-next-door shade of dirty blond, highlighted with honey streaks, straightened and flatironed with the latest technologies into a silken consistency, it is truly a rock star–worthy head of hair. The hint of time is reflected only in his slightly receded hairline. Gold-framed Chanel goggles hide his hazel eyes.

When I think of Vince, I see a trio of pictures in my head. One is this Vince, the Vince of today, the Vince I've been describing as he exits his Lambo. The second is of Vince on the (reissued) cover of Mötley's second album, *Shout at the Devil.* Who could ever forget those eyes—his expression at once so vulnerable and so totally absent. Equally memorable is the third: his leather-encased crotch on the cover of their inaugural album, *Too Fast for Love,* his left thumb applying pressure to the clearly visible outline of his penis.

As you read this book, I think it would be helpful if you keep the second of these images in mind. (Though I'm sure the third won't be far from your thoughts, either; he has spent much of his aggregated waking time on this planet in pursuit of sexual favors.) The studio photo was taken at the height of Mötley's early success, sometime in 1983, during the group's *Mad Max/Escape from New York* period of post-apocalyptic-influenced style. With his high cheekbones and full lips—the legacy of his parents' mixed Mexican and American Indian ancestry—Vince represented the male archetype of the New West's golden generation. Part James Dean, part Tony Hawk, part Jeff Spicoli, Vince was the male twin of the sun-kissed California girl.

Try to imagine what it was like to be that guy—a rock star, rich, achingly beautiful by any standard, flying around the world in a private jet during an era, before AIDS, when cocaine, quaaludes, Jack Daniel's, and wild consensual sex were the equivalent of karaoke—what you did on a night out. Even in flyover land people were partying like rock stars. Vince had a rep to upkeep and took full advantage. He had the gall of the beautiful; he never had to seek, he only had to choose. He did whatever the fuck he wanted without a thought. He plied the Strip with a vengeance, fucking girls in the bushes, getting into fistfights with undercover cops and a drunk yuppie in a Porsche. As Vince's career expanded, so did his range. He drove race cars and racing boats. He participated in orgies on yachts in the Caribbean. He traveled the world. He threw his empty bottle of Jack Daniel's out the nearest window. Sometimes, the window wasn't open. He didn't give a fuck. Nothing could be out of order. Nothing could be too outrageous. Nothing could violate the standards because there were no standards. He owed his existence, his place in the spotlight, to humankind's need for heroes and entertainment. He was the show. Excessive was what was expected of him, aided and abetted by fawning minions. Groupies lined up outside his dressing room, his hotel room, his tour bus, in the back of the jet. Groupies waited behind the drum riser, eager to give him a blow job during a drum solo—"which gives you an idea what I *really* thought of that egotist," he will later say of Mötley Crüe drummer Tommy Lee. The 1987 Aerosmith classic, "Dude (Looks like a Lady)," was written after Steven Tyler and Joe Perry spotted Vince in a bar and mistook him for a hot chick. Was it any wonder that at seventeen Vince became the first kid in high school to owe child support?

One-tenth sexiest man alive. Nine-tenths accident-waiting-to-happen.

Imagine if that dude was *you*.

In a decade defined by cocaine, voodoo Reaganomics, the discovery of the HIV virus, and rising neo-fundamentalism, the members of Mötley Crüe—Mick Mars on guitar, Tommy Lee on drums, Nikki Sixx on bass, and Vince Neil on vocals—set new standards for decadence, self-destruction, and excess as they acted out their every impulse, determined to live the rock 'n' roll lifestyle to the hilt. Their sound was an amalgam—rooted in hard rock and the bombast of KISS, glam's transgender fashion, pop's bubblegum, LA punk's effrontery...all of it slathered together with mascara and blood. Mötley's songs will never be as memorable as the band's attitude and approach. Fast, loud, and showy—but also melodic and candy coated—their music was a bridge on the rock 'n' roll time line between the theatrical dress-up bands of the eighties and the self-conscious, shotgun-swallowing grunge movement of the nineties.

Raised (or having come of age) in idyllic Southern California—the land of surfers, skaters, garage bands, and worshipers of self—the members of Mötley Crüe had no political or social agenda beyond their next high, their next fistfight, their next prank, their next piece of ass. What separated Mötley Crüe, what makes them memorable, was their inarticulated philosophy—an aggressively perverse dedication to all things darker and meaner and nastier than the rest; an American iteration of the savage, balls-out traditions of English punk, a sort of nihlism-lite. Yes, they played music. But more than that. They *were* the music. In Freudian terms, they were pure id. They did what they felt like doing, what looked and sounded cool to them, with no care for the consequences—rebels without a clue. Like Vince will later tell me: "The answer to 'Why?' was always, 'Why not?'"

Over the years, Mötley Crüe's relatively small quiver of hit songs would come to embody youthful urgency and disregard for the rules; life without fear of consequences, lived as far out on the edge as possible. As the eighties became the nineties and beyond, the fortunes of the band and its members rose and fell and rose again. Today the work of Mötley Crüe is part of the vocabulary of rock 'n' roll, a huge draw around the world. As I write this introduction, Vince and the other members of the band are making their way to rehearsals in Los Angeles, prepping for a tour of Canada. Through all of their hijinks and arguments, all of their ups and downs, they are still playing together and are relevant—though it seems, in real time, that a great bit of will is necessary to get them onto the same stage. In all the interviews for this book, more than forty hours overall, Vince was hard-pressed to find anything good to say about *any* of his fellow band members. Only Nikki Sixx could be persuaded to be interviewed. He spoke of Vince only in the most glowing terms. There are obviously many tortured emotions between them. To date, all four members are millionaires many times over, though some have been more successful than others at holding on to their earnings. All have attempted solo careers in one form or another; they are all clearly elevated by their association with the band. Finally, they all seem to grudgingly understand: Mötley Crüe is something greater than the sum of its parts. After three decades, they are like a wildly dysfunctional family, all love and hate, with not a hint of the love showing on the surface.

After the Mötley tour Vince will head south for a solo tour of Mexico, Latin America, and South America in support of the new album and book (this one), both by the same name, *Tattoos & Tequila.* Acts as varied as Papa Roach, Linkin Park, Marilyn Manson, Nine Inch Nails, Moby, Slipknot, and Belladonna have all cited Vince and Mötley Crüe as an influence in recent years, most notably for *Too Fast for Love* and *Shout at the Devil,* the band's first two hits. Mötley Crüe's early look in music videos has also been borrowed by a variety of artists, from Beck and the Red Hot Chili Peppers to New Order, Aerosmith, and the Backstreet Boys. Even today, in the second decade of the twenty-first century, Mötley Crüe is still a musical right of passage and an instant time machine. Their songs are the easier ones to play on Guitar Hero and Rock Band. Thanks to the timeless magic of digital music, keen marketing, and several successful greatest hits efforts, new Mötley fans are ever entering the fold. A Mötley Crüe or Vince Neil Band concert is today an intergenerational affair, with aging mullet heads sharing the venue with thirtysomething squares, tattooed young rocker wannabes, and slutty-looking suicide grrls of all ages, who now as then observe the time-honored ritual of baring their breasts to the band.

A few milestones for perspective: Mötley has been featured on a number of VH1 countdown shows: "Dr. Feelgood" was ranked the #7 Greatest Air Guitar Song, "Live Wire" was ranked the #17 Greatest Metal Song of All Time, and "Home Sweet Home" was ranked the #12 Greatest Power Ballad of All Time. Mötley Crüe was featured several times on VH1's *100 Most Metal Moments* and was one of the many bands featured on VH1's popular *Behind the Music* series. The band was ranked #19 on VH1's list of the most popular hard rock bands of all time. Mötley Crüe was also ranked tenth on MTV's list of "Top 10 Heavy Metal Bands of All Time." In 2008, iTunes picked "Saints of Los Angeles" as the number one song in the Rock category of their "Best of 2008"; the song was also nominated for a Grammy Award in the Best Hard Rock Performance category.

All of which has made for a pretty interesting life. Vince has been married four times, fathered three children, fucked thousands of groupies—sometimes ten a day according to numbers floating around; he won't venture a count. He has had liaisons with dozens of brand-name women, including the porn stars Savannah and Gina Fine (simultaneously) and the TV actresses Tori Spelling and Shannen Doherty (on separate occasions). He dated supermodel Christy Turlington; he dated Pam Anderson *before* Tommy Lee, when she was the Tool Time Girl on *Home Improvement;* his third wife was the knockout soap star and primetime TV actress Heidi Mark, who exemplifies most of the women in this book, Vince's "type": long blond hair, pretty face, blue eyes, large augmented boobs, visible abs, tiny ass, long legs. He starred in one sex tape (a three-way with Vivid Video girls Janine Lindemulder and Brandy Sanders), several pornos (directed by adult film legend Ron "the Hedgehog" Jeremy), dated handfuls of *Playboy* Playmates and *Penthouse* Pets, ingested every drug and combination of drugs he could possibly find, drank an ocean of booze—or so I remind him. There is a lot he doesn't remember. At least that's what he says. Says one ex-wife: "He's got a memory as clear as diamonds when he wants to. Sometimes it's just easier to say you forgot. He has a lot of regrets."

In our sessions together, Vince was always courteous; he reminded me of a schoolkid with a tutor—he didn't really want to do it, but someone had convinced him he should. On several occasions during our window, Sunday football took precedence over interview time. Occupying his usual reserved table at the sports book at the Red Rock Casino, Resort & Spa was clearly a higher priority than this autobiography. Often, as I tried to pin him down—three middle schools or two? What year did you marry Sharise?—he would become annoyed with me. I wondered if the emotion he was really feeling was embarrassment or some kind of shame. What person doesn't remember why he moved out of his parents' house for good at seventeen? A lot of clarity is lost in a haze of years and booze. Obviously there are painful truths that haunt him to this day... things we will learn a little bit about as we slog through his history and his murky depths.

Trying to chronicle such a life is difficult: Even Vince can't keep straight how many stints in rehab he's done or how many times he's been arrested. For this reason we have enlisted the voices of others. We hear from Vince's current wife, Lia, and all three of his ex-wives: Beth Neil, Sharise Neil, and Heidi Mark. We hear from his children, Neil Wharton and Elle Neil; from his parents, Clois Odell and Shirley Wharton; from his sister, Valerie Saucer; from the members of his first band, formed in high school, Rockandi. Other interviews done in preparation of this book include: Poison's Bret Michaels, rapper MC Hammer, porn star Ron Jeremy, LA Lakers owner Jerry Buss, Night Ranger Jack Blades. Making a special guest appearance is Nikki Sixx, along with a score of behind-the-scenes managers and other close confidants who've been there throughout Vince's career.

Onstage, Vince was and is undeniably the center of the Mötley Crüe circus—no longer clad in bright spandex or built like a Greek god, he still rips his signature piercing-yet-clean wail on lead vocals. Nikki Sixx , the main writer and musical force behind the group, who's never gone out of his way to compliment Vince about anything, once called him "the quarterback of Mötley Crüe." Though Vince isn't well known as a songwriter, he co-wrote some of Motley's biggest hits, including "Home Sweet Home," "Wild Side," and "Same Ol' Situation." That he has always been a multifaceted entertainer is sometimes lost in his seemingly effortless work onstage; what looks like wild abandon is really the product of decades of effort and experience. He has always been the consumate showman.

Offstage, for all their drama—Mick with his crippling ankylosing spondylitis and female troubles; Nikki with his well-publicized addictions; Tommy with his trials with fame, actresses, hairstyles, and anger management issues—none of the other Crüe members would live a life characterized by the monumental highs and lows experienced by their frontman. In 1984, Vince would be found guilty of vehicular manslaughter. Left dead on the street that rainy night, after a three-day drug party, was his good friend Nicholas "Razzle" Dingley from the Hanoi Rocks. The driver and a passenger of another car were also permanently maimed in the drunk-driving incident; Vince would pay $2.5 million in restitution and serve time in jail. Some years later, having been fired/or having quit Mötley Crüe, he would sit helplessly by the hospital bedside of his four-year-old daughter as she fought and lost a wrenching battle against cancer. The time period immediately afterwards was lost in a bottle; today there is a charity, the Skylar Neil Foundation.

Vince is still haunted by many demons, some of which I don't think he can even explain himself. He is, in his own words, "an entertainer." He needs others to write, score, arrange, and organize. "I get out there and sell the songs," he will later tell me. Like many a diva before him, he has often felt himself mute offstage, in the cold, unscripted, and unforgiving light of real life. Alone, without an audience, without anyone to keep him company, he becomes lost and uncertain. This much we know. It is the explanation for many things.

As he arrives in his Lambo, I spy on him through a door that's been left open to air out the stink of beer and pheromones from the night before. Feelgoods is a prototype for a chain. They hope to have forty places like it someday, scattered all around the country. Vince owns 30 percent. They send him a check. He can sign for food. The place is decorated with purple velvet and leather and faux leopard skin. A huge bank of Marshall amps dwarfs the moderately sized stage, where live acts hold forth several nights a week. Glass display cases hold authentic heirloom guitars, gold albums, his old auto-racing fire suit; there is a fully chromed and tricked-out chopper on the way to the bathrooms. TV screens play a greatest-hits assortment of rock videos, giving the place the feeling of a sports bar, only instead of sports, the theme is rock—a museum masquerading as a dive bar. An older couple—he with a gray ponytail, her hair dyed jet-black, both wearing leathers—dine in a booth to one side. The center of the room is dominated by a large round table full of men in identical work shirts, their names authentically in bubbles over breast pockets, some of them no doubt enjoying the $6.95 lunch special the place has recently added to the menu in order to combat the economic downturn.

Of course I was early for the meeting. (I was early the first day, too.) My mission: to climb inside a rock star's mind and bring out what I can—the memories, the sensations, the collected experiences; the sex and drugs, the exhilaration and the heartache. A chronicle of a lifetime spent in the bunghole of unbridled self-indulgence. It might be hot and tight in there, but the smell is not so good sometimes.

And so it is that I gather up my clipboard and my digital recorder (and my cute little flip cam, which will prove to be a piece of shit) and move to meet him at the hostess stand. Up close he is still a handsome man, his face maintained by a number of cosmetic procedures, some of which were famously (and excruciatingly) documented on the 2005 VH1 series *Remaking Vince Neil*. He is enveloped in a pleasant cloud of Lagerfield cologne, a discontinued scent he has stockpiled from sources around the country. He shakes my hand warmly and leads me inside.

Beyond a velvet rope there is a small VIP area. Vince proudly points out the four tables he had designed specially for the club. Taken together, the pieces form the shape of a giant guitar. Around the rounded bottom part is a leather banquette. We take a seat at the next four-top, a rectangle like the rest, this one representing the lowest part of the neck, where the highest-register notes are fretted.

"You ready?" I ask.

"Ask whatever you want," he says. His face is blank. His voice is thin and a little bit hoarse. There is a tonal uptick at the end of his sentence; his loopy Cali dialect makes many of his statements sound like questions.

Mike Sager

La Jolla, CA
3/1/2010

TATTOOS & TEQUILA

Chapter I

TATTOOS & TEQUILA

Hey—sorry about yesterday, dude.

I had my Lamborghini brought down from my house in Danville, in Northern California, to my house here in Las Vegas. I had it swapped out for my Ferrari—he took it back to Danville. It's good to keep the mileage balanced on cars like that. They're collector's items—an investment and whatnot. And the Lambo is much more fun in Vegas; they got long, flat roads out here where you can turn it out—not that I would ever break the speed limit or anything.

The driver was supposed to be here at noon, and then I guess there was all this rain and shit—he says there were fourteen different accidents driving from there to here; he didn't even get here till almost 6:00 P.M. And of course my assistant, who lives here in Vegas and is supposed to have my back on stuff like this, she was out Christmas shopping with my wife and my mother-in-law, who is here spending time with us because my father-in-law died not that long ago. So what can you do? You know how that goes, right? The glamorous life of a rock star. You get to have an assistant, but the chances are she's busy helping your wife when you need *assistance* doing something and you end up stuck doing what needs to be done, like fuckin' waiting at home for this guy to show up with my car so I can let him in the garage. And I was waiting like a long time. I couldn't leave. I actually ended up screaming at her, too. I was like, "Kelly? Why am I sitting here waiting for this guy to come when I'm supposed to be starting the interviews for my book!" And then she tells me, I couldn't believe it... it turns out she knew the *whole time* that the driver was going to be late. She knew it but didn't bother to tell me. *Nobody told me!* She was like, "I told you the guy was going to be late." And I was like, "You did not!"

Nobody tells me anything. I swear to you. When I have my tombstone they can put that on the B side. "Nobody Told Him Anything." I'm not sure yet what I want on the front. That line hasn't been written yet. You know when the new Mötley Crüe album came out, the new *Greatest Hits*? I had no fuckin' idea that was coming out. It was funny. I was doing this interview with some reporter and they go, "So tell us about the new Mötley's *Greatest Hits* album." And I go, "What are you talking about?" Nobody told me I had an album coming out. It happens that way all the time. 'Cause we could have, like... I told my assistant, I said, "Kelly, I could've gotten together with the writer earlier than we'd first planned and then I could have been back in time to get the car," or to be here for the car, whatever, because there was nobody to punch in the code on the garage door so he could swap out the cars.

The funny thing is, I really do take pride in being early. I am usually always early. I've always been early to everything I've ever done. Seriously. That's why I thought it was pretty hilarious when Mötley said they fired me that first time 'cause I was chronically late for rehearsals. Dude, I am never late for *shit*. It's like I have

OCD or something, obsessive-compulsive disorder. I'm always early. Like even going to an airport, I'll be sitting there for over an hour because I don't want to be late. When people are late I can't stand waiting for them. I fuckin' hate that. I've left people behind on my solo gigs. Band members. Left 'em back at the fuckin' hotel. Like one guy was constantly late and I just said, "Fuck it," and I left. And we just pulled out and drove to the next city. The bus pulled away from the curb without him. People should be on time—if they say they're going to be there on time, you know, they should be on time. If they can't, they should call and tell you they'll be late. But don't show up an hour late, two hours late. Or even fifteen minutes late. You know that drives me up the fuckin' wall.

So where do we start? I remember when we did *The Dirt*—the best-selling book about Mötley Crüe written by Neil Strauss—I got interviewed at the Grand Havana Room in Beverly Hills. A lot of people say I didn't get to say much in that book. It's probably true. I didn't read it. When I was young I was diagnosed with dyslexia. I never really enjoyed reading too much. It's difficult for me. I see printed stuff backwards and out of whack. It's just a struggle. I'm sure that killed my education before it even got started. If I could read better maybe I'd have been a doctor or a lawyer. You wouldn't even be reading this book. If you see me after you've read this, lemme know what you think. I probably won't read it myself.

I was pretty much done with school and out in the world by age fifteen, sixteen, seventeen—already a father, out of my parents' house for good, living in Tommy Lee's smelly van, sweeping up this rehearsal studio in exchange for time, working as an electrician, trying to make it in Rockandi, my first band. I guess another reason there might not be that much from me in *The Dirt* is because, you know, I'm not that big a talker. Nikki and Tommy—those guys can fuckin' talk. They can eat up all the oxygen in a room in no time flat. I don't tend to run my mouth. I don't like to talk about stuff—how I feel and shit. It's bullshit.

All those years in rehab and counseling—the talking cure? I can't say I really got that much out of it. All that cure and I should be cured by now, don't you think? All this talking. I'd rather just go out and live, you know? Some people have lots to say. Other people just shut up and do what they gotta do. I guess I'm the second. So forgive me if it's a bit hard for me to slice open a vein and let my blood run red all over this page for you. Somebody thinks it's a good idea for me to tell my story, so I'm gonna tell it. But remember this: I'm a singer. I let my emotions out through demonstration. I'm *demonstrative*, isn't that the word? I'll fight you or I'll fuck you, but chances are I'll be hard-pressed to sit there and *talk* to you. I'm one of those people who are more comfortable in front of an arena full of screaming fans than I am at a small dinner party. Call it socially inept. Call it quiet and shy. I am kind of shy. Women can sense that. They always want to take care of me. They like that about me. I let them do all the talking. Women love to be heard. I do listen. And I know how to look like I'm listening to a woman even when I'm not. Maybe that's the secret—listening. It probably doesn't hurt when they like the way you look and carry yourself. I've never really been the kind of guy who had to work it real hard. I never had any lines. I never needed any. From an early age, they've just come to me, a flood tide of women, all shapes and colors and nationalities, but most of them blondes, long-haired blondes with big tits and long legs and little round butts and…maybe we'll get into all that later.

Thinking about the *Dirt* interviews makes me nostalgic for the Havana Room. Man, we had some epic nights there. It's this high-end, members-only cigar club. Lots of expensive wines and scotches, and good cigars, and big swinging Hollywood dicks. You could even have your own, like, humidor/safe-deposit box where you kept a stash of Cubans or whatever. I always got a kick out of being there, living the high life, suckin' on a fat Cuban cigar, doing shit that's not readily available to the common man—and me, this mixed-breed mechanic's son from Nowhereville, CA. I remember one night in January 2000 I bumped into the comedian Tom Arnold at an LA Kings hockey game. You know the dude. He used to be married to Roseanne. Another crazy motherfucker—some time when you've got nothing else to do, take the time to Google their photo shoot in *Vanity Fair* back in the day, when the couple was hot and heavy, literally. Wow. I didn't know they allowed that kinda shit in family magazines. You know I've lived in the LA area all my life. I know people all over. Tom is the kind of people I know in Hollywood. It's small; it's basically my hometown. You get to be friends with the *fun* people. Like attract like, I guess. And what can I say? I love a good party. I love fun people. I love crazy motherfuckers like Arnold who have no public filter. Something about them makes it like they just don't give a shit. And they know other crazy fun people, too. After the game, we went to the Havana Room and we met up with the actor Mel Gibson. Mel is a cool guy, no matter what anybody says. Some people drink and a switch goes off. I know it does for me. They don't know what the fuck they're doing. Believe me, they're telling the truth. I got to know Mel a little bit during my years living in Malibu—I think we drank together a few times at Moonshadows, which was like my hangout for years, I used to drink there with all kinds of people—Kelsey Grammer, David Duchovny. All the Malibu partiers went there, all the heavy drinkers. It was there, in Moonshadows, that I rode out the dark and stormy seas of my daughter's death. I would go directly from Skylar's bedside at the hospital, out Sunset Boulevard, hang a right on the PCH to Moonshadows. There I would meet my good friend oblivion.

At this time I was with the actress and *Playboy* centerfold Heidi Mark—an amazing woman, an amazing piece of ass. I met her in her prime, twenty-four years old. When she was twenty she'd dated Prince a few times; she was with O.J. for a while after his whole deal with the murder of his wife. This was after that. We were together for a number of years before we got married. This was right before we got married, I think. My third time down the aisle. After Tom left the Havana Room, Heidi, Mel, and I kept going. Since we were regulars, the staff went home at like 3:00 A.M., leaving us to finish our cigars. We ended up at our house in Malibu. We were up all night drinking and playing pool and taking goofy Polaroids—somewhere there is a picture of Heidi riding on Mel's shoulders around our living room. It was just a howling good time, pretty much PG rated. Finally, around dawn, I passed out. Heidi put Mel in a cab.

The next day on the news we see a story about how the Havana Room had burned down overnight...after two gentlemen threw their lit cigar butts in a trash can that caught a light, setting the club ablaze.

For some reason, they never came after us for that. I've been sued so many times by so many people...assholes trying to make a buck just by fucking with me. I don't know why, but I am grateful. To somebody I owe a debt of thanks. Probably there's a lot of people I could say that about. I owe a lot of debts of thanks, I am sure. There's so much I don't remember....

So how do you like the place? Feelgoods Rock Bar & Grill. There's another one sort of like it in West Palm Beach, Florida. It's called Dr. Feelgoods. That was the first one. That's more of a club. It's got five bars; it's huge. But it only serves, like, finger food. This place has the full-on kitchen. Check out the menu. Order whatever you want. The food is great. They have these great homemade tortilla chips, I already ordered some. They serve 'em hot. Amazing. I tasted most of the stuff before we opened.

This is like a flagship store. We spent a lot of money on getting it together, on decorating, on organizing the concept. There are going to be like twenty-five or forty of these around the country before we're through. A lot of work has gone into all this stuff. I mean the kitchen was open for three weeks *before* we even opened the place. While the workmen were still working, everybody would have lunch here. They call it a "trial feed" in the business. It gave the chefs a chance to really work on their dishes and tweak the menu and stuff. See here on the menu? This thing above the tuna melt—Pete's Plate. Pete was my father-in-law, Lia's father, who passed away. That was his favorite meal—two hot dogs with a sixteen-ounce Budweiser. So we called it a Pete's Plate. There's also a Vince Platter. It's just a really good burger with a secret sauce—Thousand Island dressing. They make it real good; it's pretty amazing.

I think we'll do great here. I know you talked about doing these interviews at my house. How it's intimate there and all that. But believe me it's not. My house, you know, I've got my mother-in-law there. That's the thing. My dogs, my mother-in-law, my wife. It's just... it's too much. And if we did a hotel room—didn't somebody say a hotel room? Somebody at 10th Street had said something about getting a suite at the Rio, where there's a Vince Neil Ink. But if we get into one of those environments where I'm just, you know, like, walled up in some room... I would just feel like I wanted to get the fuck out of there, you know? You start walling me up, keeping me places... I don't know. I don't react well. I'd rather be here... you know what I mean? If this doesn't work we could always go to the studio, which has rooms above it. I have to be there every afternoon anyway. We have to get cracking on that record, too. Two weeks is all we've got. You're coming with me after this to the studio, right? This is gonna be a busy couple of weeks. You know we're also filming the video next Wednesday and Thursday, right? That'll be cool. We'll just have to find the time to talk in between, I guess.

I love this place. Like I said, a lot of thought and care went into it. It's pure rock 'n' roll. It's red lights and leopard skin, purple velvet, iron spiderwebs, button-tuck black leather banquettes. Hot little rock chicks waiting tables—suicide grrls in short skirts with lots of eyeliner. And the stage is great. Intimate. Perfect sound. But we can pack them in, too. We have national acts coming in now, which is pretty cool. One night a week my son DJs. His name is Neil Wharton; everybody calls him Neil Neil. My parents raised him for a lot of his life. We're really just getting to know each other. He sings in a Mötley Crüe tribute band. He only recently moved to Vegas to live. I got him a job working with the clothing line and stuff that we sell.

With Feelgoods, it's weird, 'cause like most of the bands that are playing in here are bands that we came up with. We got L.A. Guns, Ratt. The BulletBoys just played here. Slaughter will be here New Year's Eve—that's my guys who also play in the Vince Neil Band: Jeff Blando, Dana Strum, Zoltan Chaney. You'll meet them today at the studio. My partner's got his custom shop down there, too, Count's Kustoms. He's got all these restored cars in one warehouse. It's like a fuckin' museum. I got my '32 Ford in there, too—the ultimate hot rod, the engine's all chromed out, with flames painted on the sides. Speaking of which, tonight is bike and hot rod night at Feelgoods. The whole parking lot will be full of motorcycles. It gets packed in here; it'll be jammed. And Wednesdays, Thursdays, Fridays, and Saturdays we're usually kicking out the last people at six in the morning. This is Vegas, right? The people here know how to party.

And all I have to do is collect a check. I can sign for anything I want.

Sweet, right?

The other thing I like about this place is all the memorabilia. As you walk in there's a glass case with my flame-proof racing suit from my Formula One racing days, pictures of me and my car. There's my outfit from Crüe Fest 1, a whole bunch of platinum records, gold records, stuff like that. At this stage in life, my wife jokes that I need a warehouse. And I'm like, I do have a warehouse. It's called my garage. I have tons of old clothes and memorabilia and stuff I've worn onstage. I have tons of guitars these people keep sending me. What are you going to do? Throw it all away? Not that I'm sentimental about stuff. Absolutely, absolutely not. It's just, I don't know. I don't throw it away. Sometimes the Hard Rock buys your stuff from you and you actually make some money off the shit. Where do you think they get it? Like when you go into the Hard Rocks all around the country you see people's stuff there. That shit is all out of somebody's garage. They contact you and say, "Okay, we want such and such an outfit." You know, they want whatever you were wearing at a certain historic concert or occasion or something. Like there's a really cool outfit of mine at the new Hard Rock that just opened here on the Strip. I went to the grand opening and it's in a big display case, this big long jacket and stuff I wore when us and Aerosmith were touring together—talk about a trip down memory lane. If only my pants could talk. Maybe *they'd* remember some of the stuff I don't. (Remember the leather pants from the cover of *Shout*? They could tell a whole chapter by themselves.)

So we'll meet here every day at noon. At least for now. The only thing that might change is if it affects my singing, you know? Because we're recording this album and talking is the worst you can do for your voice. That's what I've learned over the years: It's not even singing that's so bad for your voice; it's talking. So we'll see how it works out. We might have to end up changing things around. Like I might have to rehearse and record during the day and you can come to the studio later at night. Or in between sessions, you know. The studio's not far. Just like five minutes from here, in these warehouses right behind the Strip. I could work for a few hours and then you could come there, talk for a couple hours. Whatever. We'll get it figured out.

Another reason I like the idea of meeting here at Feelgoods is because I feel like today, as we're writing this book, I'm a different person than the kid who started out thirty years ago. I'm not just a frontman, a singer, what have you, anymore. Today I'm a businessman as much as anything else. I like business. First of all, business is good because you don't have to do anything except make decisions. I mean, it's not heavy lifting. It's not digging ditches. It's not even memorizing lines. It's like: Your money works for *you* while you sit on your ass. It's a helluva lot easier than running back and forth across a stage for ninety minutes a night. You try it. I've been clocked doing twelve miles a show. Twelve miles back and forth across the stage! I remember back in Atlanta that time, I was what, in my mid-forties I guess, I think it was 2005. You think rock 'n' roll isn't a sport? Try this: I'm running across the stage, I'm high-stepping, moving at a fast clip from one side to the other, when all of a sudden, *POW!*—I feel this incredible pain in my calf. I thought I'd just been shot... or hit with a piece of metal. You take all kinds of shrapnel, bottles, bolts, what have you, when you're up there onstage; it ain't all panties (maybe a good subtitle for the book—*It Ain't All Panties*). The tour manager was up there on the stage afterwards hunting for whatever hit me. But nobody could find anything. And my calf. Jesus H. It hurt like shit. It swelled up instantly like a balloon.

But it turned out nothing hit me. I tore the sucker. Just ripped it. I got to the hospital and I got the MRI and they confirmed it. Like some weekend warrior at a fucking company softball game ripping his hammie trying to stretch a double into a triple. Only I ripped the calf muscle. Yikes. I was in unbelievable pain; they had me all doped up on Demerol. But like two days later I was back on tour and finished it out. There was another time where I had a broken ankle and I had to go on tour but didn't even have a walking cast. I ripped up an old tennis shoe and made my own walking cast. The show must go on, right?

War stories. War wounds. I know, I know.... Old rock stars fall hard. But I ain't singing the blues. Here I sit in the VIP section of my own restaurant, at this cool custom set of guitar-shaped tables. I'm not just behind the velvet rope. I own the motherfucker. I'm forty-eight years old. I'm five foot nine, 170. The spandex is over. I've had three plastic surgeries. But who do you think gets laid more, me or you? Time changes a man. I ain't twenty-one anymore. But I'm probably in better shape than I ever was. In the early eighties, we were skinny, but we weren't very healthy. It's a miracle we survived at all. We were not exactly treating our bodies very well in those days. A bottle of Jack Daniel's and a package of stolen Hebrew National hot dogs do not make for a particularly well-balanced diet. (Looking back, I don't think we even bothered to cook the damn things.) Later, when we all had money for the first time, we had a period in there when everybody in the band kind of blew up. Everybody was looking kind of green around the gills. Our problem? We could afford at that point to eat, drink, snort, swallow, or shoot up anything and everything we wanted. We were gluttons. We spoiled ourselves with any whim... and it showed. We are all very lucky we didn't kill ourselves. It might look like we were trying to do that, but speaking for myself, death was never my intent. I just wanted to feel good, you know? I was just looking for that kick, that high, that superintense orgasm. Die young and leave a beautiful corpse? Not my style. I think I'd rather take the plastic surgery route.

These days, the debauchery is done. After years of unchecked drinking, I'm pretty straight now. I don't do any drugs at all. Not anymore. And I stopped drinking three years ago. I've owned the tequila company for four years. And that's what made me stop drinking—I was drinking too much tequila. But yeah, I haven't, I haven't even tasted my own tequila in three years.

I don't miss getting high or drunk. I don't miss it at all. I have so much more productive time now. I get so much more accomplished. I get up at 7:00 A.M. and make the coffee. Who'd ever thought I would be a morning person? I couldn't have any of these businesses going if I was still that fucked up as I was for so long. Getting high never crosses my mind. Drugs are just... lame. Sobriety is cool. Well, I mean, I'll have maybe a glass of champagne once in a while. That's it, you know. But it's nothing like it used to be. I have too much stuff going on. The tattoo shops, Vince Neil Ink. My solo record. Mötley Crüe. Feelgoods. Tres Rios. Vince Neil Aviation—I'm just getting things going with that right now, but you know what? My planes are *tricked out*—I'm talking flames on the sides, leopard-skin interior, full bar. If you want to fly like a rock 'n' roller, you fly with me. It's gonna be great.

Probably all of us watch our diets—especially when our wives are watching. How much chicken can you eat? The answer is: a shitload. Not to disappoint you, but I have been known to order a Chinese chicken salad and a Diet Coke for lunch. Some of us have weight issues and stuff when we're off tour. But when you're on tour, onstage, that's different. When I'm on tour, I'm running for ninety minutes straight, sometimes longer. When I get offstage in between songs, it looks like I've been playing basketball. I am just dripping wet, drenched. And that's every night, five days a week. I always keep a towel and a blow-dryer on the side of the stage, along with my other stuff. During a drum or guitar solo, I'll towel off and blow-dry my hair. They call it Vince's World—my area backstage right with all my shit. My towel, my blow-dryer, lots of water, my throat lozenges... here's a trade secret—licorice lozenges. They really open up your throat. It used to be I kept a groupie or two waiting in Vince's World, too. Now, being married for the fourth time and all... let's just say that kind of stuff is in the past.

I read somewhere that an NBA player runs five miles in the course of a forty-eight-minute game. So there you have it. I do more than twice that five nights a week. Put me up against Kobe!

He and I do have something in common: We both have four Lakers championship rings. Just like his, my rings have my initials in them, too. I'm actually waiting for my fourth one right now. It's on order. I love the Lakers. I'm an LA boy, a huge fan. I grew up part of my life not far from the Forum, in Inglewood, where the Showtime Lakers used to play. The owner of the team, Jerry Buss, is a good friend of mine. When he gave me my first Laker ring he said he was doing it 'cause I "score more than any other Laker." How cool was that, you know? If you wonder what I have in common with a guy like Dr. Jerry Buss, a seventy-six-year-old business mogul with a Ph.D. in physical chemistry, I'll just say this: We both like beautiful women and drinking our alcohol out of the bottle. Strong friendships have been built from less.

As I'm telling you this, Dr. Buss is recovering from a stroke. I hope he's doing okay. One thing Jerry and I always talked about was business. He would give me advice (whether I wanted it or not!). No, I'm joking. When he spoke I listened—at least before I blacked out. Because a lot of things he told me really did sink in. I think over the last several years, as I've been sober, I've been able to capitalize on some of the things he taught me. One thing he used to say: With business, you always know there's going to be problems. You have supply and demand, employees, shipment problems, what have you. As a businessman, you have to learn to deal with it. You take care of problems, fix things, figure out how to make the business better. It's never been like that with Mötley Crüe. With Mötley Crüe, there's problems and nothing ever gets better. It's very frustrating, I have to tell you. I'm at a point in my life where I just don't want to fuck with it anymore. I've always said I'll stop singing when it's not fun anymore. Well, lemme tell you this. When it comes to Mötley Crüe, it's getting to be not fun anymore. It might even be a little past that.

With Mötley Crüe, it's always like the *Greatest Hits* album—I'm the last to know everything. I've always had the distinct impression that nobody in this band gives one shit about what I think. I mean, it's weird. I get no respect in that band, and it's fucked up. It's old.

I know, I know. I was the last one to join the band. I'm *just* the singer. I'm the entertainer. I'm the person in the front; I'm not the one bringing the songs. But I don't care about all that. I don't mind if somebody else writes the songs. It's my job to interpret the songs, to sell them, to sing the shit out of them. To perform them and make them memorable enough to sell 80 million copies. Who knows how many more times than that Mötley has been downloaded or sharewared or pirated or whatever? Do you think Mötley has suffered from my lack of songwriting? Or is it my singing that sells the songs? We all know what happened when they tried to replace me with John Corabi. They set up this whole fake meeting to try and get me to come back. I knew it was a fucking meeting. What do you think, I'm an idiot?

The thing is, I know my role in the band. I've never really needed to bring songs to Mötley Crüe because the songs they have are, you know, there have always been really good songs coming in. I'm not gonna say I haven't made some good suggestions. It was me who suggested covering "Smokin' in the Boy's Room." Everybody knows that song kind of saved our asses at the time. But I'm not a guy who says, you know, "If my name is not on the song, I'm not going to sing it." Fuck no. I'm not that guy. I'm the opposite of that guy. I mean, my name's been on plenty of the hits that we've had. That's fine. But that's not the biggest thing. The biggest thing is does the song sell? The biggest thing, right now, is eliminating all the bullshit in my life, number one, and number two, finding the business model for each part of my business life so that things work smoothly. 'Cause that's what I want. The same as I've always wanted: I just want things to be easy. Like *Saints of Los Angeles.* The producer knew my voice so well he would sing the scratch vocals first; I would know going in what was expected of me, what would work, you know? So when I went in to sing the record it was like totally smooth. I did a song a day and I could've done more, because each song took me no more than two hours to lay down. To tell you the truth, it took me longer to drive to the studio and back to my hotel than it did to actually do the work on the album. That was *Saints.* And *Saints* was up for a Grammy last year. So how can you argue with that?

In the old days it was sooooo…fuckin'…hard…to put out a record. Everything was a struggle. Everything was heads beating against the wall. I hated it. You know, we would spend eight months in a studio grinding it out, arguing. Sometimes it would get really nasty. It was like a rock 'n' roll cockfight, 24/7. Nikki would be in there telling me to sing a song one way and then another: "Try it this way. No, try it that way." He was always trying to lord his power over me, whatever. To this day I feel like he's pulling the strings over at the agency. And then you'd have the producer stepping in and he would tell me something *different* about how to sing the song… and I'd just go, you know, "What the fuck? What the fuckin' fuck. Fuck all you-all, I'm gonna sing it like I'm going to sing it; we didn't get this far with everybody second-guessing my voice. Remember, *you* were the ones who came to me and wanted me to sing for you."

I'm glad those days are gone. Today it's more about business. I got a contract. We handle it like business. We don't have to like each other. We just have to make music together. It's like a friendly divorce with shared custody. We do it for the sake of the music. Because what we made together, something from nothing, was valuable and groundbreaking. Today it lives, like a child all grown.

I think one of the problems is that Nikki resents me. He has always seen this band as his baby. And I think he resents the fact that, since I'm the singer, the songs are identified more with me than with him. I mean, I can go out on the road solo and sing the Mötley catalog. And I do. And people love it. One thing everybody knows: You can change the band around and still maintain your sound. If you get good musicians, they can play whatever they need to play; they can imitate anybody. But you can't imitate the singer—the front man is not interchangeable. He's the face and the voice of the band. They learned that before when we broke up. I think that weighs on Nikki and Tommy both. Because Nikki wants to be known as the musical genius he is. And make no mistake, he's fuckin' awesome. And Tommy has just always wanted to be famous. So there you have it: Everybody resents me—except Mick, who's this gnomish musical genius who's always had enough of his own shit to worry about. It's like, he was the older brother, living in the house, while we lived in the tree house out back, three younger brothers at each other's throats.

Whenever we get together to do things now, that's the dynamic. Who needs that kinda crap, right? Nowadays I pick my own band members. And I pick my own partners. I have partners in all my different things, you know, my business ventures. But it's usually me and one guy, or me and two guys who are making the decisions. Like with Feelgoods, I have one partner. At my bar in West Palm Beach, I have one partner. I have two partners that I'm gonna work with to build a bunch of these in the next two years, so they'll be all over the country. Twenty-five or forty. We're working on the numbers. But the thing I'm trying to say is... in business, there's no ulterior motives. But with Mötley Crüe everybody has an ulterior motive. Which sucks. And you have to just try and live with it. Because there's a lot of dishonesty in rock 'n' roll. And there's a lot of money in Mötley Crüe. It's like that movie *The Perfect Storm.* If you don't watch out, you can end up on the bottom of the ocean.

You'd think with Mötley it would get better over time. You'd think as we all grew up and became older things would be different. Like maybe it was just everyone's youth—we were all so young when we started out, and things just *kerranged* out of control.

It sounds like a cliché now, but when you're living it, you're not exempt. Isn't that why clichés exist? Because there's truth in there? Unfortunately, I'm telling you, it's worse now than it ever was. Like we're all getting older and even more set in our ways. Instead of wiser and more mature, like my wife suggests we should all be. But it's just the same old shit, over and over again. Like, we have this Canadian tour coming up that *nobody* told me about until the day tickets went on sale. And then of course I start getting texts and e-mails from people, like: "Oh, you're coming to Canada!" And I'm like, *What the fuck are you talking about!!!!*

So I'm pissed off. I'm going on this Canada tour and I'm pissed off. I mean, I just wrote my schedule down in a calendar. You want a glimpse into my life, here it is. Right here on my iPhone. From now till the nineteenth I'll be recording the album and working on the book with you. Then it's Christmas. I have the first week of January off. Then I'm booked solid at least until March. I have to rehearse with Mötley; I got to go to the Grand Caymans for a tequila promotion, I got to go to Palm Beach for my two-year anniversary of Dr. Feelgoods. Then I start the Mötley thing and that's till the fifth of February. After that I go to the Super Bowl. And then my birthday's the next day, and then I play St. Louis and Kansas City with the Vince Neil Band, and then we're off to Mexico and South America, where we have a huge following. It doesn't matter if they know the language; they know the songs. I actually toured South America before Mötley did. Last year was the first time Mötley ever went down there. And I've played there twice already. Argentina, Brazil, Chile. All those places. It's really cool down there. And then, you know, I'll start, I'll probably start the book tour.

With all that shit, I really wasn't in the mood to go on the Mötley tour of Canada. I told them, "Fuck you, I ain't going to go...." But then, you know, I found out I *had* to go because of our T-shirt deal. No show, no T-shirt deal.

And so, you know what? Fuck it.

I'm playing Canada with Mötley. It turns out Mötley would get sued if I didn't do it. And then I would get sued. I would have to give some lawyer all kinds of money to represent me. That's just like flushing it away; paying lawyers is like wiping your ass with hundred-dollar bills. Plus, if I didn't do the show, I would lose a chunk of change. I was like, *You know what? I'll just go ahead and do Canada.* I keep reminding myself—I'm not part of Mötley anymore. I just have to play with them. It's a better situation than before. Especially in the beginning. Back then I just, you know, I wouldn't... I felt like I was bullied around. For some reason I wouldn't stick up for myself. I just kind of didn't want to make noise. But now I'm like, fuck it, you know? I've got to have a voice. I was always the odd man out. (Another good subtitle for this book: *Odd Man Out*. That's me when it comes to Mötley Crüe. I don't think anybody would argue.)

Think about it. 'Cause Mick is Mick. Mick's always just been Mick. And you know Nikki and Tommy were always... they tried to be, you know, like Tyler and Perry when they were the Toxic Twins. They even had their own nickname and stuff like that. But it was like... they've always *tried* too hard to be rock 'n' roll people. Where me, I never really dressed to be a rock star, not offstage. I didn't go out in the street looking like a rock star. (Not since the early days at least.) I'm just... I'm a surfer guy from LA, you know? I don't have to wear chains around my waist and leather jackets and boots every minute for people to go, "Oh, that must be a rock star." That's what it was always like to be with Nikki and Tommy. They still do it today. It's like we'll be on an airplane or in Japan on the bullet train and they'll come decked out like they're going to a concert. Full rock 'n' roll regalia. And like it's like, *Fuck, what's up with that? Where are we going? We're supposed to sit on a train for three hours, man; put on some sweats, lose the makeup.* I mean, I'm as much for wearing eyeliner as the next guy, but only when I'm actually *working*. Back in the day, on tour, I'd actually try to pretend I wasn't with Nikki and Tommy. I'd try to walk a ways behind them. I still do it today. Just so that I don't kind of have to really be associated—which is bad, but that's what it's come down to.

These days I'm basically like a free agent. I have a separate deal. I got out because I just didn't want to deal with their bullshit anymore. If we have to go on tour, the corporation hires me. I still get 25 percent of everything I do, so it's not like, you know, I get a paycheck. But I have an *option* not to do stuff. This last Canadian tour is the end of this tour cycle. And what they always seem to do is piss me off about something, and then I have to renegotiate with them for the *next* tour and *next* album. *Which makes me not want to fucking do it.* They're not the cool people who they want people to believe they are, who they *represent* themselves to be. It's pretty sad. Nikki tries to run everything with the management, but they make a lot of wrong decisions and, you know…fuck. I just like keep my mouth shut and just like whatever. (Except for now of course.)

For me, the best thing for now is just to limit my contact with Mötley Crüe. It's not like working with my solo band. I mean those guys—Blando and Strum especially—we've been together for years. These guys are my friends. With Mötley Crüe, those guys are *not* my friends. And they haven't been for a long time.

But the thing is, you know, they need me to do Mötley Crüe. And unless they want to go out on their own and do their solo stuff, they're stuck with me.

Anyway, fuck the negative. That's not where I'm at right now. This book is about Vince Neil. It's about taking stock of the life I've lived and telling the tales, dredging up the good old days, and having a good laugh, maybe a good cry, too, before it's all over. By doing this I feel like I can move forward into the next chapters of my life, you know what I mean? Put some closure on the past. Open a door to the future. Nobody stays the same. We grow; we change. You have to find peace with what you do, with who you are, with what you've accomplished.

One thing I have to say, I think I'm singing better than ever. Especially the last two years. At Crüe Fest—both 1 and 2—I sang better than I've ever sung in my life. I think I moved better, too. I think I am healthier and have more energy. I keep telling myself that I want to be the best I can be. There have probably been a lot of years of my life that I wasted. I don't think I want to lose that kind of time ever again. Now I hear the clock ticking. It's easy to get older. That's gonna happen whether you like it or not. The trick is to pick up some wisdom along the way.

The point is, you got to go with the flow. I love my life. I love where I live. Viva Las Vegas. Sin City. City of possibility. To me, Vegas is like the Wild West. That's why I needed to have my Lambo here, you know? A Ferrari fits wine country. A Lambo is pure Vegas. You can do things here, businesswise I'm talking about, that you can't do anywhere else. Like with me opening up not one but two tattoo parlors on the Strip—you can't do that on Rodeo Drive. You know what I mean? The most expensive real estate in the world is the Strip. And to get on that street, that's exciting. It's funny: When I started dating my wife I lived in Beverly Hills and she was living in Northern California. She was playing hard to get. She'd fly in on weekends. By the time I finally persuaded her to move in with me in LA, I decided I was sick of LA, that I was moving to Vegas. Hollywood is a small town. I'd had about enough. But she was disappointed. She told me, "I moved in with you so I could be in LA and now you're taking me to Vegas?" I guess the answer to that is "Yes."

And it is also the answer to the question of why we have another huge house not far from the place where she grew up.

So what do I do when I'm not on the road? Check my Web site. I'm all over the place all of the time; the Vince Neil Band does a lot of touring. But when I'm not on the road I like being home. I like running our foundation, the Skylar Neil Foundation. We have a huge golf tournament every year. I like playing golf. I like being normal. I like eating good food and hanging out. I like driving my cars. I like cooking shows. You know like *Top Chef* is one of my favorite shows. *Project Runway,* I like that show. I don't like all reality shows, just the ones where people have some talent and they're actually doing something. I haven't seen *Jersey Shore* yet. I just keep reading about it—I want to watch it. It's good entertainment 'cause the people are so weird. That's sort of my guilty pleasure is all these kinds of shows. And I like *Haunted* and *Ghost Hunters,* and *Ghost Adventures,* and all those haunted shows. And I do love *Survivor.* I've loved that for a long time. Of course I was on one of the first reality shows, *Surreal Life.* It was just the very first year. There were like nine seasons of it. Unfortunately, I don't have a copy of it.

My real guilty pleasure these days is betting football. I have my own table at the sports book at the Red Rock Casino off the Strip in Las Vegas, a beautiful place. I have my own big booth right at the center in this roped-off, reserved area; it's got a separate TV, but all the huge screens on the walls are dead center front of me. I go in there every Sunday, usually at eight o'clock in the morning till about eight o'clock at night. To have a reserved booth you've got to bet at least three thousand dollars a game or ten thousand dollars a day or something like that. That's my big vice now, I guess. I like the action. Something to get your heart pumping. More healthy than a syringe full of cocaine powder like I was doing back in '81 with my girlfriend Lovey, that's for sure....

But you got to admit...those days are a lot more fun to talk about.

Chapter 2

NOBODY'S FAULT

I was born Vince Neil Wharton on February 8, 1961, in the Queen of Angels Hospital in Los Angeles County.

My mom, the former Shirley Ortiz, is half Mexican and half white. My dad, Clois Odell Wharton—know as Odie—is half Native American. Some people would say that makes me biracial or triracial or whatever. But I consider myself Californian. Even though I don't actually live there anymore, I feel like that's my home. I've always thought people from Cali should carry a special passport. We're a special breed—for better or for worse. They used to call California the Land of Fruits and Nuts. I just call it home.

The hospital is still there, a short distance as the crow flies across the 101 Freeway from Hollywood, the place where the real people live, I guess you could say. Having gotten this far, I have to stop for a second to smell the roses. Do you know how many times I've imagined writing my autobiography? Maybe we all do it at times in our lives. But how cool is this? It's really happening. An autobiography. Even though I'm not, by nature, overly reflective or deep, I realize how lucky I am to be in this position, writing a book about myself, thinking that people will actually want to spend their hard-earned dollars to buy it and read it. When it comes right down to the bottom line, I'm just a Heinz 57 from the other side of the freeway. Who would have thought all this was possible?

My mom grew up in New Mexico, I think. She was a stay-at-home mom for my early years, taking care of me and my sister, Valerie, who is sixteen months younger. When we got a little older my mom went to work to help make ends meet. I think she worked at a factory making cosmetics for Max Factor. I don't know what she did. I never thought much about it. I was a kid, you know, so I mostly thought about myself.

I never knew my mom's father, my grandfather. He passed away when my mom was little. My grandma was a Mexican woman. My aunts only spoke Spanish. Homemade tortillas are like the greatest thing in the world, especially warm on the gas burner and slathered with butter. That's the kind of food I grew up on. Thanksgiving you had a choice: either turkey or enchiladas. That was the kind of family we had. Talk about a melting pot. As a family we were like a potluck supper—different dishes from different nationalities, all mixed up and comfortably sharing the same plate.

I used to stay a lot with my grandma. I don't remember if she worked. I don't think she did anything. I think she was just my grandma and that was it. She did a lot of sewing. She might've even sewed for other people. I remember she sewed a lot. She probably made money doing that. She lived in the area of South Central Los Angeles known as Watts, and I remember when I was little and the Watts riots were going on and I was there. I was only four years old; it was pretty scary. It happened in August 1965, a large-scale race riot that lasted six days, burn, baby, burn. Thirty-four people died; more than one thousand were injured. Nearly four thousand were arrested. Thousands of homes and businesses were burned and looted, resulting in over $200 million in damages. It would stand as the worst riot in Los Angeles history before being eclipsed by the riots of 1992—another racial conflagration touched off by alleged police brutality after a traffic stop of a black motorist, which is what caused the Watts riots, too. I remember the tanks going down the street and the army men marching. I was a little boy. I was like, "Wow! We're saved. The good guys are coming!"

When I was little I also met my grandparents on my dad's side. They passed away when I was probably seven or eight. They were from the Texas/Oklahoma area. My dad was born in Paris, Texas. I think we lived in . . . I want to say New Mexico for a while, or Utah. Something like that. And then my dad got a job with Los Angeles County as a mechanic. It was a government job with benefits, nice middle-class stuff. The LA County Mechanical Division. He repaired sheriffs' vehicles. The same type I'd have to ride in a number of times myself—in the backseat in handcuffs.

My dad was a good-looking guy in his day. He and my mom are still alive and still together. They and my sister live in Utah, but I think they're gonna move to Las Vegas soon. We don't really talk—haven't talked since my wedding, like, five years ago. Some stuff went down then, too much drinking, some ugly words said—maybe we'll get into it later. With families there's always drama, I guess. My dad's up in age now, but he's still a good-looking guy. He's six foot something, you know, and he has the salt-and-pepper hair—he grayed when he was young—and this really cool Elvis hairdo, the combed-back style. In *The Dirt* they said I said he was a "ladies' man." I don't know who ever said he was a ladies' man. It says that in *The Dirt* in my own voice, but I don't remember saying it. And I don't know where that would come from. Maybe just 'cause he was good-looking. But you know my mom and my dad have been married, what, almost fifty years or so? So if he's a ladies' man he's probably the sneakiest guy alive... because my mom would have never tolerated him messing her around. She's a tough one. A blond Mexican toughie. Maybe that's where I got it. She's a fighter, like me.

Growing up I can't remember doing much with my dad. There was some stuff. We had a boat at one point. A small fourteen-foot outboard boat. We'd take it out and run around on weekends at a place called Castaic Lake. We'd go up there and fish and stuff—me, my sister, mom, and dad. Once in a while we'd do that. I think when I was small he and I got to work together on a project rebuilding my uncle's car engine. That was something we did together. We worked on it for a while. I think it was a sixties Nova or something like that. It was my mom's brother actually. His car. I remember for a couple summers working on that car, my dad fixing up this car for him and me helping. I also remember going to a music shop with my dad. He bought me my first guitar. I took lessons and stuff. Later I had an electric guitar and a little amp. After a while—as a kid does—I just kind of forgot about it and it went into the closet... until much later, of course. A few chords have served me well.

Another little bit of fact checking: When my parents bought a house and moved to Compton, it was not because they were down-and-out or anything. Maybe they had bad real estate judgment, but at the time it was supposed to be nice there. Like a new beginning for the middle class. It was a nice middle-class neighborhood. Lots of those types of housing divisions went up at the time all over the country to accommodate the continuing post-war prosperity. The homes were affordable; the schools were close. It was not the gang- and drug-infested place that it would later become. You know the first rap album by the hard-core South Central rappers N.W.A. (Niggaz Wit Attitude)? It was called *Straight outta Compton.* That and other rap music and some films like *Boyz n the Hood* have put South Central on the cultural most-wanted list. But that album came out *twenty years* after I lived there. The part of Compton I lived in eventually incorporated into Carson. I mean it was just a new neighborhood at the time. Affordable to middle-class people like us, a lot of blue-collar working people—it was close to the oil refineries. I remember I used to ride my bike to the refineries. When we moved in, it was still very open around there. There was a lot of building going on, a lot of raw land. It had the feeling of, I don't know, like a new settlement on the frontier. A great place for a kid to play—war, spy, army, survival, off-road bicycles. It was pretty fun.

When I was little, I loved baseball. I played Little League in Carson. I was good. I remember I was on the Dodgers. I remember getting my first uniform and I wanted to wear it, like, all the time. I didn't want to take it off. You know how you feel when you're that age? That jersey just felt so good. And *smelled* so good. It had this smell to it, this new-uniform smell. It's the smell of promise, I guess. The smell of a little boy's dreams.

Clois Odell "Odie" Wharton
Vince's Dad

My dad's folks were part Indian; they were from Oklahoma. He was orphaned at a young age. I think the people who kind of raised him were living in Oklahoma; they were just across the border between Texas and Oklahoma, with the Red River there in between. My dad became a sharecropper in Texas. My mom was from Tupelo, Mississippi. I was born in Paris, Texas. It was just a little hole-in-the-wall—actually my birth certificate says Lamar County, because we were out in the rural area, on the farm. The doctor had to come to the house to deliver me. My mom said he was pretty drunk when he got there.

We lived in just a little shack. It didn't even have a bedroom; it was all just one room. And I remember during the wetter weather we had tar paper up; the boards the house was made of didn't fit together real good; the wind used to whistle through the cracks when it rained. We had to put pots and pans down to catch all the water where it was dripping through the roof. And of course we didn't have any indoor plumbing or electricity or anything like that. We used to listen to a battery-operated radio.

I left there when I was five years old. I remember when we moved we had an old truck. We loaded what belongings we had and took off from Texas to come out to California. My sister and I were lying in the back of the truck. We had a mattress back there; we lay on the mattress the whole trip. This was in 1941, kind of right after the Depression. Back in the Dust Bowl there were a lot of Okies and Texans and Arkies who moved out to California. My dad's sister had gone to Los Angeles; my dad and mom decided to move out there; we stayed with my aunt until my dad got a job as a housepainter for the University of Southern California—he always wore white and had paint speckled in his hair. Later he worked at a packinghouse. My mom worked at a shoe factory for a while.

The first night I met Shirley, she was with her friend Tootsie, who had a brand-new Ford T-bird. It was a sweet little car. They cruised through the drive-in. The guy I was with knew them, so we met. A little while after that, our car club had a picnic at Griffith Park. Shirley was there. I was sitting at the table and had a beer in one hand and a cigarette in the other. When Shirley walked by, I flipped the cigarette out, and then I grabbed her and pulled her over and gave her a big smooch. I guess it was the beer talking. We dated a little bit, and then I quit high school in the eleventh grade and went into the army in 1956. They sent me to Germany. I was lucky; it was in between Korea and Vietnam. While I was over there, she'd write me letters and send me photographs of her. We rotated back to Fort Hood, Texas, in January of '58. While I was there, Elvis Presley was, too; he was doing his basic training.

When I got let out of the army in August of '58, I came home. Shirley and I dated for a few months. In November of '58 we got married. We're still together today, fifty-two years and counting.

I remember when Vince was six weeks old I had to leave town to go on a job. I was working as a fiberglass laminator. They sent me along with a crew up to Moab, Utah. We were lining these great big huge steel tanks with fiberglass lining—I think the process it was used for was called uranium reduction. We expected to get back home in just a couple weeks or so, but they liked our work so much they gave us more tanks to do. So I called Shirley and told her that I was going to have to stay much longer than I anticipated.

After her six-week checkup, she hopped on the bus and come on up to Moab. We got us our own motel room there. Vince was just a tiny baby; in the motel room we made him a bed in the suitcase—we put the blankets down there and everything. And he just slept in the suitcase.

I was working so many hours. We were trying to finish the job and get back home. I was working fourteen, sixteen hours a day and then I'd come back to the motel room and, wouldn't you know it, as soon as I'd get there, he'd start screaming his head off. He was fine all day until I got there. I told Shirley, "God, could you keep him quiet? I got to get some sleep, I'm working all these hours." I was like, "If you don't shut up the screaming I'm going to close the lid of the suitcase!" Of course I was just kidding.

When he was fifteen I bought him an old '53 Chevy pickup. It was all primered and had big black wheels; it had a split six; the manifold had the exhaust running out beneath the running boards on each side. He didn't have a driver's license yet. But we saw this truck and I liked it even myself. I only paid like seven hundred dollars for it. I figured by the time we had it all fixed up, he'd have his license. I even cut the top out and put in a sunroof; the wife made little curtains for the back window—it was what they called a five-window.

Vince had this friend of his who said he had a driver's license; I took him at his word. The two of them used to take the truck out. Come to find out his friend didn't have no license, either. So they were just driving around illegally. Then Vince hit something and smashed the rear fender on the thing.

I kept that truck for a while and then I sold it to a neighbor down the street for a hundred dollars. They came and picked it up and drove it away and I haven't seen it since. It was a nice little truck. I remember Vince had the surfboard rack in the back—I remember that guy who tried to take it from him or something. Vince was a young kid. Probably a freshman. He had the long hair and he was interested in music. I guess this other guy was a football jock, a senior. He started picking on Vince because of the hair and because he was a freshman—he was an easy target, I guess. Anyway, one day, I don't know what happened, something with the surf rack, but the guy was picking on Vince and I guess Vince had enough of it. Vince hauled off and smacked him right in the mouth. And the guy had braces, so it cut the kid's mouth all to shreds.

I ended up having to go to court—his parents sued us for I think five hundred dollars or something like that. So I ended up having to pay that. Even though the guy might've been picking on him with words, Vince had no call to haul off and hit him. That's the only trouble that I really can recall with Vince as a youngster.

One thing I'll never forget. At some point, when Mötley Crüe was starting to get pretty well known, Vince sent a limo over to our house to pick us up and take us to the concert. It was a big black stretch limo. It was the first time I'd ever even been in a limo. And I told Vince, "You know I've never been in a limo in my whole life?"

He looked at me and smiled real proud. He said, "Well, Dad, you better get used to it."

That was one of the shining moments. I never in my wildest dreams thought Vince would get as far as he has gotten. There are so many talented people out there that just never get a break, so many people who never get famous. But I guess Vince was in the right place at the right time and had enough talent. Like I say, I'm real proud—you know I bought him his first guitar, right?

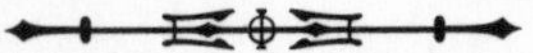

By the time I was in third or fourth grade, Compton started to change. You could see the beginnings of what would later happen. By then, it was becoming predominantly black and lower class. Gang activity was everywhere. The ruling gangs in my neighborhood were the Crips and the AC Deuceys. The brother of my best friend, Paul, was one of the leaders of the Crips, so I didn't get beat up as much as I could have. A bunch of Crips lived directly across the street in this apartment; they used it like a clubhouse. Guys in the AC Deuceys lived about five houses down the street. And then some other Crips lived around the corner. So I was right in the middle of it. The Crips and the AC Deuceys were always at war. There were shootings and drive-bys; this was way before the crack epidemic brought the gang problems into the spotlight. This was just plain old gang warfare, Sharks and Jets stuff, all about turf and pride, something that men have done for centuries, protect and defend their families and their 'hoods.

One day, I was walking home from school and I saw four kids take down this well-dressed, preppy-looking guy. They shot him, took his sneakers, and left him lying in the street. There was blood gurgling out of his mouth. Somebody called 911. It was a horrible sight to see, this guy spitting up blood. He couldn't even talk. I was only a little kid.

After that it seemed like a lever had been thrown. A few days later I was waiting in front of my house for the ice-cream man, like I'd done a hundred times before. The same four gangbangers who had shot the kid for his sneakers came out of the Crips' apartment. Even though I knew there was no way my sneakers were ever going to fit any of those huge guys, I was still pretty nervous as I watched them cross the street coming directly toward me. My only thought was like, *Jeez,* you know, *I hope they're getting in line for ice cream, too.*

The tallest among them, walking on the left side of the group, wore a black T-shirt. He had raised red lines running down his arms, like tribal scars. As they were coming toward me, he kept staring at me the whole time. My throat went dry and my knees got weak. I was maybe ten, eleven years old.

Before I really knew what was happening, the tall guy separated from the others. He grabbed me and spun me around like they do with hostages in the movies, so that he was standing behind me, holding my arms. Then he stuck his hands in my pockets and rummaged around my pockets. I only had fifteen cents for ice cream. Then I felt this, like, pressure across my throat. It was quick; it didn't feel like there was a lot of weight or force behind it. For a moment there was no pain. But then my neurons began to scream; I could feel wetness flowing down my neck. I'd been cut with a knife or razor. They say you never feel the slash of a sharp knife, only the pain after. There's this weird delayed response, like your body doesn't even realize for a moment it's been hurt.

Even though the attack came in broad daylight, not one neighbor lifted a finger to help. It's tough in gang territory because everybody is so afraid. People want to be good neighbors, I guess, but why risk your own life to save somebody else? Somehow I picked myself up, and I must have gone back inside my house. I don't remember what happened next. Someone—my mom? my neighbor?—took me to the hospital. I got stitches. I don't remember how many, but the cut was on the side of my face and on my chin. The doctors told me the knife missed my jugular vein by only an inch. That's fate, huh? I could have died that day. At the hospital the nurses all doted on me. I ended that day with all the ice cream I could eat.

When I returned to school, Mrs. Anderson, my teacher, was effusive. She was a former *Playboy* playmate. She had long, straight brown hair and a figure like Jessica Rabbit—*bada bing*! I still have her pinup in a *Playboy* anthology edition somewhere, probably in one of my garages. I think it's fair to say that Mrs. Anderson switched on the light for me. Beginning with her, my eyes opened to what has probably been the guiding revelation of my entire life: *I love women*. And when I see a beautiful one I'm like a child. I've got one instinct—gimme.

Being in Mrs. Anderson's class, in her proximity, I had this warm and gooey feeling. I didn't know what sex was yet, though I knew all the associated vocabulary words. Yet somehow I grokked that what I felt for Mrs. Anderson was what a man feels for women. It was like the first hit of crack: a rushing sensation I've been chasing ever since.

In Mrs. Anderson's class, if you behaved well and folded your hands on your desk, or read well or answered the questions she asked, Mrs. Anderson would give you the honor of walking in the front of the line to lunch and recess…while holding her hand! I can't ever remember being selected for that honor by virtue of my classroom participation—more on that later. Of course I wanted badly to lead the line, to hold her hand. But that day I came back to school all bandaged up, she singled me out. I got to walk in the front of the line. I know to this day she had no idea the kinds of things that were going through my mind. In *her* mind, I'm sure, she was playing nursemaid to this traumatized little boy. But when I was with her I didn't feel things a little boy feels. I wasn't sure if I wanted to be her lover or her son—but I felt like I sure wanted something. On parents' night, when I introduced her to my mom and dad, I said, "This is my mother, Mrs. Anderson." Talk about a Freudian slip! I wanted to dig a hole and hide.

After that, the genie was pretty much out of the bottle. Within a year's time I found myself experimenting with a neighborhood girl named Tina, sticking my hands up her skirt, feeling around up there for the first time, getting an idea, so to speak, of the lay of the land. I didn't know what I was doing or why or what came next. I only knew I felt compelled to keep touching.... What is it about females that makes you just want to feel them all the time?

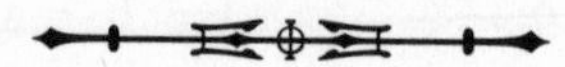

Shirley Ortiz Wharton
Vince's Mom

My mom was raised in Albuquerque, New Mexico, one of five kids. She and my dad moved to Inglewood when we were kids. My dad went to work as a machinist. After he died of cancer at forty-two, we moved to a smaller house. I think he had some life insurance—I don't ever remember my mom going to work. There were six of us. I graduated high school in 1965. My mom lived there pretty much the rest of her life. We used to visit her in the little house—I remember during the Watts riots we all went to my mom's. Vince was like four years old. The sky was orange. He was fascinated with the National Guard troops.

After high school I became a hairstylist. I went to cosmetology school in Hollywood and junior college in Del Amo, California. That's where they always parked the big Goodyear blimp. I met Odie one night while I was out with some girlfriends. He was in this car club called the Shifters. He had the great DA hairdo, all combed back slick, and he wore a green and white Shifters jacket—he had a green and white Chevy, too. I was put together pretty nice; I was a blonde but not by birth—you know, it's cosmetic. Being a beauty school girl, I liked to experiment. I met him at a drive-in, actually. Everybody went at night, it was in the neighborhood, down there on Manchester. Odie's dad was a housepainter, but he was pretty much retired when I came around. They said he was part Indian.

I remember moving to Carson, to the house on Dimondale Drive. Odie and I had the two kids by now. They were only sixteen months apart. Just to set the record straight, it was not a ghetto. It was a nice development when we moved in. Vincent took ice-skating lessons with his sister when he was little. It all started with Valerie. She was a pretty good skater and he went to see her at a show once, and after that he said, "I want to do that, too." So I gave him lessons and he did a solo. He was very, very good. He will die when he reads this—he hates for me to talk about it. But I've got pictures of him in the whole skating outfit and everything. I still have his ice skates. He took dancing lessons, too, and he played the guitar. He was very much an extrovert on the stage. But by himself, no. With people he was very shy. He would never get up and sing in front of you unless there was a stage.

Later I remember he started lip-synching. He'd do Rod Stewart songs like "Hot Legs." He was a little bit of a ham. He liked to be up in front. Girls chased him. Starting in junior high he would bring them over to the house. We always told him, "You can't go into the bedroom and close the door." It was hard to supervise him all the time because I worked. When the kids were real young, when we lived in Carson, my husband worked during the day and I worked at night. I worked at Max Factor. I packaged lipsticks and makeups and stuff to ship all over the United States. It was a fun job. After we moved to Glendora, I worked at Ormco. We manufactured orthodontics. I was in charge of getting orders out to the doctors all over the world. Believe it or not, they even made braces for dogs.

I don't remember Vince being a bad student. He never got in trouble at school. His grades were average. He turned out good, but he went through a lot with his—you know, I didn't realize that he was smoking marijuana when he was young. I had no clue. Valerie told me that he used to do it, but she was no angel, either. They both used to sneak in through the bedroom window if they came in too late. Vince would close the window on Valerie so she couldn't get in. They were just typical kids I guess. Sometimes, when we were asleep, they would take the car . . . well, Valerie would. Vince would tell on her.

He started bringing Tami around. She was older than him. She was seventeen and he was sixteen. An absolute sweetheart. She's my favorite to this day. I don't remember if it was Vince or Tami who told me about the pregnancy. She was just crazy about Vince. But Vince was seeing another girl named Shani. So it was hard. We felt so bad for Tami. Because we really liked her. I said, "Tami, don't chase him. He doesn't need to be chased. Don't do that to yourself." After she had Neil, Vince was just too young. We moved her in for a while, and Vince moved out. But he held Neil; he brought him gifts—a little tricycle and everything. But he really wasn't around for him like he should've been. Me and Odie made sure that Neil went to a lot of concerts and saw his dad whenever he could.

I guess everybody always tells the famous story about Rockandi's big party at our house. It wasn't a secret. We weren't away. We knew all about it. The only thing we didn't know was that Vince was going to advertise it on telephone poles throughout the city. We had a swimming pool in the back, and an enclosed patio, all screened in. The band was set up in there—the party was going to be inside and outside, just a regular house party, from what we knew. Vincent said it would be fifty or sixty kids at most.

Before things even started, Odie goes to a couple of the neighbors and says, you know, "Why don't we go down to this local place and shoot some pool while the kids are having this little party." So we all left before anybody had even gotten to the house yet.

When we came home there were *hundreds* of cars. They were parked on the grass, on the sidewalks up and down the street. Tami was at the back gate with a cigar box and she was collecting the money. We didn't know they'd charge money to let people in; I can't remember how much it was. Finally the police came with big bullhorns and made everybody leave. Oh my god. For months after that we were finding bottles of liquor in our yard, in the bushes, everywhere.

One thing I'd like to correct from *The Dirt* is the part about Odie dancing with all the girls and stuff. He was a grown man. He did not dance with the little girls.

After that party, we were there for every concert that we could possibly go to. We went to the Whisky, the Roxy; we went to every place in Hollywood Vince played. We were excited for him. We were thrilled. I remember thinking to myself, *He can't really sing, but he's singing.* I was pretty amazed, you know, because he'd never really sung before. I asked everyone, "Does he sound good to you?" Because, you know, I wanted to know if it sounded good to other people. . . . I'm just his mom, of course it sounded good to me. He's got that high, raspy voice, and he's got a lot of charisma onstage.

Over the years we got to know Tommy's parents really well—they went to all the shows, too. The last time I saw Vincent, I asked, "How's Tommy doing?" And Vincent turned around real angry and he said, "Mom, how come you always ask about Tommy? I don't know what in the hell Tommy's up to, okay?"

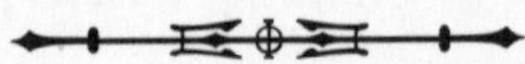

As the empty lots filled up with warehouses, the neighborhood went into further decline. Even the way we played was a little rough. My friends and I would meet in a deserted lot and play army with BB guns. Or I remember they were building this gas station, with huge, deep holes for the tanks, and we'd play there. We'd actually shoot each other. No goggles or protection or anything. I would come home bleeding and full of welts. My mother would yell at me as she dabbed the blood from some wound on my head or thigh. "You're lucky you didn't lose an eye!" But really, the BB guns were nothing. A lot of the kids I knew were more serious than that. Many of them were already joining gangs. I shit you not, by sixth grade kids were carrying knives in their lunch boxes. Several kids I knew had real guns. Everybody knows that kids around that age—thirteen, fourteen, fifteen—make the best foot soldiers. Look at those kid soldiers in Africa and Cambodia. I saw shows about them on TV. Ruthless. They become totally brainwashed. Same thing happens in a street gang, believe me. I've seen it happen. A guy you thought was your friend can change practically overnight.

For the most part, the kids I hung out with were pretty much normal rowdy kids. You know, just typical kid stuff. We'd throw rocks at cars going down the street. I remember people stopping and getting out of the car and chasing us. I actually got caught once. My dad was so fuckin' pissed. This was a time when Evel Knievel was big, you know, so we would build ramps on the sidewalks and take our bikes and just see how far we could actually launch ourselves. Or we would make go-karts and tie them to the bikes and fly down the hill. Going from my house to school you had to walk up a big hill. You know—it was hard to get to school, but coming home was easy. We would launch the karts behind bicycles and then cut ourselves loose. The karts would come flying around these corners and down the hill. Or sometimes we'd use those old-fashioned skateboards. There wasn't really the whole modern skateboarding thing going yet. Our skateboards had metal wheels. But we had no regard for anything, you know, 'cause there could've been a car coming around the corner at any minute and we would have just slid right underneath the car and killed ourselves.

One day when I was in sixth grade, four other kids and I—three black, one Samoan, and me—decided to pull a caper. We climbed this barbed-wire fence and snuck past two security guards into a warehouse full of souvenirs. There were giant conch shells, sponges, coral—all the expensive junk they sell to tourists at the beach. We took whatever we could carry in our backpacks and sold it on the street and at the Compton swap meet. I put some of the proceeds toward buying my first cassette tape, *Cloud Nine* by the

Temptations. My parents were not particularly musical, but they played music a lot. My dad loved Johnny Cash and Creedence Clearwater Revival, you know, so I grew up listening to that a lot. My obsession with soul came from growing up listening to my mom's Motown collection: Stevie Wonder, Marvin Gaye, Al Green, the Four Tops, as well as earlier stuff such as Mable John, Mary Wells, and Barrett Strong. I guess maybe you can see some early soul influence in my singing, too. All those groups have a tradition of great falsetto singers. I'm not sure you would call what I do falsetto, but it's up there in that range. Maybe you could say that the classic rock power singing is a little like the soul falsetto... something to think about. It's definitely up in the higher registers. Soul music is pretty much mainstream now, but back then it really was ghetto music. Of course everybody in the neighborhood listened to it also; it was a good thing to have in common with the other kids. My musical knowledge was expanded by listening to the radio, and before long I had a pretty impressive singles collection, cassettes and vinyl. I had Deep Purple, The Guess Who, Paper Lace, all kinds of stuff. Remember, I was only in like sixth grade. Thinking back, I remember my other obsession at the time was Matchbox cars. Pre-adolescence: You're so all over the place. Thinking about sex, playing with toy cars. You're in two worlds at once. So much can influence you. Most of it bad.

While some of this collecting was supported by my five-dollar-a-week allowance I got from my dad for washing the car and doing chores around the house—you could get a lot for five bucks at a swap meet back then—the rest of it was financed by my life of crime. My mom and dad were both working by now to help make ends meet. They really had no idea what I was up to. Things got pretty out of hand for a while, culminating with the time the police caught me running out of a warehouse in broad daylight with a box of stolen gardening supplies. They handcuffed me, threw me in a squad car, and brought me home. I know my parents were not pleased. I have no recollection of what happened. I'm sure I was punished big-time. I just don't remember.

By this time, my sister and I were the only white people in the school. Things in the neighborhood were getting worse and worse. Whenever we left our house, my mother would cross herself and pray that none of us got shot by a stray bullet.

One evening my mom's worst fears almost came true. There was a bullet shot through my sister's bedroom window. She had the room facing the street. It was one of those houses with like the little porch out front. I still remember the name of the street. Dimondale Drive, right between Wilmington and Del Amo. I'm taking out my iPhone right now. I'm looking it up on Google Maps. I know *exactly* where it is. You go up 405 into Carson. There it is. Wilmington! There it is! And there's Del Amo right there. And there . . . is . . . Dimondale. That's it! *Shit, I can show you my house!* Here's where I used to walk to school. Here's the cul-de-sac near our house. I lived in . . . I think it was 1836 Dimondale. This house right here! No, it would've been 1832. Maybe it was *this* house? Eighteen thirty-four? Honestly, I don't really remember the number, but I think it's one of those houses. And moving across the map . . . this is my elementary school right here, Broadacres Elementary. It wasn't very far. It was only a few blocks away. Wow. Shit's still there; I'm shocked. Across the street was a giant open field—we would ride our bikes in there, until they finally built, like, an industrial complex on that spot. And once they built all that, that's when me and my friends started breaking in there and just stealing shit. That's where all those warehouses were. Right across the street. Talk about a target of opportunity.

So the night of the bullet, we were in the kitchen playing a board game. All four family members. The house was like you walked in and the garage is here to the right, front door is here in the center, and the bedroom would be front left. The living room was behind the kitchen toward the back, leading out to a sliding glass door. There were three bedrooms. As a family we liked to play board games like Monopoly. Or we played cards. My dad and I would play this football game on the table sometimes, like it was this old-school electric football game, with the green metal field and the little guys on it that would like vibrate. My family was just a normal well-adjusted family, I guess. Maybe there was some drinking. I think my mom and my dad both liked to drink.

And then we heard gunshots. They were close. We heard them all the time, actually, but not usually that close. We turned off the lights and went in the living room because there were no windows to the street. We ended up all sleeping on the floor in the living room. It was pretty scary. I don't remember myself being that scared, but I remember being really scared for my parents. Then the next morning we all went in my sister's room and you could see there was a bullet hole in the window.

A couple of days after that, there was a news item or something in the paper or on the TV news about a couple of kids at the local high school throwing a teacher out of a third-floor window. That was it for my parents. They didn't want us to go to junior high school in the same neighborhood, you know? When it's so rough that the teachers are getting beaten up and thrown out the windows, who wants their kid to go there? So my dad and mom said "That's it, we're moving." They put the house up for sale, but we finished out the rest of our school year. That summer, my parents sent me and my sister to West Covina to live with our aunt.

I started seventh grade using my aunt's address while my parents looked for a house. This place where they'd moved me was way out north and east from where we'd lived, east of Pasadena, between the 210 Freeway and the San Gabriel Mountains. Halfway through the school year, my parents finally moved to this house in nearby Glendora. So then I transferred over to that school, Sunflower Junior High. This also corresponded with my mom getting a better job at a dental brace factory. The housing prices were higher in Glendora, I guess. I didn't have a clue about stuff like that in those days. What kid does?

Basically, I confess, I was always a terrible student—with the exception of Mrs. Anderson's class. As you could imagine, classes at the school in the better neighborhood, at Sunflower, were a lot harder than I was used to at Broadacres. To be honest, I had a hard time even writing a simple sentence. I found out eventually that I have dyslexia, but not really bad—I can read okay, though I don't prefer to. I'm just so slow when it comes to reading. When I write it's worse. When I go to write something down it really takes me a while because I will mix up numbers and it's just, it takes me forever; it's difficult. If somebody says to write a letter, it's tough. It takes me forever to do it. And I mix up my writing and cursive or printing—I combine the two, which makes it even worse. But instead of getting tutored or something, or working on my problem, I reacted by avoiding the unpleasantness...probably people would say that that is my MO today, too. I just chose to skip school. What kid wants to admit he has a learning disability or whatever, you know? The school didn't do much about it, either. They just kept on passing me to the next grade. Kicking me upstairs, I guess you could say.

One highlight in my new neighborhood was I actually joined a football team. It was flag football. Even though I was always better at baseball, I enjoyed it. I played special teams and defense. I think I was a cornerback. Moving to the school meant all new people. At the time I had a couple friends. But not a whole lot of friends. I just kind of went through the motions, you know what I mean? I didn't really know anybody.

This was the time, I think, when the Beatles' White album came out. I remember I had a music class and we were all fascinated with the Beatles back then and whether Paul was dead. We'd get into huge debates and discussions, looking for the clues, playing albums backwards and stuff, trying to find the supposed secret messages that were rumored to be on there. It was pretty fascinating. I remember to this day. I was already kind of going the music route even then. I was like one of the first people in my class to really grow my hair. I just dug the look, you know? People wore jeans and puka shells and that kind of stuff. I don't remember ever trying to follow any trend or anything. It's just kind of like what everybody wore—you know, what your mom got you at the store.

Walking to school one day in seventh grade I found this porno book. It was basically a sex manual with photographs, a paperback. The models, or whatever they were, appeared to be very straight-looking people. They were naked and all and they were doing the positions, but it just seemed like they were doing it for demonstration purposes—they looked grim, you know, like they were just doing it for a job, not enjoying it. It was weird. But of course everybody at school wanted to see the book, all my friends, all the guys in class. I decided I wasn't just gonna give it away. I stashed the book in a pile of junk inside my neighbor's shed. Every day, I'd rip out, like, ten pictures, then replace the book and go sell the pages to the kids at school for a quarter each. After about seventy pages being sold, the word was out all over school. A couple of idiots even taped the pages they bought from me to their lockers in the boys' locker room. Of course the gym teacher had a cow; the kids caved immediately and ratted me out. Within an hour, I was suspended. On the way home, I came up with a plan. I was going to retrieve the book and make a final score—I'd sell what was left for five dollars; then my days as a pornographer would be officially over. I even had an idea in mind who I was going to sell it to. But when I got to my neighbor's shed . . . the book was gone. Another of the great mysteries of childhood. My days as a pornographer had ended . . . for now.

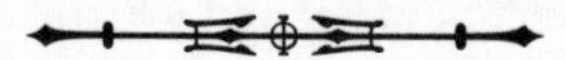

Valerie Wharton Saucer
Vince's Sister

My grandma's maiden name is Ortiz, but we're not Mexican. We're Spanish. My grandma spoke Spanish, but only to her sister. It's funny because in one of Vince's interviews he used to say that he was Mexican and my grandma got really offended and said, "What is Vincent doing? I'm not Mexican; we're not Mexican. I'm Spanish!" Vince, I don't think he really knew there was a difference. From way back they came from Spain. They might have immigrated to New Mexico. But they were from New Mexico, not *old* Mexico.

Vince and I were sixteen months apart. Everyone always used to think I was older. And I'm like, "No. Wrong. I'm *younger*." When I was growing up my mom used to always say we were eighteen months apart. Then one time I did the math. And I'm like, "Mom, you know we're sixteen months apart, we're not eighteen." And she's like, "You are?" I think they call that Irish twins or something. But of course, we're not Irish, either.

When we were little growing up, our little neighborhood was a nice neighborhood. We used to go outside and ride bikes and play hopscotch, just normal kid stuff. Later things got bad. I remember that time they shot into our house. I remember the gunshots; I remember us ducking in the living room. I don't remember an actual bullet coming into the house. That doesn't stick out in my head. But I just remember hearing it. My mom was home and my dad was at work. My mom yelled for us to get down and we lay down on the floor in the living room. When my dad got home and heard about it, he was like, "We gotta get out of here." Because we basically had, like, a gang that lived across the street in this rental house. They would bother us all the time. My mom couldn't even walk outside. She was a blonde. Like white blond hair. They would make comments to her and whistle at her and, you know, like flirt with her. She was scared.

My mom used to work nights. We would come home from school and she would just be leaving for work. We were home alone every weekday for probably about an hour or two. We used to fight over TV shows and what to watch, stuff like that. We weren't allowed outside. We had to stay inside until my dad got home from work. So we had to do stuff together; it was just the two of us, so I guess we were close. We fought of course. But I think every brother and sister do. Especially when you're that close in age; he used to try and boss me around. It seems like to this day Vince likes to always be with somebody. He doesn't like being home alone. I don't know why. I don't know—maybe he's just insecure that way. He just needs somebody with him.

Vince has a big heart. Well, when I was in the sixth grade and Vince was in the seventh I wanted to go to the sixth-grade dance that was held at Sunflower Junior High. My girlfriends were supposed to come to our house and pick me up and we were all gonna go to the dance together. My girlfriends never showed up and I was crying so hard 'cause I wanted to go so bad. Vince said, "Val, come on and I'll take you." We walked into the dance and he made sure that my friends were there before he left. He knew how much that dance meant to me and it hurt him to see me so upset.

First he was in this thing where he used to go to this roller-skating place and they would have lip-synching. I used to go there and watch him sing—I remember I used to steal my mom and dad's car at night and go down there to the roller-skating rink and watch him sing. And one time Vince came home and he was like, "Val, did you take the car?" And I'm like, "Yeah, please don't tell Mom and Dad!" And he kinda got this grin on his face and he goes, "Val, just get in the house." And I think that's when the time came that Vince thought I was cool. 'Cause I used to be the goody-goody little sister. Now he was like, he thought, *Well, shoot, now I have something on Val. She's not a goody-goody.* He was happy to finally have something to hang over my head.

In the beginning of Rockandi, Vince wasn't this cool rock guy yet. They were just like a garage band, you know? They practiced in my garage. I think my dad bought him a microphone. In the beginning I think people . . . people always . . . you know, they said, "Oh, he sucks," you know, "His voice sucks," and stuff like that. Of course you're going to get that with everybody. You know not everybody can like everyone. But I thought it was cool. You know, a couple of the songs I was like embarrassed. I think the very first song, the very first time I heard him, was at our party that we had at our house. And I was, I was actually embarrassed. And I thought, *Oh man, he can't sing very well.* And I thought, *Well, he's having a good time and it's fun.* And, you know, everybody else seemed to be having fun, so I was like, *Okay.* But I did think, *Oh shoot. He can't sing very well.* That was my first impression. I think I was just being judgmental. You know I was just being picky because . . . I don't know. He was my brother. I was thinking, *What's he trying to do now?* I honestly didn't think anything would happen—I didn't think he would become famous. Hell no. Uh-uh. I never thought that for one minute.

Growing up and being his sister is . . . Over time, I got to know that you don't tell people who you are. I *don't*. Well, I do have this thing on my e-mail signature line for my real estate business that says "Homes For You and Your Crüe," but I don't really go out of my way to explain it, unless somebody asks. Because you never really know if people like you or if they like you just because of who you are, you know, Vince Neil's sister. I learned that really soon. And now I keep my mouth closed. I don't say anything to anybody and I've been that way for years.

One time Vince gave me this amazing ring. It was like a ruby ring or something like that. It was cool. I mean, it wasn't my style. But it was beautiful. And then he gave me this really cool pair of sunglasses. And a couple of times I've needed money and I went to him. Not for very much money, but I was kind of at my wit's end and I needed money and I went to him and he helped me. I'm not a person who's going to ask for stuff. I don't need anything—we're doing just fine here in Utah with my parents right nearby to help take care of the kids. I don't ask for stuff. I don't need anything. I don't ask him for, like, people say, "Well gosh, why don't you ask him to buy you a car?" Or, "Why don't you ask him, you know, to buy you a house?" Since I'm a Realtor and all. But I don't do that. If Vince wanted to give it to me, then that's fine, but I don't ask for it. I mean, he gave my mom and dad a car. That was cool. He's a good person. He's a good person.

I wanted to tell you the story of when I approached Vince and asked his permission to give my daughter her middle name. My daughter Samantha was born June 19, 1997. When I found out I was pregnant and decided to name her Samantha, I wanted to have her middle name Skye, you know, after Skylar. I was at Vince's house with my husband, Guy, and my parents. And I asked Vince if I could have his permission to name Samantha after Skylar. Vince looked at me with tears in his eyes and he said, "Of course you can, Val. You can even name her Skylar if you want." And I said, "No, I would never do that to you. I just want to name her middle name Skye."

Vince came over to me and said, "I would be honored." That felt really good.

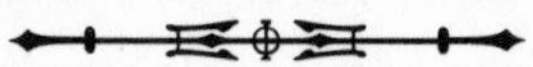

When I was fifteen my dad gave me a '53 Chevy pickup truck. I would actually work on my own; I did all the work on it myself. It was kind of a tease, you know? At fifteen you didn't have a license, but you had a car. It was sort of fucked up. Like who puts that kind of temptation in front of a rebellious fifteen-year-old boy? But being a mechanic, I guess, my dad came across this deal on a truck that was too good to turn down. I will forever love him for giving me that truck. It was cherry. I mean, it needed a lot of work, but the guts were sound.

The deal I made with my parents was that I wasn't supposed to drive. But my mom and my dad both worked during the days. While they were at work I often drove to school. Even before I got my truck, I remember a few times I stole my mom's '68 Buick Riviera—a beautiful, classic car—and drove to junior high school. *Nobody* drove in *junior* high school. The parking lot was just for teachers.

I loved my truck. I worked on it for years, adding improvements. It had running boards on it. It had no color; it was primer color—not gray but primer brown. And I had attached these chrome Thrush pipes, you know, side pipes under the running boards. It was a five-window pickup; my mom had made me some Hawaiian curtains for the back window. The upholstery was redone real nice—the side panels I did myself with button tuck, just like here, in the banquette at Feelgoods. I mean, I went and bought the foam, I bought the leather, I bought the buttons. You drill it out, take it up, stick it back, pop it on. And I had a mural on the tailgate of, like, an orange sunset. It was a stick-on. Right on the tailgate so everybody could see it when they drove behind me. Then I had my surf racks across the back of the bed. And big slick tires. It was a really cool-looking truck; the engine was a straight six, it had a three on the tree. Eventually I took that out and mounted a Hurst shifter on the floor. I mean, I did all this shit myself. I attached the pipes. I hooked up the linkage transmission. I was fifteen, sixteen years old. I'd ask my dad questions now and then, but I pretty much did everything myself. I was always good mechanically, always good at figuring out stuff. If something isn't working, no matter what it is, I can always get it fixed. Around the house my wife likes that.

Charter Oak High School was literally a block and a half from Sunflower Junior High. There was a huge park directly across the street—Charter Oak Park. They had a bunch of baseball diamonds, you know, one diamond here and then another baseball diamond facing the other way. It wasn't like a forest, but there were trees and grass and fields and then like benches under the trees. Your standard suburban park, I guess. But this was where you hung out when you went to the high school.

There were different cliques. There were the park stoner guys and another whole surfing clan. And then you had the high school jocks, the preppies, the cheerleaders—the socials, you know, the so-called in crowd. There were all these different cliques; each group had their own turf in the park. On the other side of the park was a continuation high school for kids who'd had to drop out of other schools for various reasons. (Eventually I went there, too, and so did Tami, the mother of my first child, more about whom later.) Those kids were also in the park; they were a wide assortment, none of them exactly on the straight and narrow, sometimes for no fault of their own, it's just the way it was, the breaks. Believe me, I understand that plenty of people had a worse childhood than I did. If I had to pick a clique that I belonged to I would say I was a park hang-out stoner guy. But part of the reason I was even in the park all the time was because I had to actually cut through the park to go to and from school. My house was on the other side.

I think the first time I got high on marijuana I was with a girl. She was kind of like my first girlfriend. Her name was Penny Panknin. We were at her house. And I think we had a joint or a couple joints or something and smoked them and fooled around. That was the first time I got high.

The second time I had pot mixed with PCP, a horse tranquilizer known on the street as angel dust. I remember the first time I tried it. I was with four friends in a car at a drive-in theater, watching

Silver Streak, a hilarious movie with Richard Pryor and Gene Wilder. My friend John Marshall handed the pipe to me; I didn't know how much to smoke. And I sure wasn't gonna be a puss wad and ask. I just toked it down, big-time. I ended up getting so fucked up that I could hardly move or speak. Honestly, that was one high that I *wanted* to see come to an end. I remember we all freaked out when a security guard came up and knocked on the window. John rolled down the window and the smoke billowed out.... I was sure we were going to jail.

But all the guard did was ask John to take his foot off the brake. His red brake lights were disturbing the people behind us at the drive-in.

After that I got out of the car and staggered toward the snack bar, which was located at the rear of the drive-in. Even though I was fucked up, I was totally munched out, hungry as hell. The girl who served me must have thought she was dealing with an idiot, because I could hardly speak. I ended up having to point at the stuff I wanted. I got a big box of popcorn and some sodas, but I ended up spilling everything on the endless walk back to the car. It felt like I was on one of those primitive plank bridges over a gorge. I was lucky to even find the car. The next day I smoked more. Mostly because it was there.

Soon after that I got turned on to white cross pills, a pharmaceutical brand of speed, I think it was, a little white pill with a cross on the top. It came in a little foil packet. I think they used to sell them to truckers and shit back in the day when they called speed goofballs. When combined with angel dust and pot, the white crosses made me into a frothing maniac. Totally incapacitated.

I was fifteen. I was a freshman. We'd get fucked up on something every day. We'd do it in the park after school. I don't ever remember having to scour around for drugs. Everybody was doing it, you know, it was kind of there. It was the times, the mid-seventies. It was like whoever had something, they shared it with you. You just tried it. I don't even really remember paying for it. Maybe five dollars here or there. Or I would just buy joints and they were like a dollar or something. You'd spend your lunch money on drugs. And then you would go to English class, like, lost in space. The teacher would ask me something and I'd stare back at her. *Hello?* I remember smoking angel dust before school one time and just walking the hallways and not knowing where I was, bouncing into things, 'cause you hallucinate on that shit. Once I got sent to the principal for being too fucked up in class. They found me a couple hours later walking aimlessly around the football field.

When I met Tami, I had broken my leg at a skate park in Glendora—for some reason she found it cute or sexy or whatever that I was a crip. We ended up having sex in my truck in the parking lot one afternoon. It was really hot that day. I still remember the feeling of the sun shining down on my ass. I actually didn't really like her at first; I liked her friend. A group of us hung out at the park. I liked this girl Laurie. Laurie Ruck. Tami was her friend. I don't know how, but somehow I ended up with Tami and not Laurie. But I ended up dating Tami for a while. Seeing her. You know, we were having sex on a regular basis. I dated a bunch of girls in high school. Since my trusting (or disinterested?) parents were at work all day, I'd take girls home during lunch break. This one girl was named Candi Hooker—I shit you not. Her father had invented Hooker headers for racing cars. What was the guy thinking when he named her? I always wondered.

Meanwhile, my friend John Marshall and I started going to this roller-skating rink not far from school. We would try to pick up girls there. For some reason we got it in mind to sign up for this lip-synching contest they had. We really got into it. We dressed up in bell-bottom flares and polyester shirts. Some people say we wore huge wigs, but I don' t remember that part. We did a Bachman-

Turner Overdrive song, "Let It Ride." It was like air guitar–type stuff. That's when I realized I liked to perform. I jumped around onstage, danced, threw the microphone around. The crowd ate it up. Particularly the girls. Not only did we win our first contest—I got laid that night.

Next we went to another rink in the Valley. We wore different outfits and did "You Really Got Me" by the Kinks. And we won again! Soon we were lip-synching all over—there was a rink in Rancho Cucamonga, a mall in Diamond Bar; all these different places held contests. I've always said, "I'm an entertainer." There is a bit of ham in me, I guess. I remember when the first Van Halen album came out. It was Halloween; I dressed up like David Lee Roth and did "You Really Got Me." I came in second. It was all lip-synching, no singing. But the crowds were real. They weren't exactly showing their tits yet, but the seeds were definitely sown. Later I remember Van Halen came to town; they were playing at the Long Beach Arena on their very first tour, and I was selling T-shirts outside to make money. But I could hear them playing inside. And I remember saying to myself, *God, I wonder what they're doing in there right now. I wonder what's going on.* And I remember fantasizing about being inside that arena and wondering what it would be like to be up on a stage that size, with a real band, really singing.

Two months after the last time I hooked up with Tami, she came to me and told me she was pregnant. And she said she wanted to keep the baby. Just like that. It hit me in the gut. I mean, I felt a responsibility for the whole thing. It's burned into you, you know, you have to *do the right thing.* I felt like I was supposed to love this girl I hardly knew and make a family. I didn't really love her. I didn't even want a steady girlfriend—I was having way too much fun (and success) fucking whoever I wanted.

But when I realized that she was really going to have the baby, I tried to make it work; I tried to be just a regular doting boyfriend.

I spent a lot of time with her; I was there for her when she was kicked out of school—they didn't allow pregnant girls in class in those days.

My son, Neil Jason Wharton, was born October 3, 1978. My own birthday is February 8, 1961. You can do the math yourself. I was a junior. No matter how you look at it, I was a kid with a kid.

I was working as a roadie to make some extra money, loading equipment for a Runaways concert, when my mom wheeled into the parking lot and told me it was official: I was a dad. The reality didn't really set in, however, until I actually saw this little life I had made. I couldn't believe the sensations I was feeling. It was way too intense to even believe. I looked at him and fell instantly in love. And then I think I probably went out somewhere and got really fucked up. I can't remember. I couldn't fuckin' believe it. I didn't know what the fuck to do with a kid. It was a big joke around school: I was the only kid at Charter Oak High paying child support. Only it didn't feel like a joke to me.

In the beginning I really tried. I tried to be the boyfriend, husband figure, whatever. Father figure. I was so young. Tami was cool. We always got along. She never did anything wrong to me, *ever.* She was a cool girl. I liked her; I did. I just wasn't ready to be a dad. Looking back, I wish I had been there more. But I couldn't be. When Neil was born, it was hard to have that responsibility. Actually, my mom kind of took that responsibility on for me. For a while Tami lived at my parents' house. Eventually I moved out, started living somewhere else. I mean I did try to make a go of it for, for a little while. But it just, I just couldn't do it.

As an escape, I guess, I started surfing more than ever. It was so peaceful. The drive to the beach, a couple of joints, and then it was just you and your buddies and the waves, the adrenaline rush of surfing. If you're not from the coast and you've never surfed, maybe you've snowboarded. It's something like that, I imagine.

Going downhill fast on a board. The ocean was a long way from where we lived. We had to be dedicated. We'd pile in my truck or somebody's car and drive to the coast. It took like an hour, depending on traffic. Sometimes I wouldn't even go to school. I would actually throw my surfboard behind my back wall and I'd be like, "Okay, Mom, I'm going to school." And I'd just go around the back of the house, pick up my surfboard, and then drive off. I'd pick up my friends; we'd go down to Huntington Beach, Seal Beach. I didn't ditch class every day. I didn't miss school for weeks at a time. It was more if like it was a particularly beautiful day, a great day for surfing. And we'd be like fuck it. It was like a *Ferris Bueller's Day Off* situation.

I wasn't really that good a surfer, but I was good enough. There was a surf team from the school, too. We'd surf against other schools and stuff. It was informal, but it was still a team. After the meets or anytime really we liked to drink. I remember taking a thing of orange juice and a pint of vodka and pouring out some of the orange juice, pouring in the pint. One time I passed out from drinking too much. I actually woke up several hours later on the beach. When I'd passed out I had my hand across my chest. By the time I woke up, I was all sunburned . . . and there was an image of my hand burned into my chest. I got so sick that day. To this day I still can't stand the smell of vodka orange juice. I mean it stuck with me that long. I got so sick. It was, like, traumatic obviously.

A big milestone of high school for me was the time, during freshman year, that somebody stole my surfboard racks. His name was Horace. He was an asshole. A football player. This one time I came out to my truck at lunchtime and I noticed somebody had stolen my racks. I'm pretty sure I was amped up on speed and dust at the time. This was just, like, before shop class. Being pissed off, I obsessively looked in everybody's car until I found my surfboard racks in the back of this guy Horace's car.

Horace was a barrel-chested muscle head who was constantly victimizing underclassmen and anyone else who came within range of his beady eyes. I went looking for him and found him inside school, walking with a bunch of the football players in the hallway. I confronted him, you know? I was, like, "Did you fuckin' take my surf racks, you fuckin' asshole?"

He looked at me and lied to my face. He was like, "No. Fuck *you.*"

So I go, "You know what? Fuck you, motherfucker." And *boom*! I fucking punched him in the face and knocked him out cold. I can still see his eyes rolling back in his head. And then he dropped to the floor like a slab of meat and banged his coconut. It was just this sickening hollow sound, you know? Like *craaaak!* And this was a big, big football guy, you know? And he went down like a ton. And all his friends were in shock.

I just stood there. I think I was shocked, too. And totally tweaked.

Then the bell rang, so I went to class.

Not even ten minutes later, here comes the principal. He looks at my hand. My knuckles were bleeding. It was an open-and-shut case. They actually had to call an ambulance for the guy 'cause he was unconscious when they found him. He had a broken nose and a broken jaw.

I was suspended for two weeks. But when I got back...The funny thing was...all the football players actually liked me after that. They hated that guy. I became, like, an honorary jock. One of the players came up and said, you know, "I wish I did that a long time ago." Nobody ever, ever fucked with me after that.

Partially because of some of the new jock friends I made, when spring came I decided to go out for the varsity baseball team. To everybody's surprise, I made it. I was pretty proud of myself. I mean I came from nowhere; people are serious about their baseball in

California—all these kids had played club ball for years. I played center field and first base. I was an okay hitter, but I was a *great* fielder. No ball could get past me. Everybody was proud of me, talking about what a great asset I was going to be to the team. Even my parents were proud of me. Baseball was something they could understand. Maybe their son was gonna turn out okay after all, you know? Maybe this would be just the thing I needed after venturing down the path of drugs, surfing, and girls.

But then the coach told me I had to cut my hair if I wanted to play.

I thought about it. I really did. But my hair was pretty important to me then, as now. It was long, down below my shoulders, a sandy blond color. I wanted to play ball, but I didn't want to, you know what I mean? What I *really* didn't want was to become one of the jocks. I didn't want to alter my appearance. I didn't want to have to change the person I was. I just wanted to play ball. (Not to mention the fact that I was good enough to make their team, right? And as a *freshman*.)

But I wasn't going to cut my hair. No way.

So that was it. I quit the team.

Who knows? If I decided to cut my hair I could've been a pro ballplayer. Maybe my life would've went that way. Maybe my life would have been a lot different. But I decided to keep my hair—I made the choice about what was important to me.

And wouldn't you know: It was literally my hair that ended up getting me into rock 'n' roll.

Chapter 3
BEER DRINKERS AND HELL-RAISERS

Growing up, I never thought for one minute I'd end up in music—I had no idea what I wanted to be. I never even thought about it. Sure there were daydreams. What kid in those days didn't imagine what it would be like to be Magic Johnson, Buzz Aldrin, Mick Jagger? But me ending up where I did? I would have bet a million dollars against it. I know all my teachers would have, too. And probably my parents if you asked. Let's face it. I was going nowhere fast.

It all started when James Alverson showed up in school. He was a transfer. This was the beginning of my junior year at Charter Oak High School, a month or so before my son, Neil, was born. James was a long-haired rocker guy—he looked like a surfer, you know, with blond curly hair. He fit right in. I'd seen him in the hallway, but that was kind of it. Never talked to him. Never gave him one minute's thought. He was just the new kid in school, you know?

He was obviously a guitar player; he wanted everyone to know. He carried his axe with him wherever he went; he was always playing it. One day he comes up and starts talking to me about forming a band. He didn't know anything about my history of lip-synching. Nobody really knew about that; it was a while ago. I had no reputation for singing. I had no reputation at all, really, for doing anything. (Except that people knew not to fuck with me, like I said, since my fight with the football douche bag.) I was a stoner park guy, popular with the chicks but pretty much under the radar. But right out of nowhere James just walked up and he asked me, "Would you like to sing in a band?"

And I'm like, "Why did you ask?"

And he's like, "'Cause you have the longest hair in school."

It *was* long. I mean, longer than it is now. A lot more volume. And maybe because I had made the choice between my hair and baseball, I was definitely letting my freak flag fly, if you know what I mean. My hair was a statement I proudly wore—*I'm gonna do whatever the fuck I wanna do.* There weren't that many long-haired people in school, so I guess I kind of stood out—most people's hair was just maybe touching their shoulders.

So there you have it. Had I decided to play baseball, maybe some other guy from Charter Oak would be writing this book.

Next James recruited our classmate Robert Stokes for drums. I can't remember the name of the bass player. There were a couple. The longest one was Joe Marks. Both of them were surfer dudes with long sideburns. Beginning with our first jam, in somebody's garage, I can't remember whose it was, it felt pretty good; we just clicked. We were a tight little band. James modeled his playing after Eddie Van Halen; he was quirky and animated. Somehow my voice complemented his driving, high-octave licks—maybe because I sounded like Robin Zander with his balls being pinched. James was the unquestioned leader. He owned the PA system. He came up with the name Rock Candy. In typical sixteen-year-old-style, he thought it would be cooler to spell it weird. Thus, Rockandi was born.

People ask me all the time how I became a singer. It's a good question. I never sang in the school choir. I don't really remember ever going to church. I never even sang in the shower. Nobody in my family sings. I never took a lesson. I never knew what I was doing. Basically I faked it from the jump. When I think about it now, I guess I just built on the lip-synching—I had the act down; all I needed was the voice to go with it. It was all about the attitude. What they call "selling the song." Out of that came the voice—not that this was conscious on my part. I didn't even think about it; I just did it. That's pretty much another subtitle for this book; it kind of defines my whole life. I didn't even think about it; I just did it. So it was with singing, too. What came out is what came out.

At first I was just imitating other singers. I think I have a gift for mimicking. Like if I'm singing a Cheap Trick song, I can sound like Zander. It's not me singing—it's me trying to impersonate somebody else. Now of course, after thirty years, I have my own style. I have this instrument—it's my voice. I'm a professional. But back then I was just singing in other people's voices, you know? That's sort of the evolution you go through as an artist. You start with imitation and it leads to your own individual style. It's the same in classical music and in jazz, probably in all the arts. I never even *knew* I could sing until I actually tried it at that first practice. And then it was like, *Wow, I'm not that bad!* Then I remember after that, sitting in my truck with eight-track tapes, writing down lyrics. Now that I think about it, that was probably more writing than I'd ever done in my life. I don't think I had any problems with it, either.

Once we'd gotten an entire set together we started playing people's backyards. That's really how we learned to play together. That's the best place to practice, playing in front of people. It's never the same in the garage or the rehearsal studio. We'd get someone to throw a party at their house—we'd find out whose parents were going to be away for the weekend. We'd tell them we'd play at their house for free if they would get some beer and stuff. We'd take care of the music and the chicks, because all the chicks would come to hear the band; there wasn't much else happening in Covina, let's face it.

We charged a dollar a head to get in, all you could drink, whatever. We'd spread the word at school—we designed flyers; me and James would go out in the streets and stick them to anything that didn't move. We played AC/DC, Zeppelin, Bad Company, Black Sabbath. "I Want You to Want Me," by Cheap Trick; "Sweet Emotion," by Aerosmith; "Smokin' in the Boy's Room," by Brownsville Station (which, along with the power ballad "Home Sweet Home," really ended up saving our asses on that piece-of-shit *Theatre of Pain* album). We also did some songs by the English glam-rock band The Sweet.

The parties would be packed. There'd be like four hundred kids—four hundred bucks for the band, a hundred bucks each for doing what we loved to do. We'd keep on playing until we ran out of songs, and then we'd call the police on ourselves and complain about the noise. The cops would arrive, shut the party down, and toss everyone out into the street. And we would take off with the money (and some of the chicks), leaving whichever poor kid whose house we'd commandeered with a disaster area on his hands.

Back then, at these weekend parties, we weren't doing it because we imagined someday we'd be rock stars. At least I didn't. James wanted to be a rock star and he made no bones about it. But for me, in high school (and really, in a way, for the rest of my life), being in a band meant free beer and a steady supply of girls. That's why I was into it. Girls wanted to get with the guys onstage, especially the singer. That was pretty much it. What else was important in high school? That was my *entire* reason for getting into a band. Fate has obviously been at work on me. To some degree, I'm the object lesson: What happens to someone who always takes the path of least resistance? I have always been someone who absolutely goes with the flow. I've never been the type to swim upstream. It's just too much effort. I don't want to hassle. I'd just as soon cut bait.

One time *my* parents went away for the weekend. I decided to stage a Rockandi gig in our backyard. Performing was like a drug to me. Nothing else was as important. It was the gateway to everything good in my life: getting high, getting lots of attention, getting laid. As it happened on this night, things turned out like the plot of some B movie we've all seen a million times. Just as the party kicked into high gear...my mom and dad decided to come home early from their trip!

There were like four hundred kids partying in the backyard when they pulled up. I thought they would kill me.

To my amazement, they didn't break up the party.

They joined right in.

The next thing I knew, my mom was serving drinks; Dad had a great time dancing with the girls. If I had to explain the whole thing I'd probably say that maybe they were pretty impressed with my band. They'd never heard me sing before. I'm sure they thought we were just a bullshit garage band or something. After the party, they never said a word to me about it. But I've always wondered if that was it, that they were actually proud of me. I guess they would have told me if they were. Who knows? Some people aren't good at telling their feelings. I guess I get it honestly. I wasn't about to ask them or to fish for compliments, you know. That's never been my style.

I played with Rockandi for almost three years. I'm surprised James never made it to the big time. As a guitar player he was as good as a lot of people I know who are famous now. I think maybe his problem was he never committed to himself. He tried to change with the times instead of sticking to one clear vision. Like for a while he tried to imitate Eddie Van Halen—he even had the striped guitar and stuff—and he was amazing. Then when New Wave came in, he cut all his hair off and wore skinny ties. And then New Wave went out again—you know what I'm saying? It's like he didn't know who he was. If he'd have stuck with rock, he probably would've been in a big band.

Say what you want about me, I've always stayed true to the music I love. I never tried to change with the times; I never rode the trends—well, there was that solo album with the Dust Brothers, but that was more a case of "before its time." Just because it's popular doesn't mean it's for you—you know what I mean? I know who I am as a performer. I sing rock music. That's what I do. I knew it then and I know it now. Like somebody once said: "Keep it simple, stupid." It works for me.

James Alverson
Rockandi Lead Guitarist and Founder

My dad was a technical writer for the aerospace industry, but he really wanted to be an actor and a photographer. He did a lot of little theater. He played bagpipes. I grew up going to Disneyland and all the local fairs; he played in a bagpipe band; he'd do funerals. I'm real familiar with bagpipe music. He also played guitar and banjo. He was a musician, a self-taught artist type. I sort of think of my parents as beatniks, like they were hippies without the drugs.

I took guitar lessons in first grade. Then I quit because it hurt my fingers. Then my brother started playing, and I got jealous, so I started playing. This was in '72, '73. I was twelve or thirteen. I'm one year older than Vince, almost exactly. At one point, three of us in the band all had birthdays in February.

My folks owned this house in the La Puente area. It was a really shitty neighborhood, near El Monte, but we had lots of toys, you know, everything we needed as kids, and we would go away a lot on vacation. So it was kind of the trade-off—by living in this shitty neighborhood we could have a higher standard of living. But in like '76, '77, my dad was suddenly, like "Fuck this, I'm going to pursue an acting career full-time." He up and sells the house. And we all move to this rented place in Covina. And he pays up one year of rent and he goes, "Okay, we have one year here. And I can't tell you what's going to happen after that." He wanted to pursue the acting and writing thing. This was his last big shot. I was seventeen, going into my last year of high school.

I transferred to Charter Oak High School. Boy, what a change. Where I was from it was the closest thing to an inner-city school. There were a lot of gangs, a lot of violence. I mean I'd seen a lot of stuff. People getting knifed and beaten up—I got chased myself; I had guns pointed at me.... I was in this gang-infested neighborhood and that's for three years of high school.

And then I move to this all-white neighborhood and it's like culture shock. Most of the kids were white. There was probably only one black kid in the whole school. And there were no Mexican gangbangers. All the Hispanics, if there were any, were you know, assimilated, I suppose you would say. So that was weird for me just from the beginning. Because here I am, my senior year in a brand-new school. I didn't know anybody. And I was kind of shy, so I only talked to people who talked to me. I ended up always talking to these strange outcasts—which I was one, too. I had this long blond hair and I dressed probably a little differently, and I was from the bad side of the tracks. Plus I was the new kid in the senior class. It was not a recipe for success.

I remember seeing Vince walking through the hallway. He had longer hair; most of the kids didn't. And I had long hair. And I was always looking for a singer because that was always one of the problems of getting a band together—it was impossible to get a singer. I saw Vince in the hallway and we probably nodded at each other or something because we both had long hair, but probably both of us were too shy to break the ice. At some point somebody introduced us, or they told me about him; they told me that he played in a band or sang or something or had a guitar. I remember the first time we spoke... there was this park right across the street where all the kids would go and smoke pot. It was called Charter Oak Park, and he was over there and he was going to show me his guitar in the back of his 240Z. He was with his girlfriend at the time, Tami. It was one of those cheapie little guitars. And I go, "That's nice, that's nice," you know, trying to be friendly, even though he had this bullshit toy guitar. And that's how we kinda like started talking.

Vince told me that first day that he played in a band, but I didn't believe him. My brother had been in bands—I was pretty savvy to who was what. I'd seen a lot of bands. He just didn't seem like he was talking the talk. It was really one of those little beginner guitars. So I knew he was making it up, whatever. But it didn't matter. I needed a singer. I asked him if he'd sing, and he said he would sing, and I said, "Well, let's get together." So we probably exchanged numbers; I don't remember the exact thing. And I put together some songs; he brought this drummer named Robert Stokes. I brought Danny Monge to play bass. I knew him from my old school. He was from Nicaragua. He was a character; he got on my nerves. It was hard to find a bass player at first. We went through a couple before Joe Marks ended up taking over. He was Vince's buddy, too. I remember the first rehearsal. I remember playing "Hot Legs." That was like the first time I got to hear Vince's voice.

He was a little bit of a natural; it was obvious to me he wasn't a singer, but I thought he could be a singer, you know? He was really timid, real quiet. I thought his intonation was pretty good. And I thought he looked pretty good. He had long hair and he wasn't completely hideous—you know, like a lot of guys are. The thing was, I was a huge Van Halen fan, right from the early days, before they were big stars. I remember my brother taking me down to the Whisky and watching Eddie Van Halen and David Lee Roth and the whole band. Roth was just phenomenal. I mean he was just the greatest frontman. It was a fun band to watch and they didn't take themselves too seriously, which is something that always bothered me about certain musicians. They kicked ass. That was my model. And I thought Vince even looked a little like Roth. I remember trying to teach Vince how to sing, basically. I remember I told him, "Just pretend like you're yelling at your sister, or your parents, you know. Just *scream*." I thought he had it in him. I don't think Vince had ever sung before, anywhere. Probably in the shower, or something. But he was a pretty quick study and he was dedicated.

Rockandi was the first real popular band I was in. The other bands I was in were just kinda like I was just learning. This band, I had a plan; I knew exactly what kind of material we needed to do. I had a focus—it was quite successful. I mean, I wasn't a big Led Zeppelin fan, but I knew that's what everybody wanted to hear. We played a ton of Zep and Vince did it okay. We also did some ZZ Top and some Aerosmith. I remember we played the school for our first gig. It was at lunch hour. We played, like, three or four songs. It was really cool. It was really, really cool. As a seventeen-year-old, lemme tell you, I thought I'd found heaven.

When I met Tommy Lee he was playing in this band called US 101. We used to rehearse at the same studio down in Covina; the owner used to put on these showcases for local bands. Vince and I worked around the place in exchange for rehearsal time. I think Tommy's parents paid for their time. US 101 was absolutely horrible. We used to make fun of them 'cause they were so shitty. I mean they were just like, they were like some church band where the parents put them all together, right? So they could all barely play and it was just—oh my god. And Rockandi, we were like these bad kids, you know, the juvenile delinquents or whatever.

Tommy was maybe a little bit spoiled. His parents were definitely upper middle class. He always had all the stuff. They were pretty horrible. We used to just laugh at them. They were maybe like what you call soccer parents today. They were like all involved. My parents supported me, but they didn't follow me around. Vince's parents supported us, but they didn't follow us around. But you know in Tommy's band their parents would take the equipment for them and help them set it up. It was just—it was just the opposite of us.

Tami fuckin' hated me. I was dragging him into this world where he was going to get a lot of attention. She wasn't a bad-looking girl, but she wasn't a great-looking girl. She had a lot of attitude and that may have been what attracted Vince. There were definitely prettier girls at school. Way prettier girls. Our school had some very beautiful women, some of whom probably would have never ever had anything to do with him because he was a stoner guy—a lot of the pretty girls were cheerleaders and that type.

I remember when he found out Tami was pregnant. That was horrible. I remember him sitting on the curb just bumming out. He was sick for weeks. He was just physically sick. It was just bad. I felt so bad for him. He didn't say much about it, though. Vince was an introvert. He really doesn't talk much about stuff. But he thinks a lot about stuff and you could tell it was really bugging him. And I just remember thinking, *Oh shit, he's done. This is over. He's done.* Because I knew he wasn't too serious about Tami. He wasn't ever serious about one girl. I can't even see Vince staying with one girl for any amount of time, ever.

We played all the backyard parties and we really got popular. We made money and we had some experiences that to this day I think about and it makes me chuckle. I'll tell people the stories about the lines of cop cars coming to bust our party, or all the bass players we went through, 'cause we went through quite a few, or how one of the guys got arrested one night. Our band ruined backyard parties in that area for any band after that. We'd have a thousand people at a backyard. One party we played in Covina, we were in this fair-sized backyard. By the end of the party, all the fences around the backyard were flattened. People had climbed up on the roof of the garage and fell through the roof. Somebody jumped off the roof onto my mom's station wagon. When I walked out to go get in my car and start loading stuff, I remember looking down the street and seeing this line of cop cars rolling toward the house. I mean there must've been fifteen, twenty, thirty cop cars—a line of them that stretched all the way down. After we'd been playing around for a while, there was a rumor that whenever the cops found one of our flyers they'd put it up in their precinct station and mark "BYOB" across it, meaning "Bring Your Own Billy club."

I know Vince always says he never wanted to be a rock star, but he was pretty dedicated. I look back fondly on some of the things that him and I did to push that band forward. You know, we would cut class and go at lunchtime with a thousand flyers that we had made up—there was a kid at another school that would make them for us in his shop in his printing class. He would draw these elaborate flyers. We would drive all over the place, going to other high schools, plastering all the cars in the parking lot—*every* car would get a flyer. We were *dedicated* to making this work.

In those days, I don't remember him drinking or drugging much—he probably would have a beer or two maybe at some of these parties, but I never saw him drunk. I can't even ever remember one time he was drunk. I would've frowned upon it, especially while we were playing. He was pretty serious. He wanted to succeed as much as I did.

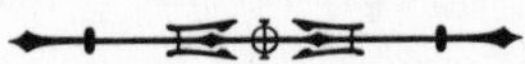

After the baby was born, Tami moved into my house with my parents and tried to make a go of it. I lived at home for a while and then I would leave for a while; I was basically crashing here and there. I just wanted to be out on my own. Sometimes I would go to my parents' house for meals and shit, or to see the baby, but basically, I was outta there. Who said eighteen was a magic age of maturity? And it's not like I moved that far away. I was literally just blocks away from my parents' house. Like here's the high school, and here's the house I'm living in, and here's my parents' house. All I had was my clothes—everything that I owned was in a Henry Weinhard's beer case box. That was it. That was sophomore year. By the end of the year I'd basically dropped out of school.

My junior year, I really stopped going to school. For a little while I went to the continuation school—Tami was going there, too. Then for the start of my senior year I transferred to Royal Oak High School, which was the next school over. I was sweeping up this recording/rehearsal studio in exchange for Rockandi being able to practice there. It was through them that I got the occasional roadie gigs, too. I used the rehearsal studio address as my legal address, so all my official school mail went to the studio. My parents had no idea what was going on because all notices and report cards went there.

As everybody knows by now, Tommy Lee was a student at Royal Oak. His name back then was Tom Bass. He was born in the Greek capital city of Athens while his dad was serving as a sergeant in the U.S. Army. The family moved to the States and settled in Covina while Tommy was still a baby. His mom had been a beauty queen and a model, Miss Greece 1957. They didn't use the term MILF in those days, but she was one. When she and Tommy's dad first began dating, the story goes, they could only communicate by drawing pictures. No doubt they found other ways, too. She cleaned houses now to help make ends meet; she didn't speak very much English. Like my dad, Tommy's father was a mechanic. For a time he worked for the LA County Road Department, repairing trucks and tractors.

I'd known Tommy even before I transferred. He was in a rival band. They called themselves US 101, after the freeway that bisected greater Los Angeles. Later that band semimorphed into another band, Suite 19. When Rockandi started playing backyard parties, Tommy's band was also playing backyard parties in our area. That's how we met, how we first started hanging around. Eventually we also played the couple of clubs in the area. There was one called the Wood Sound in Monrovia—once or twice I think we even played on the same bill. We were like friendly rivals from two different bands. We would play one party and they would play another party. We were like the only two bands in the area.

By the time I went to Royal Oak, I think I was already living with Tommy. Maybe that's one of the reasons I decided to go there. Tommy and I were really close at that point. Really close. Literally. At first I was sleeping in his van. And then I was sleeping on the floor of his bedroom. What happened was his mom found out that there was some guy sleeping in her son's van and she came out and said, in her broken English, "Why you don't come sleep in house?" I will never forget her doing that. Her kindness is something I will always remember. In later years my mom and Tommy's mom would become superclose as they circled the globe following our concerts.

Tommy and I hung hard. We were tight. We'd ditch school and go to the recording studio and hang out or jam. We'd sit in his van with *Highway to Hell* cranked to the max. Another of our favorites was the *Lovedrive* album by the Scorpions. ("Another Piece of Meat" is covered on *Tattoos & Tequila*.) Tommy was a year younger than me. His mom made us meals. I thought of him as a sort of little brother.

My relationship with Tommy is, well, um . . . it's funny . . . It makes me a little bit sad thinking about this right now. 'Cause nowadays me and Tommy are so far apart. And I don't really know any way to bridge the distance. Tommy's an egomaniac. He has to be the center of attention; if he isn't, he'll leave. If he's somewhere and there's someone he thinks is a bigger star than himself and they won't talk to him, he'll leave. That's why he marries and hangs out with the girls that he does. Think about it. Heather Locklear? Pam Anderson? He loves fame; if he didn't have the fame he would slice his throat; he couldn't live without Tommy Lee being Tommy Lee. Down deep he's a fucking great guy, a sensitive, nice guy, but you really have to peel the layers that he's built up over the years to get down to that niceness that he used to have when he was a kid, when we used to fuckin' sit in his van and crank up the music. That was the *cool* Tommy. Now he's the *too cool* Tommy. If you watch him through the years, he's one of those guys that has to fit into every trend. He had to have a Mohawk when everybody had a Mohawk; he had dreads when everybody else had dreads. Whatever's in, that's what he wants to be. He's a year younger than me, but he still tries to fit in like a teenager. It's like if a mature lady walks into a bar and she's trying to compete with the twenty-two-year-olds, she starts looking ridiculous, you know what I mean...?

Whatever. Another thing I wouldn't have imagined in a million years: that me and Tommy would be estranged. If there's some way back from the quagmire, I don't know.

From there, basically, my high school career sort of fizzled out. I just sort of stopped going. Between rehearsing with Rockandi, getting high, going surfing, hanging out with Tommy, and dealing with Tami and Neil, there wasn't much time left over for classes. I was young, foolish, and headstrong. I thought I already knew everything. I was anxious to get on with life. The fact that I'd fathered a child was more than I could register—it was a nagging pain that needed to be blotted out. Thinking about stuff hurt, in other words, so I just tried not to think. I guess I summed it up pretty well in *The Dirt*, when I was quoted as saying this:

> I did not think that I'd ever get taught a lesson, because I had no use for lessons. I didn't read, I didn't write, I didn't think. I just lived. Whatever happened in the past happened;

whatever's going to happen in the future is going to happen anyway. Whatever is happening in the present moment was always what I was interested in.

Joe Marks
Friend, Rockandi Roadie, Rockandi Bassist

Vince and I went to Charter Oak High School together. He's a year younger than me. I think his birthday is this week. I lived in Covina. My dad ran a drilling and blasting company—it was my uncle's company and my dad ran a good portion of it. He was in charge of the crews and he did all the blasting. At the time, economically speaking, we didn't know what we were. We all had enough, but none of us were spoiled.

I was the kind of guy who was friends with everybody at school. I didn't have any clique. I played some football, so I had those kinds of friends, but I also went to the park and smoked weed with all the stoners. But senior year I got kicked off the football team for—well, it was an indiscretion. I was taking a leak out on the football field and one of the cheerleaders walked by and they saw, you know, little Elvis. And that was the end of my football career, which I was kinda losing interest in anyway. By then I was really starting to get into playing my bass.

Charter Oak Park, across from the high school, was like the drug capital of the world. That's where everybody went back then and bought, like, five-finger lids for like five bucks, and everybody would go there and get stoned. I wasn't a big stoner, but all my friends were, so I kinda went over there. I was more of a drinker. Vince was there. I'd run into him there a few times—I think we had the same PE class, too. We really didn't start hanging out together that much until *The Rocky Horror Picture Show* craze got started. They used to play it at midnight every weekend at the theater downtown in Covina. I bumped into Vince there and that's when we started talking. Rockandi had already started. I think they'd just done a gig at our school. I think it was the first time they ever played out in public and they played at our high school.

And they had this bass player, he just didn't fit in. Vince and James were these long-hair guys, and the bass player had a big 'fro of hair—he looked like an old hippie, you know? He kinda didn't fit in.

After I met Vince officially at *The Rocky Horror Picture Show*, we became friends. I said, "Hey, I like the band," and he said, "Want to come down and check out the rehearsals?" So I did and I even started you know, helping with the equipment or whatever—whatever needed doing I'd help them. Finally, after they went through another bass player, I started playing with them.

Vince and I became friends out of the band, too. At that time life was just absolutely nothing but fun. He skateboarded; I skateboarded; we surfed. We were the California guys. Vince was kicked out of Charter Oak and ended up going to Royal Oak High School. I had a Volkswagen Bug. It was a '69. And I used to pick him up from there. I'd have both of our surfboards on my car. And then we'd just go straight to the beach and he'd miss school. Or I'd pick him up in the morning behind his house. And then he'd go home and he'd pretend that he'd been in school all day.

The truck by then was broken down. He left it in his driveway forever and then he got the Z. It was like a 240Z. And he used to, he just tore that car up. The boy liked driving fast from like day one. He was like Ricky Bobby in the movie *Talladega Nights*. He always enjoyed driving fast. It was a little scary to be in the car with him. He handled the car well, though.

Once we did a battle of the bands at the place that we used to rehearse. Rockandi played and Tommy's band US 101 played. All they played was like Journey and Boston and Styx and stuff like that. We were more Van Halen, grungy, bluesy stuff—we were two different kind of bands. But I think Tommy really wanted to be in a band like Rockandi instead of US 101. He was having fun, but the parents were all in it. US 101 seemed like Little League.

I kinda liked Tommy. We actually got along pretty good. He was like two years younger than me when we met; then I saw him play a couple years later and I started thinking, *This guy's pretty good, he's improved a lot, maybe we should audition him.* And so we did. There was this time when Robert Stokes, our drummer, wasn't doing anything with the band—there was some sort of downtime. So we auditioned Tommy for the hell of it. He actually even helped us kinda write a song, but James and Vince didn't want him, so they said no.

And check this out: Tommy's mom got so pissed off that Tommy was auditioning with us and possibly quitting whatever little church band he was with at the time, US 101, that she threatened to kick him out of the house. Tommy's mom hated Vince. Vince had this reputation of being like a coke dealer or something. When he got kicked out of Charter Oak they all said it was because he was a coke dealer. But he wasn't. All he was, was just a guy who didn't show up to school and you know smoked weed at lunchtime. I think after his mom kicked him out; he was living in his van—I think she kicked him out and let him keep the van. I remember that he was kicked out of the house and he ended up staying up in the hills with Vince and his girlfriend Leah.

Vince's mom loves him the same as ever. From the first day I ever met his parents, it was clear they thought he was the greatest thing ever. They cherished him to death. They weren't too happy with his choices as far as being in a band. And it was hard with him being a father and all. There was a time when his parents were saying either go back to high school or get a job. And if he couldn't do one of those, he had to stop living in their house.

So Vince and I both joined the carpenters' union together. I guess Vince's mom knew someone in the neighborhood who could get us into the carpenters' union. We joined as apprentice carpenters. Our first day on the job was on a freeway build. It was like an overpass where they built these giant forms for the concrete. The company I think was called Kasler.

On our first day, we were carrying scaffolding that had dried concrete on it. You can picture us with our long hair, our hard hats, our T-shirts with the sleeves cut off. We thought we were the shit. And the jeans. So we're still rocking it, but we're getting our ass kicked all day in the heat. I think we lasted about three or four days and then you know we were just wiped out. One day, I'm picking Vince up for work at five in the morning, and we just looked at each other, like, *Do you even want to do this?* And the answer was, *Fuck no*.

We pulled over—I think we went to a Winchell's Donuts, and we sat around and talked about it for maybe ten minutes. And then we agreed. We were like, "Fuck it, we're done. We were so fucking done with being carpenters." 'Cause we were swinging hammers up over our heads, trying to hit these nails that were above us; our arms hurt so bad we kept missing. The supervisor on the job was telling us, "Next time bring a skillet so you can hit those fucking nails." You know, and we were just getting pounded all day—and we were just like, "Forget it. We're done." We waited for his mom and dad to go to work and then we went back to Vince's house; we'd watch *Green Acres* and Vince would make fried-egg sandwiches. And then we'd just sit around and, you know, maybe a couple hours or an hour before his mom would get home we'd clean up the house and split. Then we'd put on our construction clothes and go out and get dirty and then walk back in later, like, "Oh boy, what a rough day. *Whoo!*"

I think that lasted a couple of days. And then Vince's mom figured it out. She goes, "I'm done with you." I remember she said that. She's like, "You're done, Vincent."

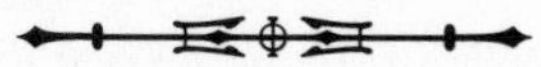

By seventeen, I was out on my own. At one point, me and the bass player, Joe Marks, got jobs with the Kasler Corporation, which built freeway bridges. We'd get up at four in the morning and drive to the site. Building freeway bridges is a lot of work. A *lot* of work. I mean it was a tough, tough job. Climbing up there. Lugging all this heavy stuff into place. It's form work, you know, getting things precisely into place to pour the concrete so they can build these huge bridges in the sky. I was the guy building those things. It was dangerous work, man. We worked there for maybe a couple months.

One day me and Joe got up at four in the morning, just like usual. Just like usual we went and got donuts and coffee. As we headed to the site, something hit us, like, simultaneously. Suddenly we both just looked at each other. And like, simultaneously, we both said, "You know what? Fuck this job." I don't remember what had happened, but something had. It was over. We just made a U-turn and went home. I went back to bed. I remember, I actually went back to bed. It was sweet.

Around that time I met this girl named Leah Graham. I don't remember how I met her, but I have to say one thing: Throughout my whole life, women have always been there for me, even though I have not always been there for women. It is my blessing and my curse, I suppose. Women have always done things for me. They have loved me and put me first. And in return, I have disappointed them in their expectations. But those are *their* expectations. Not reality. It's always been complicated. There are two sides to every story, to every couple, to every coupling. No one tells the truth about themselves, not totally.

In any event, Leah Graham is the girl who had the nickname Lovey in *The Dirt*, which was given to her a few years later by the guys in Mötley Crüe. When I first met her she was hot; she looked like a young Rene Russo. But she was a real druggie. She was shooting up cocaine when nobody was doing that. She was the first person I'd ever heard of doing it. She showed me the first needle I'd ever seen—at least the first one I'd seen outside of a doctor's office. Over time she became pretty haggard looking; that's why the Mötley guys called her Lovey. It referred to Mrs. Howell on the TV show *Gilligan's Island*, the old lady—her husband called her Lovey.

Leah's dad owned an electrical company. She got me a job with him as an apprentice electrician. It was good-paying, union work. And I lived at their house with her in Covina. She was wealthy. The house was up on the mountain, overlooking the whole valley. During the day, especially in the summer, there was a lot of pollution and haze. But at night it was amazing.

I dyed my hair platinum blond; Leah liked to help me fluff it up by teasing it and using Aqua Net hairspray—it would be just *towering*, six to eight inches high, a huge tower of hair. Back in the early days with Rockandi, I was really into white. White satin pants, white leg warmers, white slippers by Capezio, a white T-shirt ripped up the sides, sewn together with lace. It was also Leah who bought me my first pair of leather pants. They set her back five hundred bucks. I ended up wearing them on the cover of Mötley's first album; I had them long enough that wife number three still tells stories about trying them on. Say what you want about leather pants. They fuckin' last.

Leah functioned (when she was functioning) almost like manager of Rockandi. She put ads in papers, got us gigs at Gazzari's, the Starwood, and other places on the Strip. She actually did some really good stuff for us, you know? And of course I was living under her parents' roof, eating their food, fucking their daughter. We spent a lot of time in her bathroom shooting up coke. She had, like, this bedroom suite with its own bathroom. We'd hang out there for hours and hours. She was a stone junkie. After a while she got me hooked, too. We'd be in the bathroom for what seemed like days. Or we'd go to these other people's house. I can't remember their names. It was a whole junkie sex scene.

I liked shooting coke. I mean the rush is great. The whole thing of doing it, you know, the ritual of it, was exciting—just the anticipation of it, waiting my turn, you know? And she was like a big hog, too. 'Cause she'd always be the one doling out the hits. And she'd always make her hits bigger than mine. And I'd be, like, "Waitaminute!" I'd be pissed off. I'd be like, "How come my hit isn't as big as yours?" And she'd be like, "Because I've been doing it longer!"

Wait a minute. Thinking back, the *shooting-up* part didn't come until a little later, when I joined Mötley Crüe. During the Rockandi era, Leah was shooting it, but I'd just be snorting it. I think I was taking a lot of speed then, too, because working as an electrician, you know, I would... well, *everybody* on the crew was taking speed to do the jobs. There is no way you could be shooting up cocaine and still going to work, as I would later find out. Speed was something you did on the job at that particular company at that particular time. Maybe a lot of other companies, too. I tell you, I really needed it. I don't know how I would have survived those days *without* speed. Because I was basically working forty hours a week as a union electrician. And then I was going out at night and playing gigs with Rockandi. Or if I wasn't playing, I'd be out seeing other bands, keeping up with the scene, partying. There was never any time for sleep. I'd go straight from a gig to the job (after changing first, of course). I didn't think the guys on the crew needed to see me in my Capezios. TMI, as they like to say today.

The electrical work was hard. Sometimes I'd be digging ditches—the ditches to put in the underground pipes and stuff that you pull the wires through. Or sometimes I'd be wiring a house or whatever. It was a lot of hours. As the low man on the totem pole, the youngest, I did everything—all the lifting and the bullshit nobody else wanted to do. This was right at the time when drive-thru windows were just getting popular in fast-food restaurants. Leah's dad had this contract to retrofit all of these older McDonald's. Sometimes we would build McDonald's from the ground up. Sometimes we would renovate an old one and put in a drive-thru. Like for one contract we did every

McDonald's in Palm Springs. It took us six weeks. During that job we actually lived down in Palm Springs. I remember we slept during the day and worked at night because of the heat. It was like six dollars an hour, something like that. It doesn't sound like much now, but it seemed like a lot at the time.

As history records, it was just about this time, in the first months of 1981, that Nikki Sixx—born Frank Carlton Serafino Feranna, Jr.—went to the Starwood to catch a band called Suite 19. He needed a new guitar player for his new band...which didn't yet exist. For the moment, he was a band of one, a guy with an idea, a few songs, and a need for at least three other people to make his vision complete.

Nikki was three years older than me. I knew *of* him, but I didn't really *know* him, if you know what I mean. We were both on the scene. Like me and Tommy, he was also from Cali, born in San Jose, CA, to a single mother with a rep for being a little wild. She toured as a backup singer with various artists, including Frank Sinatra. Raised primarily by his grandparents, Nikki became a teenage juvenile delinquent, breaking into neighbors' houses, shoplifting, expelled from school for selling drugs. Like me, Nikki was out living on his own by the age of seventeen. He moved to LA and worked various jobs—a counterman at a liquor store, selling vacuums over the phone—while he auditioned with bands in the hope of becoming a rock star.

After he got turned down by Randy Rhoads, his version of Quiet Riot, and then by Sister, with Blackie Lawless of W.A.S.P., Nikki joined the LA-based glam rockers London, whose major claim to fame was that their singer, Nigel Benjamin, had sung with a late version of Mott the Hoople. Careers have started on less. Nikki is a talented guy, he would have made it somehow or another.

I don't think Nikki has changed much over the years. He still likes to portray himself as the Messiah. Everything is *his.* Everything is his idea. I'll look at him and think, *Fuck! He just loves playing that persona.* And my sentiment is: *I don't really care one way or the other. If he wants to be that, fine.* I do my job, and I fucking have fun. That's how I live my life. But in Nikki's world, he has to be known as the "thinker," or the "creator"; he needs to be seen as Mr. All-Important. Nikki Sixx, tortured soul. And like Tommy, he's another one of those guys who just love the whole fame thing. He wouldn't have been with the tattoo artist Kat Von D if she wasn't famous. And Donna D'Errico before her; she was a huge star at the time he married her. He just really likes to see his face in the paper. He likes the press buzz. He likes being that guy from the band with the famous girlfriends.

I mean, you should read the e-mails he sends about Mötley. He goes: "I've crunched the numbers, and we should do this. . . ." And I'm like, *What? Is he my fucking accountant now? I mean, what the fuck?* He makes these decisions for Mötley Crüe that I think are just stupid. I call him up and I'll be like, "You're the worst businessman in the fucking world. You're a fucking idiot!" And he'll be like, "How can you say that?" And I'll be like, "Because you are a fucking idiot." Just because something looks good on paper with your name on it doesn't mean it's going to work."

I guess what it comes down to is I'm not the same as these guys. Probably I never was. I never aspired to all this. I mean, in my perfect world, I'd be on a beach somewhere drinking a Corona and renting out Jet Skis to the tourists. That's my dream job, by the way. I would be the guy that rents you your Jet Skis at a resort, like say the Caribbean or Hawaii. All I'd have to worry about is to ensure those Jet Skis are running that day. What a great job. That's my retirement plan.

Of course, things get blown out of proportion. I mean me and Nikki; we love each other like fuckin' brothers. He was the best man at my wedding. Come to think of it, I think he's been to all my weddings.

We've been together for so long. It's always been like that with us. Maybe I don't know what I think of Nikki. I love him and I hate him, just like Tommy. (And they feel the same, I'm sure. It is a pattern in my life, as I'm sure you'll hear from the others in this book.)

Getting back to '81—Nikki went to the Starwood to check out Suite 19's guitarist, a guy named Greg Leon. But what really caught Nikki's eye was the drummer, Tommy Lee.

A few days later, when Nikki called Tommy to set up a meet, Tommy totally freaked. As Nikki's voice came booming through the phone, his image was simultaneously staring down from the poster on the wall of Tommy's room. They arranged to meet at a Denny's in North Hollywood; from there they went to Nikki's apartment, where he played Tommy some demo tunes. I guess it was like love at first sight with those guys. Within a few days, Tommy had moved his drums into Nikki's living room/recording studio; the pair started jamming with Leon on guitar. To this combo was added a singer, an overweight guy named O'Dean—his first name has been lost to the ages. Although he was a passable singer, Nikki disliked his vocal pitch. O'Dean had this quirky habit of wearing white gloves everywhere. It was really weird. When he refused to take them off during a recording session—so that he could clap properly on the record—he was let go.

Nikki has always been a stickler. He wasn't particularly happy with Leon, either. He was a passable guitarist, yes, but he was kind of a boring guy. Nikki let him go, too. He went on to play in Dokken, then DuBrow, which became Quiet Riot. He eventually formed the Greg Leon Invasion; he would end up selling the name "Invasion" to a post-KISS Vinnie Vincent. While looking for a new guitarist, Tommy spotted a classified ad in the *Recycler* newspaper, placed by a dude named Mick Mars, a journeyman axe player who was growing tired of playing covers with his band Spiders and Cowboys.

Born Robert Alan Deal, on May 4, 1951, in Terre Haute, Indiana, he was the eldest of the group by seven years—clearly a man of a different generation. After his family relocated from Indiana to California, Deal dropped out of high school and began playing guitar in a series of unsuccessful blues-based rock bands, taking on menial day jobs to make ends meet. After nearly a decade of frustration within the California music scene, Deal had recently changed his name to Mick Mars and dyed his hair jet-black, hoping for a fresh start. "Loud, rude and aggressive guitarist available," he wrote in the ad. He sounded perfect to Nikki. He called and invited Deal over.

When Nikki opened his apartment door, the story famously goes, the gnomish guy standing there reminded him of Cousin It from *The Addams Family*. Neither of them remembered having met a few months earlier, in a liquor store on the Strip, after Mick's set at the Stone Pony. Tommy and Nikki went ahead and showed Mick the opening riff to a song called "Stick to Your Guns" that Nikki had written.

Mick was hired on the spot. He has always been a kick-ass guitar player, second to none, the real virtuoso in the band. To celebrate, they bought a gallon of schnapps.

Now all they needed was a singer.

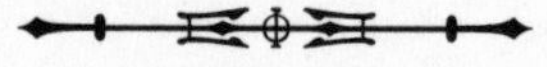

Robert Stokes
Rockandi Drummer

Me and James Alverson just started talking. He was new in school. He had longer hair, I had long hair, and I just asked him if he played. And he said, "Yeah, I play guitar. How about you?" And I said, "Drums." And he said, "I'm looking to get a band going."

He had a bass player from his old high school, but we had to look for a singer, so we just kinda talked for a little while and just kinda let it go. One day we were hanging out in the parking lot at Charter Oak Park. I had this van and I was parked over there; this was my senior year. It was a huge green park, with baseball fields, some trees, some picnic tables, a playground, the whole bit. People would go over there after second period, on break, and then again at lunchtime. You'd sneak over, ditch classes, and smoke cigarettes and hang out.

I was there one day, parked in the van, talking to James. We see Vince cruising through in his blue Datsun 240Z. It had a surfboard rack, you know, and surfboards. He was a younger kid. I didn't actually know him—he was just a guy in the hallway I would kind of nod to. We weren't friends, but we knew each other existed. I guess it was a long-hair thing or something; not many of the kids in school looked like that. Anyway, that day he drove by and we just kinda looked at him like, well, "Let's hit him up. He's got that David Lee Roth look to him."

So we just started talking to him and he said, "Let's try it." He said, "I can't sing, but I can probably get my dad to buy me a PA." He was all gung ho, you know. And he was right. His dad *did* end up buying him a PA.

We did a couple little jams in his garage; we tried to kind of feel each other out. At first James wasn't really happy with Vince at all. It went on for a couple of practices and finally I talked to James; I go, "Let's give him a shot. Maybe his parents will pay for a vocal coach." We practiced in Vince's garage for a couple weeks. And then we ended up switching to Tami's sister's house—we started rehearsing in the living room over there.

We started jamming more. We went though a couple of bass players. The first real bass player we had was this guy named Greg Meeder. He lived in upper Glendora, which was our big rival high school, Glendora High School versus Charter Oak High School—but of course we were the long-haired kids, so of course it didn't bother us. We started getting into cover tunes—Cheap Trick, Led Zeppelin, some old Pat Travers, stuff like that. Over time, we built a repertoire of songs, a couple sets.

One word I could use to describe Vince would be "shy." Real, real shy. A lot of times he'd have his back toward the audience when he was singing. He was very self-conscious about his voice. Tami helped a lot on clothes. Buying him clothes, making him clothes. I guess she could sew. I remember a backyard party this one night. We had just learned "Immigrant Song" by Zeppelin. We're in the middle of playing the song, and you know that famous part that goes, "Ah ah ahhhhh Ahhh!"—you know, that real high part? Well, it's just kind of funny 'cause I remember Vince back then, obviously microphones weren't cordless. They had cords. And I remember we were playing that song and we got to that part and he... he could hit that note, but he couldn't hold it. So right at that point, he would kinda jiggle on the microphone like something was wrong with the microphone. That always stuck in my mind for some reason.

Of course, over time, he gained confidence. You go from small backyard parties, like ten or twenty people, to huge backyard parties, to playing clubs. You start gaining that little bit of an ego character boost, if you will. We got really popular. And Vince just worked at it. He started getting the showmanship, picking the mic stand up, not just holding the mic but picking up the whole mic stand—that became one of his little trademarks. Over time, he became an incredible showman.

We probably did backyard parties for about two years; then we started venturing out into Hollywood. That went pretty well. We were doing, like, New Year's Eve night at Gazzari's, selling out the place. It was tough getting people down there at first, but after a while we started getting quite a big following. At first we were totally a cover band. Then we started throwing in a few originals. Probably one or two maybe, that was about it. We did a couple recordings, but our originals weren't killer; we were a cover band at that point—later we would evolve. But at that point, well, everybody knows you can't make albums doing other people's songs.

At this point, James was still living at home. I was still living at home. Joe Marks was in the band; he was still living at home. Vince was living with his girlfriend Leah, up on the hill.

One night we played the Starwood. It was a Sunday night showcase-type thing. I guess Nikki and Tommy were looking to start this new band, this new project, this idea that they had come up with. And of course Tommy knew Vince. I guess he talked to Leah during the set and Leah approached Vince, and then they all came backstage and asked Vince, you know, "Would you like to come and check out what we're doing?"

Vince was pretty committed to us. He thought we'd be really hurt. He wasn't really sure what to do. Then he came back and he said, "Hey, they're willing to pay me two hundred fifty bucks a week just to be in a band." And here he's struggling with Rockandi—we're passing out flyers to try to get people to come down and stuff like that, but at that point in time we weren't exactly on fire. We just told him, "Hey, this business is about making money; if you can make money at it, go for it." He didn't really want to do it at first, but after it had been a couple weeks, maybe a month, I think he decided to go check them out.

He was a loyal kind of guy. He was a good friend. He really was. He didn't want to leave. He really dug what we were doing. There's no doubt that Nikki and all them were older than us and more experienced. Vince had a shot and he took it. I'm proud of him.

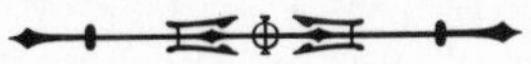

At some point Tommy told them about me. I happened to be playing with Rockandi at the Starwood; the three of them came together to see the show. Eddie Nash owned the place. I used to get my quaaludes from him. He was an amazing guy, a Palestinian emigrant who had started in LA with a hot-dog stand. He now owned several famous clubs, including a strip club in the heart of Hollywood. He would later become infamous as one of the defendants in the Wonderland Avenue murders, also known as the Four on the Floor Murders, involving the porn star John Holmes. There have been a couple of cool movies and documentaries covering the subject.

The Starwood wasn't on the Strip. It was on Santa Monica Boulevard, which was just down the hill. The Strip back then was full of cars and crowded with foot traffic. It was like *American Graffiti*, you know, except everybody looked like rock stars. There were a million posers roaming the streets, all of them dressed like they were in a metal hair band. And there were a million hot girls, each one trying to hook up with somebody in a band.

Gazzari's was, like, at the top of the Strip, the farthest west on Sunset Boulevard, closest to Beverly Hills. And then, moving eastward along the north side of the street, came the Rainbow Bar and Grill, the Roxy Theatre, the Whisky a Go Go. That was the main part of the Strip, all on the same side of the street. And then the Starwood was around the corner. The Troubadour was around the corner. There were also a few Valley clubs. Filthy McNasty's was a big one to play; the Country Club was one of the better places. Those were kind of the main clubs back then. If you go into the Rainbow today, when you first walk in there's a big wall—right before the cash register—and it's full of pictures. Those photos have been there for thirty, forty years. There are still pictures of me, you know—probably five, six, seven, pictures of me mounted on the wall. It's like a time warp. It's fun to kind of revisit sometimes. Some of the same guys still work there. Like Michael and Mario at the Rainbow. They used to let me in, even though I wasn't twenty-one. Good dudes. You should look them up. Many of those places are still there.

There were a lot of great bands playing everywhere back then. Randy Rhoads was known as a great guitar player on the Strip. A lot of people have heard of him of course. But a lot of people you never heard of. Who knows what happened to these people? A lot of bands that I kind of looked up to never even made it. It's weird. Like there was a band called Yankee Rose; this guy named Donnie

Simmons was the guitar player. He was amazing. I actually lived at his house for a little while, too, I remember. I slept in the bathtub, which was the only available space. Then there was this other band Blue Beard. Who knows what happened to them? A lot of these bands actually had record deals, but they were small things; they never went anywhere. Another band called Smile I thought was a great band back then. And Rockandi was right up there. We were just as good as anybody else, absolutely.

The Starwood was great. I remember you'd walk in and to the left was the bar and then the disco. And then to the right was the live venue, where the stage was. The Starwood was where everybody played and everybody wanted to play. You'd made it when you played the Starwood. At the time Rockandi was a well-known local band. But at that point nobody was really worried about being well known or not. Nobody was thinking about becoming famous. At least not me. Maybe James was. But I wasn't trying to be a rock star. I wasn't trying to be anything. I didn't care. It was just fun. That's all it was. Just like high school, it was just having fun; it was girls and booze. I was good at it and it was fun. We were getting popular—which made it even *more* fun. But we were never on the verge of doing anything. There was no record deal; there was nothing but what it was—we were a local name on the scene.

With every band, I was learning, there are problems. It was kind of weird. Like girlfriends, I guess. You have your honeymoon period. Then you have your problems. You have to start "working" on stuff. With Rockandi I'd be in for a while and we'd fight and I'd leave and then I'd come back and we'd do it again. And then I'd leave again. At one point I think I was even going to change bands and go sing for Tommy's band, US 101. Or maybe it was Suite 19 by then, I can't remember.

After the set at the Starwood, Tommy, like, corners me in the bathroom. He's like, "What's up, you blond-haired bitch?" I hadn't seen him in a while—he was fucking with me. He hadn't seen the platinum—it was the first time he'd seen me so white blond. He was lucky I didn't kick his ass. Because I hardly recognized him, either. In fact, I *didn't* recognize him at first. He was totally glammed out, in bright leather pants, stiletto heels, dyed black hair, a ribbon around his neck. I swear I almost went after him before I realized who it was.

Thinking back now, I probably looked just as freakish as Tommy. I was wearing all white, like always. I had my shirt open to my waist, a bandana around my neck, and this belt with all these studs and chains hanging off of it. That was cutting-edge in 1981, what can I say? All I had to do was wear one thing onstage one night and every poseur on the Strip would be rockin' the same look. It seems embarrassing now, but I guess the eighties are really *in* right now. That's what they tell me. To me, the eighties were like, well, if somebody tells you they remember everything that happened during the eighties, they weren't really there.

We go out of the bathroom and Tommy walks me over to these two guys. They were like, "Hey, nice to meet you." I recognized the tall one as the loser bassist from London. The other guy looked, like, *old*. He was kind of frail looking and crooked. He seemed to be appraising me from behind his spectacles. That was pretty much it.

Tommy called me I think the next day or two days later. He was like, "What do you think? Would you want to join the band? We're looking for a singer."

I didn't even think about it. I told him no.

I didn't know these guys as a band. I didn't *want* to start all over again with something new. Rockandi was fun already. It was together and we were having a good time—most of the time. And we were playing on the Strip, you know, which everybody wanted to play. I felt like I'd have to start over with these guys.... In my mind, joining them was kind of taking a step down.

At the time I still had my day job, working as an electrician; we were doing a McDonald's retrofit in Baldwin Park. I was still living with Leah. By now, I'd stopped snorting cocaine with her; I'd graduated to the needle. One morning I was headed to work at 7:00 A.M. It was probably a Monday morning; I'd been up shooting coke with Leah for three or four days straight. On the ride down the hill, I vomited all over the car. I was there but not there, you know what I mean? Shaky. Anyone who has ever been on a drug binge for a few days knows what I mean—it's just this terrible edgy, uncomfortable feeling where you don't feel right in your own skin. They don't call it coming down for nothing.

Once I got to the job site, it only got worse, I started hallucinating. From what I've learned, after about two and a half days without sleep you generally start to hallucinate. I was hearing voices clear as you can hear me right now. I was seeing, like, trails and the ghostly images of people who weren't there. Imaginary dogs ran past; shadows lurked on the walls. I don't know how, but I made it through work that day.

I came home that night and slept for nearly an entire day. Then I woke up and shot up some coke. That's when Tommy stopped by.

He had a tape of songs for me to learn. My eyes were bugging out of my head. As I listened, I didn't know whether to vomit or laugh. There was no way I was going to play with this lame band, if you could call them a band. Just to get rid of him—when you're shooting coke you need a hit, like, every fifteen minutes—I told Tommy I'd come over to Nikki's for the next rehearsal.

A week later, when Tommy called to see why I didn't bother coming, I didn't know what to say. I mean, this is my old friend, my bro. Even though we weren't hanging out together every night anymore we were still brothers under the skin, so I felt bad. I told Tommy I'd accidentally washed the pair of jeans that had his number in them. (Not that I couldn't have driven over to his house and asked him. I knew *exactly* where Tommy lived. Fucksake, I'd lived there myself.)

Another week or so passed. I got into another fight with the guys in Rockandi when they didn't fuckin' show up for a gig. We were scheduled to play at a house party in Hollywood. I showed up (early like always) in my full white satin costume. But James and Joe Marks didn't show up. There I am standing like a fuckin' overdressed idiot, along with the drummer, while a whole houseful of pissed-off partiers got drunker and madder, waiting for a band that was never going to play. When I called James that night, he told me he was done playing rock 'n' roll—he'd already cut all his hair off. "Rock is finished," he said. "I'm going into New Wave."

The next day I called Tommy and asked, "Do you still need a singer?" And Tommy was like, "No, we already found somebody."

I was, like, *Fuck*, you know? For the first time in like three years, I didn't have a band.

And then Tommy called me back and said they'd gotten rid of their singer. Would I come audition?

For a moment I almost said no.

Audition? Wasn't it *them* who had come to see *me* singing? Wasn't it them asking *me* to sing for them? I had to audition?

For once I held my tongue.

Chapter 4

NO FEELINGS

Tommy, Nikki, Mick, and I started practicing every afternoon at a rehearsal studio in the Valley.

Needing a handle for this lofty enterprise, we started throwing names around almost immediately—the idea was to find a commonly used word or phrase, something we could kind of turn upside down, you know, something that would have some shock value, or so Nikki conceived, another one of his high-concept ideas.

We considered XMAS, Trouble, Bad Blood, Holiday, Suicidal Tendencies, a zillion more. Then I remember one time we were drinking Löwenbräu beer; the more lubricated we got, the raunchier and more hilarious the suggestions became. At some point, Mick suggested Mottley Cru. He'd been saving the name for, like, five years; it had come to him one night like a vision as he was rehearsing with his old band Whitehorse. We *were* a motley crew, there was no doubt about it, a foursome of high school dropouts dedicated only to partying and music. Nikki took to the name immediately, but he *hated* Mick's spelling. Instead he made it

"Motley Crue," which he felt was more symmetrical or something. Inspired by the typography on the logo of the beer we were drinking, this friend of Mick's, a guy named Stick, suggested adding an umlaut over the *o* to give it a militant, German feel. Nikki took it one step further and added the umlaut over the *u* as well.

Mötley Crüe was launched.

To celebrate, instead of breaking bottles over the bow, we emptied them down our faces.

At this point, Nikki was living with his girlfriend in Hollywood. Mick was living in Redondo Beach with his girlfriend. Tommy was still living at home. At first I was living with Leah, but she was really stressing me out. Shooting coke was not my scene. I mean, it was my scene for a while. People do some wild shit on coke. There were some dark times, some of it painful, some of it fun—in the way that the people in the movie *Caligula* are having fun. Cocaine is the devil's playground. It affects the sexual part of the brain—it can get pretty wild. I'm not sure Leah would have been bisexual if she'd never done the white lady. But before you know it you cross that line and you end up like one of the rats in an experiment, pushing the lever all day and all night for your reward. I've done every drug you could think of, but my basic drug of choice has always been alcohol. I mean, over the years, I've done pot and coke and pills and heroin and everything else, whatever was generally available, but usually it started with some kind of alcoholic beverage as a foundation.

After a while, the whole junkie scene with Leah was getting kind of heavy for me. Plus, the guys in Mötley were giving me limitless amounts of shit about her. They called her Lovey because she was starting to look old. (To tell you the truth, I don't know where Tommy had the room to give me shit at this point. The guys had nicknamed *his* girlfriend Bullwinkle, which was not a tribute to her good looks. It is well documented that Tommy loved Bullwinkle like crazy, partly [if not totally] because of her extreme sexual sensitivity. Today, with the luxury of the Internet, we know her type. They call them squirters. Hypersensitive, they come multiple times and with extreme force, making you feel like a superman. The gusher is pretty novel—I've been with squirters myself, though never at my own home, way too messy. The truth is [how to say this gently?]...the whole squirting thing yields a solution that kind of smells like piss. After Tommy had been dating Bullwinkle some months, his van began to smell like a urinal.)

Eventually I met this girl who was a cute surfer chick. She was the complete opposite of Leah. Just wholesome and outdoorsy and athletic, with a killer little body. And I really...I really liked this girl. I can't remember her name. While I was with Leah, I kind of started seeing her on the side. It's always been like that. I've always gone from one main girlfriend or wife to the other, kind of like swinging vine to vine—at some point, you've got hold of both vines at once. Tricky. I've never been alone in my life; I've always had somebody. Since I was young, I've always had a girlfriend or a wife, someone to ground me a little bit. I've been married four times—I think being married is my way of always knowing that I'm not going to go home to an empty house, that there's going to be somebody there. It's a structure that in my mind I need. Some people don't need that structure, but I do. I'm really a romantic. I like being in a relationship. I love it. If I have strong feelings, I want to marry this woman. And then, you know, then I get...maybe not *bored* easily...it's just kind of...sometimes something happens and it's just kind of time to move on.

Finally, I'd just had enough with Leah. I was sick of the whole scene and I wanted out. She'd done a lot of great stuff for me, so I felt bad. It was just over, you know? There was only one problem. I couldn't leave. At the time I didn't have my own car. It was like I was stuck up on the side of the mountain in this big house where she lived.

So I made a big plan with Tommy to escape.

One day I packed up all my clothes and I secretly left everything out on the driveway, behind some bushes. I had two boxes of belongings; it was not a whole lot of stuff. Probably people thought I was putting it out in the driveway for Goodwill. Tommy met me at a certain time. I told Leah I had to go outside or some shit, and I left her in the bathroom and just went out…outside into the light. Tommy pulled up and I put the shit in his van. And that was it; I got the fuck outta there. I remember the feeling of giddiness as we pulled away. Like this uncontrollable laughter that used to bubble up when I'd snatch something out of a warehouse and run like hell—just pure evil joy. I never saw her again.

From there I think I went back to Tommy's house—back sleeping on the floor of his room. The van was out of the question. It was too putrid with the scent of eau de Bullwinkle. Just riding in it was difficult enough—luckily the smell in the front was not as bad as in the back, where the action generally took place.

We didn't have any money. That's why I always preferred rich chicks. I basically always had a chick with a nice place and a nice car and a little money. Chicks always had friends with drugs and alcohol. As for the cover charge at the various clubs, we got in for free 'cause we were Mötley Crüe—or not Mötley Crüe; nobody knew who we were yet as a band, but they knew me from Rockandi and Nikki from London, and so forth, we'd all been playing these venues for two or three years now; we were sort of the local royalty, maybe a second tier behind guys like Randy Rhoads, who of course was most famous for being Ozzy Osbourne's guitarist.

I was still only twenty years old, one year under the legal age to drink in the state of California. Sometimes I used Nikki's birth certificate, which said "Frank Feranna." Unfortunately, free admission did not include free drinks. There was no way we could afford the pricey booze inside. Instead, we would put our money together and go to, I think the place was called University Stereo and Liquor Store. It was right by Turner's Liquor, and we'd buy like, you know, fifths of schnapps and then sit and drink with the bums out of paper bags. Then we'd just walk across the street and go to the Whisky or whichever club we'd decided on. Sometimes when you were inside, people would buy you drinks. I can't ever say I spent much time sober.

As for our wardrobe, we got our look from the hardware store. We were big into the fuckin' hardware store. I would have a leather jacket or something and you'd cut the sleeves and you'd put chains on it. You know, stuff like that. After Rockandi, I started to get away a little bit from the white, but I still stood out because I was the platinum blond guy in the middle of all the jet-black dye. Nikki was always into the big hair and the heels in his band London, so when we got together it just happened to fit that we were into that, too. I still had my leather pants from when Leah bought them. I wore those all the time. And I had a white pair, too. But it's not like we ever sat down and said, you know, "This is going to be our look." Nobody said, like, "You're going to wear this, and you're going wear that." It was not like KISS or some shit, though that definitely influenced us. Everybody just got dressed how they felt comfortable and it worked. So it was everybody's instinct to just be who we were. I think it was kind of organic. We were who we were and it went together well.

When we weren't practicing, we were making our presence known on the Strip. It was an amazing place, more entertaining than anything you could imagine, like going to a countercultural zoo. In the years I was there, the general atmosphere took a dark, downward turn, moving from hippie to glam/punk, from pot and quaaludes to cocaine and speed and junk. The coke in those days was rocky and crystalline, fresh from Bolivia and places like that. It wasn't like the milled-up, manufactured stuff you'd start seeing by the late eighties and nineties. This shit was rocks. You had to use a razor blade to slice it. Like that scene in *Goodfellas*? Where the mobster in prison slices the garlic with a razor blade? That's what you had to do with the rocks at that time. You'd slice off these pieces that looked like quartz crystal. And then you could begin chopping it up with your driver's license or whatever.

Drunk and stumbling in our stiletto heels, we paraded the street with everyone else. I wore red nail polish, hot pink pants, and full makeup. Everybody in the band, as you know, had their kind of signature look. The sidewalks were crowded with spandex prostitutes and clusters of punks, New Wave hipsters, hair metal poseurs, a few retro hippies—that scraggly look would eventually come back at the end of the decade with grunge. The lines outside the clubs could be a block long, sometimes around a corner. All kinds of celebrities and quasi celebrities were hanging out to see and be seen.

One of my favorite scenes was at the Rainbow. Like I remembered in *The Dirt*, "the place was set up like a circle, with the coolest rockers and richest deviants sitting at the center tables.... The guys would sit at their regular spots and the girls would walk around the ring until they were called over to someone's empty chair. They would keep circling, like dick buzzards, until you filled your table with them." That's a great phrase, by the way, "dick buzzards." A perfect description. Somebody out there needs to use that name for an all-girl band! I'm not sure if I said it exactly that way or if Neil Strauss did, but here's a shout-out to him. He kicked ass with *The Dirt*; it was a *New York Times* best seller. I understand he's gone on to become quite an expert in pussy himself with his book *The Rules*.

Our first official gig was March 24, 1981.

Though we'd never yet run though a complete set in practice, Nikki landed us two nights at the Starwood—I think he used his connections from his old band, London. Some people say he was working days at the Starwood at the time. I don't remember that; I can't imagine what he was doing there. When Nikki told us the news, everybody was stoked—except Mick. He didn't think we were ready yet. The rest of us didn't agree. We three were all cliff jumpers. Fuck it! Are you kidding? A *paying* gig at the fuckin' Starwood? Two sets on a Friday night. On Saturday we would open for a well-known band from Oakland called Yesterday and Today, later known as just Y&T.

Leading up to the evening we plastered the Strip, and what seemed like all of Los Angeles and the Valley, with flyers. If there was one flyer for another event, we'd plaster over it with our own posters, totally obliterating any competition that night. We wanted everybody in town to come. I don't remember where we got the money for the flyers. Probably somebody was fucking some girl in a copy shop. The act wasn't quite so well organized. We didn't even know what the set list was going to be until Nikki taped a handwritten sheet of paper to the stage floor at the last minute.

Our first song was "Take Me to the Top." Nobody in the crowd knew who we were. "Motley who?" They were yelling at us and flipping us off. Then some guy spits on me and the next thing I know, I'm jumping off the stage—fifteen minutes into my new career with my new band and I was having my first fight. I grabbed the dude and put him in a headlock and started whaling on his face. Nikki followed me into the crowd. He had my back in those days—didn't think nothing about it, didn't hesitate. He swung his large and solidly constructed Thunderbird bass guitar over his head like Paul Bunyan and brought it down on some guy's shoulder. Tommy wasn't far behind. He hit some guy between the eyes with a drumstick. I didn't even know he knew martial arts! In years since, a lot of people have said that this whole thing was a publicity tactic. You can judge for yourself if you want. To film the gig we'd hired this chick who was the girlfriend of Randy Piper from W.A.S.P. She got it all from the club's balcony. Black-and-white videos of that night are still available in bootleg circles, or so they tell me.

Somehow, the fight ended and we all picked ourselves back up and continued playing. And by the second set…we'd converted the crowd into fans. The next night, even more people came out to see us as the warm-up band for Y&T. In fact, more people came for us than came for them. By the end of our set, the people were screaming for more. And then, when we got off the stage, almost the entire crowd left! The next time we performed with them, it would be Y&T as the opening act for *us*.

There were plenty of big names hanging out on the Strip, but the first big name to call himself a fan was David Lee Roth of Van Halen. Later David Lee would become a fixture at our apartment—known as the Mötley House—he was there all the time doing coke and trolling for an easy fuck. There's one story about him doing blow in our bedroom and this mirrored door from our closet fucking fell off and landed on his head…and he didn't flinch; he just kept on snorting. That reminds me of the time, years later in New Orleans I think it was, that Ozzy snorted a line of ants. It's a well-documented story, just what you'd expect from the wizard of Oz.

David Lee came to a lot of our shows at the Troubadour, the Whisky, wherever. He was a huge star. I think he had some ulterior motives, though. Unlike a lot of rock bands, our crowd was always, like, a majority of women. I swear it was sometimes like 90 percent girls. So he would come to the gigs and introduce the band. Clever boy: Before we'd even started playing, everybody in the club knew he was there. Then he'd just kick back and collect pussy the rest of the night. It was a good deal for everybody. We got the boost. He got the blow jobs. Of course we never suffered, either. There was a bountiful harvest of ripe fruit to be eaten at will. There was so much that sometimes you just took a bite and threw the rest away.

One night David Lee was like, "Vince, I want to take you out to breakfast and tell you about how things are." For somebody that was that huge to take me under his wing was really cool. It was an honor. Even to an irreverent fuck like myself.

We met at Canter's Deli on Fairfax. When he drove up he was in his black Mercedes with a big skull and crossbones painted on the hood. I was like, *That's pretty fucking cool.* He talked all about business. What I should do and not do. Who I should avoid. He was basically trying to give me tips to help me get started, so I wouldn't get ripped off like everyone always does. It was stuff like "you have to watch out for this or that." Or "make sure you have distribution, you know." He was talking about national distribution and deals and things—I didn't know what the hell he was talking about. It was a little bit, at that point, like, *Oh my god!* I kind of got what he was saying, but I didn't, I didn't understand a lot of it. Obviously I do now. But back then, I mean, I knew you had to make a record and I knew it had to be distributed across the country, and he was saying, you know, make sure you go with one of the two biggest distributors, because if you're not with them you're not gonna have your record distributed everywhere and things wouldn't work out well, stuff like that.

I walked out of Canter's with a list of managers to look at and consider, totally convinced that David Lee was right, and that I needed to get the right person to handle my affairs and the right distribution deal, all that stuff. I couldn't wait to let the other guys know what I'd learned. I felt like a light had gone on, you know, like professionally speaking. There's always more to shit than you'd figure.

But then the very next day the guys told me that we were going to sign a ten-year management contract with Allan Coffman, a man who'd never even managed a band before. As it turned out, he knew even less about the industry than I did. And, as it would turn out, it was just one of many decisions I went along with because Nikki, Tommy, and Mick thought it was a good idea. If you ask me, it was a disaster.

It had all started with this guy Stick—the one who suggested the umlaut over the *o* in "Mötley." I think his real name was John Crouch. Basically, he was a nobody. Mick's friend. A hanger-on. He used to drive Mick around and do stuff for him. Sometimes Stick also brought his sister. Her name was Barbara. She looked exactly like Stick—not an attractive package. Even Tommy wasn't interested in fucking her, and it is well known that Tommy will fuck just about anything.

Soon we met Barbara's husband—Allan Coffman. He was thirty-eight years old, a rail-thin guy who owned a construction company. He and his wife lived in a place called Grass Valley in Northern California, where he served as a member of the county board of zoning administration. Barbara, it turned out, was also a local muckety-muck, a member of the Grass Valley school district board. Coffman looked like he was on acid—his eyes were always darting around the room as if he was seeing shadow people in the corners. When he got drunk, the weird would kick into high gear. He'd start obsessively searching bushes we passed on the Strip to make sure no one was hiding in them. It wasn't until years later that we learned he had served as an MP in Vietnam. He probably had post-traumatic stress disorder. What motivated him to want to get into the rock scene is beyond me. Clearly, he was not all right in the head.

After it was decided we would sign with Coffman, we demolished five bottles of schnapps. It's funny to think back. That night, we were so grateful to each have a bottle for *ourselves*. We felt like millionaires. Eventually, we entered into an exclusive management agreement with the hastily formed firm of Coffman & Coffman. Stick Crouch was named the representative on the ground in Hollywood. The ten-page agreement detailed aspects such as the duration of the agreement, upfront loans, commissions, and weekly allowances. Each band member received an advance of $250.

Of course, we went out and spent the entire wad on cocaine and booze. A weeklong bender ensued.

Because I didn't have a place to live and Tommy didn't want to live at home anymore and Nikki had just broken up with his girlfriend and had no place to live, Coffman said he'd rent us an apartment. Being an older guy, Mick already had a life. He was in Redondo Beach living with his girlfriend, so only the three of us moved in.

Even though it's always been called the Mötley House, it was actually a two-bedroom apartment—one unit in a small building, maybe twenty or thirty units. There was this open courtyard; we lived right on the corner on the bottom floor, which was great for easy access. Ten units downstairs and ten units upstairs, something like that. It was probably three hundred bucks a month. Coffman paid the rent in addition to twenty dollars per week per band member. It was really close to the Whisky. It was like here's the Whisky and you go up the street, up the hill, and behind...and it was right there.

With three of us living in two bedrooms, two had to share a room and one got the single. We flipped for it. The deal was supposed to be that we'd rotate like once a week or once a month or something, so that everybody would get the chance to have the single. Nikki won the first toss, but he never moved out; there was never another toss. So me and Tommy had to share the bedroom. One of the first things I did was go up on the roof and rewire our unit for cable TV. It was part of my training from being an electrician; I just spliced into somebody else's service and reran it. Tommy brought his TV from home; Nikki had one, too. We were hooked up—though I really can't remember spending a whole lot of time being a couch potato.

Basically our apartment became like the ultimate party place;

there was shit happening 24/7. Most of our neighbors were just young people. There were a couple of good-looking girls upstairs and down the hall, and a guy and his girlfriend across the way—it was pretty much the rock apartment building. There were some older people who lived in there, too. They would always be calling the cops. I think they were kind of scared of us because we were so out there, just wild and crazy and setting things on fire and wearing leather and blasting the music and doing whatever the fuck we wanted at all hours of the day and night. It was great because it was so easy. We could just walk with everybody back to our place. We'd drink, do blow, smack, Percodan, quaaludes, a little acid now and then. There was a spirit of sharing. People just brought shit to the house. I don't remember doing a lot of buying. Liquor we had to buy. But drugs were plentiful. The crowd was funny because we were like nondiscriminatory. There were punks like the guys from 45 Grave and the Circle Jerks and new jacks like the guys from Ratt and W.A.S.P. Not to mention a constant steady supply of fresh females. There'd be girls coming in the front door and going out the back door. They'd be climbing in and out the windows—another good selling point for being on the ground floor in those days.

No matter when it was, day or night, there were always girls. I mean, *always* girls. Maybe the truth is that pussy is my drug of choice. I was awash in it. There'd be girls at the club, in the bathroom, backstage, back at the apartment. It was just kind of the thing that you'd do—if you came to our place, you knew you were going to get fucked by somebody, and probably somebody who was pretty decent looking. I was choosy, you know, 'cause I could afford to be. What I didn't have in dollars I made up in pussy. If I could have spent it (or invested it) I would have been a billionaire by now.

The bedroom Tommy and I shared was to the left of the hallway; we each had a mattress on the floor. Nikki's bigger room had a set of French doors that led to the living room. He nailed them

My first gig. *(The Neil family)*

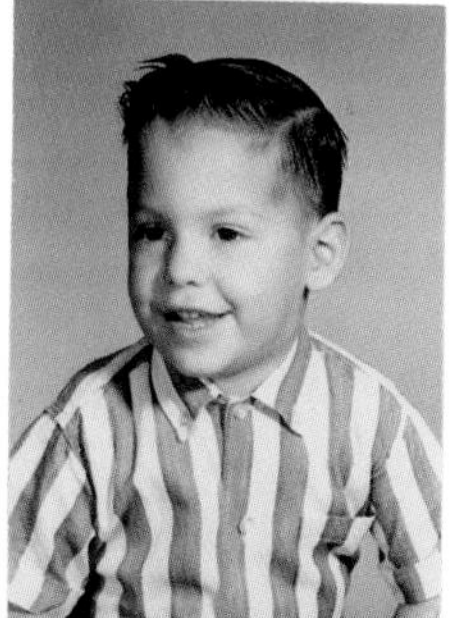

The early 1970s, with my sister Valerie. *(The Neil family)*

Me, Val, and our dog Daisy. *(The Neil family)*

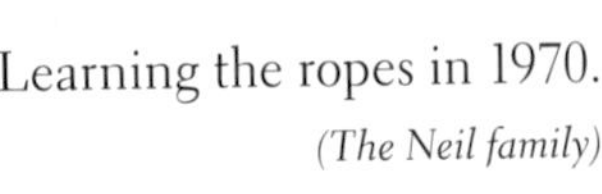

Learning the ropes in 1970. *(The Neil family)*

I win! *(The Neil family)*

So what? Everyone has an awkward phase. *(The Neil family)*

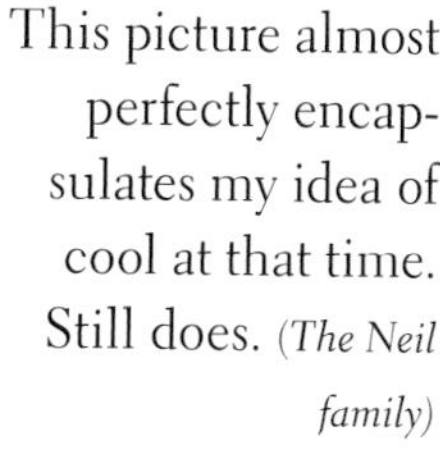

This picture almost perfectly encapsulates my idea of cool at that time. Still does. *(The Neil family)*

One of the earliest Rockandi pictures. That's me in the middle, James Alverson on the left, and Joe Marks on the right. At the Woodstock in Anaheim, California, 1980. This picture was taken by Leah Graham (Lovey), RIP. *(Leah Graham)*

Playing the Starwood with Rockandi, 1981. This was the exact night that Nikki and Tommy came to see us and tried to convince me to join up with them. *(Freddy Longoria)*

MÖTLEY CRÜE
MICK MARS
TOMMY LEE
NIKKI SIXX
VINCE NEIL
STARWOOD
APRIL 24-25 FRI-SAT
INFO 656-2200

I think Nikki made this flyer. It was for our first official show together as Mötley Crüe, April 1981. I stapled it to Rockandi's rehearsal studio door.

Me and Val backstage in the early days. *(The Neil Family)*

Image Recording studios, Hollywood, 1985. Recording Night Ranger's 7 *Wishes* album. We had all just gotten back from the Rainbow Bar and Grill (the Bow). Left to right: Brad Gillis, guitarist for Night Ranger; David Sikes, bass player for Boston; Me; Kelly Keagy, singer and drummer for Night Ranger; Jack Blades, lead singer and frontman for Night Ranger; Mark Newman, guitar tech for Night Ranger; Tommy Lee; Kevin Smith; Jim Viger; and Rich Fisher, Mötley's tour manager. *(Mark Newman)*

Beth and me in 1984, at Joe Marks's son Taelor's first birthday party. *(Joe Marks)*

Glamsformation complete. From a studio session in Hollywood. *(William Hames)*

Live in 1985—Theatre of Pain. *(William Hames)*

In my management office in 1986, holding the multiplatinum award for *Theatre of Pain*, which had just passed 2 million copies sold in the U.S. *(William Hames)*

Hot tub time machine, 1986. *(William Hames)*

Seal Beach video shoot, 1986, with Tommy and Michael Berryman. *(William Hames)*

If only all beaches were like this all the time. *(William Hames)*

In the studio in 1987. *(William Hames)*

In 1987. This was the press day for *Girls, Girls, Girls,* as you can see on the woman's underwear. Tommy and I were having a blast. *(William Hames)*

Alive in 1990.
(William Hames)

Sitting outside my hotel in London in the early '90s. *(William Hames)*

Backstage at the Donington Festival in 1991. Tommy and Mick in the back. *(William Hames)*

There's just nothing like that view. *(William Hames)*

With Doug Thaler and one hell of a jacket. *(William Hames)*

Here I am on the set of a music video in 1991 with Tommy. *(William Hames)*

With beautiful Skylar in 1992. I miss her every day. *(William Hames)*

In the studio in '95.
(William Hames)

With the boys and the legendary Larry Flynt, 1997. *(William Hames)*

With Joe Marks for the Rockandi reunion at Feelgoods in 2009. We are wiser now. *(Janelle Marks)*

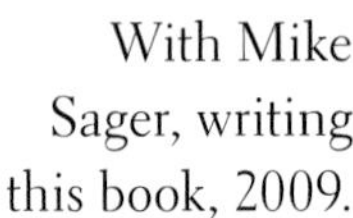

With Mike Sager, writing this book, 2009.

shut for privacy. He had his own TV in there, too. He'd sit on the floor working on songs while everyone was partying around him—not that he didn't do his share of big-time partying. It's just that sometimes his concentration was amazing to me. As fucked up as he was or whatever, doing whatever drugs, he was always composing songs and coming up with ideas.

It didn't take long before the place was trashed. The brand-new leather couch in the living room, a Christmas gift from Tommy's doting parents, was filthy and torn. The carpet was stained with blood and alcohol and ulcerated with cigarette burns. There were charred footprints from the time we were experimenting with setting Nikki on fire with this pyro gel we used in our act. There was construction stuff all over the place from when we built drum risers and other stuff for the stage—I helped by wiring all the electrical. All that shit lit up and blew up because of me. We liked to put on a good show. Like I keep saying, it's all about entertainment. About having fun, you know? We'd do all kinds of theatrical shit onstage. Condoms filled with fake blood, lighting Nikki on fire, one time we even used this chain saw to cut off the head of a mannequin/nun—though that would come a little later. But we were into the theater of it all. We'd put this gel stuff on Nikki's boots and I'd put it on this sword and we had candelabras and I'd light my sword and then light his boots. It was cool experimenting with that stuff. We were twenty, you know? It was a lot of fun. We would experiment: *How long can we let Nikki burn?* One time, lighting Nikki's boots on fire, we used too much gel and we ended up lighting the back of his hair on fire. I mean, the flames jumped straight up his back!

The walls of the apartment were blackened from our roach control efforts. We used to chase cockroaches with our hairspray—you know, we'd light the stream of hairspray with a lighter and you'd torch those suckers up. (We were known for lighting a fart now and then, too.) The ceiling was covered with broom handle and guitar head dents—whenever the upstairs tenants banged on the floor to complain about the noise, we'd bang back.

It's true what people say—the door had been kicked in by the police so many times that it wouldn't shut anymore. We had to put, like, a wedge of folded-up cardboard underneath to keep it in place. The apartment was so putrid no robber would have come in, anyway, even if the door was wide open. What amazes me is that nothing was ever stolen. We had instruments, the TVs, Tommy's stereo. (I think Tommy was a little spoiled as a child. His parents loved him and gave him everything he needed, which worked out well for me, 'cause he was always willing to share. I didn't have shit, no possessions, usually just my clothes.) I guess a burglar would take one look at our door and walk away thinking we were less well off than he was.

The bathroom was pretty much what you'd expect—sink black with hair die, bathtub blackened with personal dirt, toilet a disaster zone, tampons and toilet paper and magazines and socks strewn everywhere. The kitchen was even worse, if that was possible. Of course none of us could cook anyway. We'd steal food or sometimes we'd take advantage of these groupie chicks who worked at the grocery nearby. We also had this older couple who kind of adopted us. They'd bring us over big bowls of spaghetti.

Nobody could be bothered to take out the trash. Take out the trash? Are you kidding? Every kid knows: The trash is the first big fight you have with your father. It's always about a lot more than the trash. But it starts there. "Take out the trash!" "Fuck you!" I swear to god, if you asked ten kids in jail what they first fought with their parents about, one thing they'd all mention was the trash. It's like not wanting to take out the trash is the gateway drug to a whole range of antisocial behaviors.

The kitchen had a sliding glass door that led to a patio. We'd just toss our trash out there. It was like our own personal landfill—though nobody was covering it over with dirt. There were bags full of beer cans and liquor bottles piled up to chest height. The neighbors started complaining about the smell—you could look outside and see rats and rat shit everywhere; it totally gave me the creeps. By March of 1982 it had become so bad that the LA County Department of Health Services left us a notice of official violation. It kind of cracks me up to look at the summons, reprinted in *The Dirt*. We were fuckin' disgusting. Just clueless kids. The warning included instructions. The trash was supposed to be put out at least once every seven days. Thanks for the info. We'll get right on that.

In the beginning, everything was pure and uncomplicated. There was no fame. There was no money. It was all about rehearsing and going out and hitting the Strip, you know, advertising ourselves. We'd be hanging out; we'd be passing out flyers, we'd be picking up chicks. It was a perfect synergy. Coffman had paid to press one thousand seven-inch vinyl copies of our 45 rpm single—the A side was "Stick to Your Guns"; the B side was "Toast of the Town." At the end of gigs we'd fly them into the crowd like Frisbees. The cover art was a Mötley Crüe logo that Nikki designed. On the back was the photo of the four of us that would eventually be used on *Too Fast for Love*. I had a black eye that day, but as we all know, they ended up using a different part of me for the cover when the album was eventually rereleased.

Over time we just got really big. We became the biggest band in Los Angeles. Everything sort of sprouted from there. We played a lot of different places. Sometimes they paid us like seven hundred dollars; most of the time you just played for free. Or you'd give out tickets and however many people used the tickets you gave out, you got paid for them. Sometimes you would make fifty bucks, sometimes a hundred bucks. I mean we played this one place called Pookie's, which was a sandwich shop in Pasadena. It probably only held forty people, but we didn't give a shit; we're still fully dressed and playing and stuff—we just kind of went for it, you know? We all just wanted to play. We all wanted to get up there in front of people and do what we did best. I think at Pookie's the story goes that we drank up way more than they were paying us.

Little by little, you start having ambitions. I still wasn't thinking about being a rock star. I just wanted to, like, keep going up the ladder. First you want to play the Starwood—and then you play the Starwood. Then you want to play the Whisky a Go Go—and you get that gig. And then it's not just enough to play there—you want to headline…for a *whole weekend.* And then it happens and that's huge. And then once you accomplish that, you know, then you want to play the Civic Center, and we did, and then you want to go on a national tour, and we opened for KISS. And then you want to *headline* a tour, and of course we did that, too. So it was just all steps, you know. It was steps that we just wanted to conquer, rungs on the ladder. But it all started out just wanting to play in the band, in front of people. Like when we went from practicing in the garage to playing in people's backyards. It's a long road. One step at a time. That was our only goal—to go to the next step. Because it's such a rush to get up there in front of as many people as possible and do what you do best.

Onstage might be where I am happiest. That *is* where I am the happiest. It's definitely where I am the most comfortable. Some people are great one-on-one-type people. They make small talk and jokes; they like meeting people. They say stuff like, "Oh, I'm a people person." Not me. When I'm in a small group, I'm just no good. It's not my thing. I've always been pretty shy. I'm not that comfortable around people—unless I'm drunk. Then I don't care. But I basically like to keep my thoughts to myself, to keep my own counsel, I think they say.

But being onstage is something different. It's like an arena of ten thousand is just perfect for me. Intimate strangers. I don't really have to deal with anyone's specific responses or emotions. I just have to entertain. Of course, not every show is a great show. Drunk people throw stuff on the stage. Weird shit happens. Sometimes, when you're having a bad show, it can be merciless. I mean, maybe the monitors aren't right and you're struggling to hear yourself and every note you're singing is registering and it seems like you're up there forever—you want to throw your microphone at the sound guy because you can't get it right, you're so frustrated; I've thrown my guitar at a guy before because I held him responsible for me not being able to do my best. I don't like when people are just irresponsible. If you're hired to do something, do what you're hired to do, you know? Do your job like I'm doing my job. It's their job to make it easy for me, you know? Don't tell me why you can't do something. Don't tell me your dog ate your homework. I don't fucking care. Do your job. Make it right. 'Cause I'm doing my job as best as I can do. I'm standing up there in front of a shitload of people. The spotlight is on me.

On the good shows—and there are many more good shows than bad ones—when the sound is right and you're just powering through the set... you feel like you've only been onstage for five minutes. If I'm singing great and having a great time, I'm thinking about my laundry, I'm thinking about the pussy I'm gonna have later, I'm thinking about *anything* but singing. It's like you're on some kind of trip—an out-of-body experience. You're there, but you're not there. The people are roaring and then they're gone. You're in a state of suspended animation. It's bliss.

And then you look up and you just did two hours. They're hustling you offstage.

Chapter 5

HE'S A WHORE

At the end of 1981, we started to record our debut album, *Too Fast for Love*. Because we still hadn't been signed by a major label, we decided to create our own: Leathür Records.

It was cool to say we had a label—with a cool name and a cool umlaut—but what we didn't have was a distribution deal. Just like David Lee Roth had warned, *no one was gonna hear the fucking thing*!

D'oh!

Coffman drove around town in his big rented Lincoln, going to record stores and trying to talk managers into buying a couple of copies. Luckily I was pretty oblivious to all this at the time... if I'd given a shit about anything besides music, pussy, and getting high I would have been totally pissed that *this* was the marketing plan for our debut album—an expensive rental car and a Vietnam vet who sometimes found himself, in his mind at least, back in the steamy jungles, facing invisible foes.

But there was no denying our shit was good; like they say, the cream rises. Eventually we got a distribution deal through Greenworld. *Too Fast for Love* has since gone platinum—which isn't bad when you consider it only took three days and six thousand dollars to record at Hit City West Studios on the corner of Pico and La Cienega Boulevards in LA. If you know LA, you know the neighborhood. Pico is kind of a line of demarcation, where glitzy Hollywood stops and the gritty real world of South Los Angeles begins, a place some people call Soweto South of Pico, making reference to the shantytowns and the race and class separations in South Africa. Like everywhere, there's always the castle here, and the wall here, and the peasants over there, outside. That's LA for you.

The studio was a dump. Just a total dive, with all these tiny rooms. Funny to think that later, with all the rising egos, politics, demands, and intervening circumstances, it would take us almost a year and hundreds of thousands of dollars to make most of the rest of our albums. Life was simpler then, to be sure. There were no real distractions. No demons to elude. We couldn't afford a lot of studio time. We just got right down to the music and did it. We were purer then, I suppose. Things were so much less complicated. We were motivated only by the music.

When the album was released, we threw a party at the Troubadour; that's where Nikki hooked up with Lita Ford from the Runaways. A beautiful long-legged British-born blonde, she could chop up a guitar solo with the best. We sold twenty thousand copies pretty quickly. That's why Greenworld stepped up. They pretty much realized it was a no-brainer. We were good at what we did. And we had the groupies to prove it. You know how a football team says its fans are like the twelfth man? Well, females were our fifth man. Everybody knew that if Mötley was going to be playing somewhere, all the hot chicks would be there, too. I know that had no small impact on our draw.

All of a sudden there were several major labels interested in signing us. An A and R guy from Richard Branson's Virgin Records showed up at our show at the Glendale Civic Center with a suitcase full of one-hundred-dollar bills—Branson was offering ten thousand dollars to sign the band. We'd never seen so much fucking money. For a moment there we almost caved. But then somebody told Coffman that Virgin didn't have a distribution deal in America—most of their UK artists at the time had full-blown USA deals with Warner. David Lee couldn't have been more right. Distribution was the gold standard.

Tom Zutaut, Elektra's top A and R guy, caught one of our sellout shows at the Whisky; he liked what he saw; he was determined to land us. His pitch was that even though Elektra couldn't match Virgin's offer, it would make more sense for us to sign with an LA label. (Little did we know the label was in the process of relocating to New York. One truth stands now and forever: All these record company motherfuckers are manipulative liars.)

Zutaut tells the story of his boss laughing him out of his office when he declared his intention to sign Mötley Crüe—at the time, Elektra was only interested in signing New Wave bands. But Zutaut stuck to his guns. He said he just knew from watching the kids inside the Whisky going mental that we had a tremendous upside. He was supposed to be interviewed for this book, but I think the whole thing about me fucking his date at the Us festival (well documented in *The Dirt)* has sort of put a damper on our relationship.

To celebrate our agreement, Zutaut took the band, and Coffman, to Casa Cugat in West Hollywood, one in a chain of popular Mexican restaurants owned by the rumba king Xavier Cugat. We'd just inked a recording contract with the label that had been home to the Doors and the Stooges; it's hard to explain how that felt. Like the first hit of some drug, maybe, just pure, with no comedown. The margaritas were flowing freely. I guess Zutaut and his people were kind of expecting us to go pretty wild, but nobody was expecting our *manager* to flip out.

Usually, we didn't hang out with Coffman. Not ever. I don't think anybody in the band did. He was just the guy with the money that was taking us on our first steps, not somebody you wanted to hang out with. Having a manager is like a necessary evil. In the business world, nobody will do business with you as an artist unless you have a manager. It doesn't matter who you are, you could be Mick Jagger or fuckin' Paul McCartney and they're like, "Yes, you're the greatest, I love you, now lemme talk to your manager." They don't take us seriously. I don't know if it's a good ole boy system or what it is, but that's the way it is.

As it happened, on this night at Cugat, our esteemed manager, the owner of 10 percent of our souls, drank one or two or five too many margaritas or shots of tequila or whatever the fuck had gotten him totally shit faced. He started running around jabbering in Vietnamese, convinced, I guess, that he was back in Nam and that we were under attack by the North Vietnamese army. It was weird. Too weird. I mean, we didn't feel like taking care of the fuckin' guy—he was supposed to be taking care of us, you know? Not the other way around.

Since Zutaut was the suit, we let him take control of the situation. That was his job, right? The suits take care of shit. He took Coffman home. We kept partying.

On the way back to Coffman's hotel, at a stoplight on Santa Monica Boulevard, Coffman leapt out of Zutaut's car in the middle of traffic and started low-crawling along the asphalt like he was on recon.

Even *we* never got *that* fucked up.

You don't know this at first, but no matter what, life *always* becomes a fuckin' movie. Or a soap opera. Or an *E! True Hollywood Story.*

In other words: The other shoe always drops.

You just don't expect it to happen quite so fast.

No sooner did we have the amazing exhilaration of signing with fuckin' Electra and getting an *advance* and having *our first album*... the next thing we knew we had to stand by and watch our baby get royally fucked in the ass.

At first we thought—I don't know what we thought. I guess we thought they'd simply rerelease *Too Fast for Love* as we'd recorded it. We thought it was perfect. Everybody loved it. That shitty little studio had given it just the right amount of reverb and rawness to make the sound unique.

Then we heard that Electra wanted to bring in the well-known producer Roy Thomas Baker. When I first heard about it, I couldn't fuckin' believe it. None of us could. I was, like, what, twenty, twenty-one years old. And I was going to be working with Roy Thomas Baker, the guy who'd produced classic albums with Journey, Foreigner, the Cars, and Queen. Wow. That seemed sooo amazing.

But nobody really worked it through—if we already did the album, why would we need RTB? What could he *possibly* add? The album didn't need a thing... did it?

It turned out the answer to that was complicated. We were caught in a cross fire of politics. Annoyed that Zutaut had gone over his head to sign the band, Elektra's head of A and R, Kenny Buttice, complained that our album was not up to radio-play standards and demanded it be remixed before release. From the jump, all of us were against any remix. We thought it was a waste. I mean, remix? What the fuck is that? Redo the songs, maybe. But remix? When you get right down to it, I don't even know exactly what RTB did to the album—*other than make me rerecord every one of my vocals.* Half the time he wasn't even there in the studio when he was supposed to be there. I mean, he'd show up, listen to what the engineer did, and then leave, go take a nap or some shit, or go fuck some girl, because he was always partying.

That was part of the problem. The studio was at his house.

As you would imagine, based on all the big hits he'd produced, and all the money he made, the word "house" was an understatement. He had a fuckin' palatial spread. And the party was ongoing. We'd go up there anytime, day or night. We'd do blow with him and his girlfriend and whoever else was there. They had this, like, snow cone machine and we'd make these whiskey snow cones. Being there, you really *felt* like a rock star. We'd been partying our ass off for years on the Strip but had always been pretty low-rent, brown paper bags on the curb. Not that anybody was complaining at the time. We were young; we didn't care about living in all that filth. But you could sure get used to the other side in a hurry. There is nothing wrong with luxury, we were quick to learn. There was no end to the coke and the girls and the name-brand booze. Fuck the schnapps. Hand me that bottle of Jack. The party was always first-class with RTB.

We had enough rope to hang ourselves. Things got pretty crazy. We partied at RTB's during the entire remix and then on and off afterwards. The stories are pretty well known by now: Nikki doing lines of cocaine off a glass-top grand piano. Tommy getting blow jobs in the Jacuzzi from his new girlfriend, a *Penthouse* Pet named Candice Starrek, as a dozen others looked on. Tommy offering Candice, his future wife, to others—a display of his true spirit of sharing.

One night at a party people got so fucked up that RTB locked down the house and demanded everyone's keys. He actually wouldn't let anybody leave. Of course, nobody can tell Nikki what to do. In his highly intoxicated state, he decided he had to see Lita. After looking unsuccessfully for his clothes, he climbed naked over the wall of RTB's acreage and drove off in his Porsche—he'd left *his* keys in the ignition. Spotting the naked bassist, two groupies, who hadn't been allowed into the party, jumped into their own car and gave chase. A high-speed pursuit ensued, with speeds hitting 90 mph. At one point, Nikki looked back to see if he had lost the girls—and promptly slammed his Porsche into a telephone pole.

The girls fled the scene. Naked and bleeding, with a dislocated shoulder, Nikki extracted himself from his car and hitched a ride to a hospital. He was in a lot of pain. They gave him lots of Percodan. It was the shoulder injury, I think, that would eventually lead to his heroin use.

The partying at RTB's was obviously great. The problem was the album. He fucked it up. It sucks.

When you listen to Queen or the Cars, the sound is very polished. But Mötley Crüe didn't need to be polished. You polish it up too much and it loses the rawness. I think I can honestly say that we made up for not having the greatest talent in the world with having great attitude and delivery. It's that entertainment thing again. A lot of the critics say—and I agree—that the first album we did ourselves was better. It had real emotion to it; RTB took all that out of it. I just felt his production techniques were way too polished for how a Mötley Crüe record should sound. And I still think it sounds terrible to this day. Sorry, Roy. Fact is fact, man.

On top of that, I don't think Elektra went to any great lengths to promote the album. Maybe that was an omen, too, because we've always sort of had to swim upstream to get the proper attention from our record companies, if you ask me. Zutaut told us that he was in the office one day and overheard the head of the radio department telling one of the other guys how he didn't give a fuck about any radio stations that were showing interest in our album. At the time, the label was really pushing this Australian band called Cold Chisel. Zutaut blew a fuse and went to tell his boss what was going on. The radio asshole got fired. And as for Cold Chisel . . . if you hear anything about them and their shining career, please feel free to drop me a line.

Mostly by word of mouth, *Too Fast for Love* entered the *Billboard* chart at #157. It sold over one hundred thousand copies right out of the gate. The record company fat cats might not know what fucking day it is half the time, but the fans vote with their wallets.

In Tommy's bio, somebody once told me, he spends the entire first chapter talking to his dick.

I'd like to spend a few moments addressing my own crotch, if you don't mind.

As we've well established, it's *my* leather-encased junk adorning the front cover of *Too Fast for Love.* I am wearing the black lace-ups that Leah/Lovey had bought me a couple years before. (A few years later she would be killed in an alleged drug deal gone awry, stabbed sixty-six times, according to police reports.) I have signed many copies of the album over the years. Everybody always asks me about the "double meaning" of how my right hand is positioned.

Some people say I'm making the sign of the devil, aka the sign of rock 'n' roll. The truth is, I don't even know what the so-called devil sign even means. Ronnie James Dio is the one who started it. Everyone always throws the devil sign, but I don't know what the fuck it means, you know. Does it mean I'm giving you the evil eye or something? Am I casting a spell or whatever?

Other people insist I'm forming the American Sign Language symbol for "I love you."

In Texas, the same sign stands for "Hook 'em Horns!" the slogan and hand signal employed by fans at UT, Austin.

To tell you the truth, I'm more interested to hear what you think about the songs. You can interpret the hand signal however you want. Maybe my finger was itching at that moment and I went to scratch it on my belt, thus making it curl under in a weird way. Maybe I had a bet going on the UT game that day? (A lot less likely back then, though a good possibility today.)

And all I can say is this:

Why doesn't anyone ever think to ask me about what my *other* hand is doing?

Some more trivia for collectors: The first pressing of *TFFL* was two thousand copies. The album cover had white lettering. The second pressing was four thousand copies. It had red lettering on the cover and a white label on the vinyl. Five thousand copies were also produced on cassette. The third pressing was twenty thousand copies, with red lettering on the cover and a black label on the vinyl. (The distributor, Greenworld, went bankrupt in 1986; out of the ashes grew Enigma Records.) When Elektra reissued the album—we got a $28,500 advance, split four ways, minus Coffman's cut—a few changes to the album cover were made. The front photo and logo were enlarged and the rear album photo was reduced. A new band picture was included on the lyric sheet inside, and the song "Stick to Your Guns" was omitted. For some reason, Elektra released the original Leathür version of the album only in Canada.

Also, about my hair in the back photo:

It was airbrushed. It's fake. The back of the Elektra record is one way and the back of the Leathür record is another. My dad's got the original version, the one with the superimposed giganta-hair. People call it the big-hair album. What happened was Coffman's photographer took the shots with us standing against a white background. And being that I have blond hair, it kind of disappeared and looked like shit. In the proofs it looked really, really weird. I should have insisted on another shoot, but this photographer had already left town, so I stupidly allowed Coffman to convince me that the guy—one of his buddies, it turned out—could rectify the problem in the lab or whatever. When I saw the finished cover I was really fuckin' pissed off. It looks like I'd borrowed Elton John's beehive wig or some shit! There's a clear, like, *line* going across where you can see they've superimposed more hair on top of the other hair. By the time I saw it, it was too late to change. At least I wasn't the only one. Apparently Mick was also unhappy with the picture—he thought he looked like Joan Jett; he had a good point, though I wasn't gonna be the one who told him. Funny how things come around: On the night my son, Neil, was born, I had been working as a roadie for Joan and her band the Runaways.

Now my bandmate was fucking their guitar player.

It was just another night on the Strip.

I can't tell you *what* night, exactly.

You got a problem with that?

I suppose *you* can remember the exact date or year of everything you ever did?

That's what I thought.

By this time, things were a blur. We were living in the moment. Shit was happening. Other than being at the gigs on time, I didn't know what day it was. Night became day became night. A blur of gigs and girls and places and people. And maybe a little blackout time; when my drinking was bad I would black out and lose time. It's like this switch would go off. Later people would tell me what I did. Or maybe they haven't told me a lot of it, I'm sure. Maybe that's the reason some people have gotten mad at me over the years. There is a lot of stuff I don't even remember. There are a lot of people who wouldn't speak to us for this book.

But some things you never forget; this time was one of them.

Nikki and I were leaving the Rainbow with our girls. Things were different then. We were all brothers in arms. Like guys from the same team or army squad, you know? We partied together; we played together; we fucked the same girls . . . sometimes at the same time—like they say, our swords crossed. We were *that* close.

At this point Nikki was with Lita Ford. It was easy to see why he liked her—she was different from the other groupie-type women, like an idolized version of a musician's girlfriend, a true rocker who could shred. (It was like a regular guy finding a woman who likes to drink beer and watch football.) When she got up on the stage, Lita was not fucking around. She was as good as any guy on guitar. She had no problem keeping up with Nikki—within moments of their first meeting she'd broken a quaalude in half and fed him one part. They were a true match from the jump.

I was with my new girlfriend, Beth Lynn. She was beautiful—of course. She had a small, round ass and a nice rack—of course. She was blond and blue-eyed—or maybe her eyes were green. It is hard to remember; it's been a long time since I last saw her.

Some people say that if you lined up all my wives and girlfriends, you'd have a row of Barbie dolls—replicas of replicas, in descending order of age, older models replaced occasionally for new, and so on down the line.

I guess I'll admit: I have a *type*.

A bit of an understatement?

But you can't say I don't have excellent taste. Shoot me: I like wholesome-looking blond California girls. Who doesn't? In the contest for what kinds of chicks are the best in the world, I'm gonna vote for my hometown fave, the wish-they-all-could-be Cali blonde. Once you've found what you like, what the fuck, you know what I'm sayin'? Why change? Yes, my mother was a blonde. And so was my first crush: Mrs. Anderson. I don't know what it is about blondes. Maybe the brunettes are, you know, maybe they're too smart for me.

I do admit it's a little weird how Beth and I met, but like I said, that was how things were at the time. Originally, Nikki was the one who knew Beth. She was a groupie type, but she was also superhot. I guess what I'm saying is that Beth was like a groupie who was a cut above all the other groupies... the kind who becomes a rock 'n' roll wife.

Nikki met Beth at the Troubadour one night; she was hanging out with the guys in Ratt. She was a rich girl from San Diego, sweet and hot at once, like Chinese food. You could tell she'd had an expensive upbringing, just the way she carried herself. Let loose on the streets, she was like the rest of us at the time; we were all walking on the wild side. One night, after partying hard at the Rainbow, we all three headed back to the Mötley House, she and Nikki and I. On the way the talk got pretty hot; there was mention of a threesome. We got to the house, but then I think Nikki passed out.

I was still wide awake. And so was she.

From that night on, Beth was my new girlfriend. She wasn't the first girl I had shared with Nikki or Tommy. Like I said, it seemed perfectly natural. We had that spirit between us.

On this night, we four—Nikki and Lita and Beth and I—were walking from the Rainbow to the Mötley House when these biker dudes started yelling shit in our direction. Back then, there was a lot of static between bikers and the rockers—especially the sort of hair metal/glam variety like us. To them we looked like "fags." (Lemme tell you. I've never known a gay guy in hair metal. [Other than Freddie Mercury.] You have to be a real man to wear makeup. And I guarantee you no biker has *ever* gotten as much pussy as we got—and certainly not more beautiful. Have you seen those Hell's Angel biker chicks? Ohhhhh. *Skanky!* Some writer once called our music Glam Cock Rock. I think that says it pretty well. We might have teased our hair and used Aqua Net, but we were as macho as anyone.)

Things quickly escalated—obviously the biker boys were drunk and spoiling for a fight. Before I knew it, they jumped us. Nikki removed the chain from around his waist and started swinging. As I'm sure you're learning, I've never been one to back down from a fight, either.

We dove right in, the four of us going toe-to-toe, everybody throwing down. Suddenly these two other dudes appeared out of nowhere. I figured they were friends of the biker dudes. In an attempt to get the chain off Nikki, one of the new guys grabbed his wrist. Nikki whipped him across the face a few times before the new guy clamped down on Nikki's hand with his teeth. He looked like a pit bull trying to tear Nikki's hand off his arm.

Then the other new guy pulled a badge and a gun.

Undercover cops!

As the cops focused on Nikki, the bikers scurried off into the night—as did I. There was nothing I could do. If we both got arrested, who would, you know... I was better off on the outside to help get him released. And besides, I'd just been arrested the week before at the Troubadour for hitting a chick who didn't like the U.S. Marines getup I was wearing. I didn't want to get arrested again.

While "taking him into custody," the cops hit Nikki seven times in the face, breaking his cheekbone and giving him a black eye. He was transported in a squad car to the West Hollywood police station. On the way Nikki must have said something to someone—he's never shared exactly what he told the cops that made them stop in an alley, pull him out of the car, and repeatedly beat him about the stomach and face.

After spending two nights in the lockup, Nikki was bailed out by Lita, who hocked her Firebird Trans Am for one thousand dollars to raise the money. In the end the charges were dropped—I think there were too many witnesses to the obvious police brutality... they were really whaling on Nikki. After his release, the lovebirds walked the three miles back from the police lockup to the Mötley House—just in time to change for our show that night at the Whisky.

That night Nikki wore exaggerated makeup to cover his bruises. For fun and camouflage he added the two swatches of black beneath his eyes. He liked the look so much that he continued to wear it even after he'd healed.

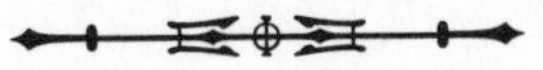

Beth Lynn Neil
Vince's First Wife

I moved to San Diego in 1979 for my junior year of high school; I began dating Robbin Crosby from the band Ratt; we both went to La Jolla High School. I'd been raised on a lake about an hour and a half outside Chicago. I was pretty naïve and innocent and country—I showed up wearing like cowboy boots. I was hungry for exposure to things that I hadn't been exposed to, I guess you could say.

Eventually I met this group of girls and we would drive up to LA every weekend. We'd go to Gazzari's and the other clubs on the Strip. When I graduated high school, Robbin was moving up to LA, so I went with him. He's dead now and it absolutely breaks my heart. He was probably my best guy friend, ever. You know how you start out in a relationship with somebody and you think you're in love and then you figure out you're really just good friends? He was that guy for me.

I met Vince briefly for the first time back behind the Troubadour. I pulled up in a Datsun 240Z. Vince was in a blue one, the same kind of a car. And one of us said, like, "We should race or something,"

something really cheesy to that extent. And then he goes, "Hey, I'm Vince. I'm playing here tonight." Which is typical for him. Vince was such a gregarious, outgoing, funny, charming guy. He was so outgoing and so just full of himself. He was spectacular, really. He's like, "Come upstairs; I'm playing tonight." So I went upstairs to the backstage area.

It was early in the night, like maybe seven. We started talking and hanging out and I was meeting everybody. Vince introduced me to Nikki and Tommy. Robbin showed up at that point; we were all, like, pretty heatedly talking, just into it, having a good time. And Vince leans over and says, you know, "We're going to have a party after the gig, you should come over," blah blah blah. And right about that time a girl came in the room. Well, not a girl. She was much older. I was like nineteen. I had a fake ID. I had like five of them. I'm actually almost exactly one year younger than Vince. My birthday is February 10. So anyway, the woman was Leah. I had no idea who she was and she came over and just started yelling at me, "Get away from my husband," blah blah blah, "I'll kick your ass; I don't know who you think you are," and I'm like, "Hey, no problem. I'm out of here. That's fine with me. I don't even *know* him; I just *met* him." She was maybe thirty-eight, thirty-nine years old. She seemed ancient to me at the time. But in any case, that was his girlfriend.

Vince was pretty amazingly gorgeous. But honestly, there were a lot of little boys running around in those days that were amazingly gorgeous at nineteen and twenty. It was more than just that with Vince. I absolutely adored him because he was fearless. He was absolutely courageous onstage. Like when they wouldn't even pack the place—it'd be like twenty people there or something, and he would have this fantastic all-white leather or all-red leather outfit with the crotch stitched up, from North Beach Leather, this really expensive store where Leah bought him stuff. I mean, the place might only have twelve people in it, but he would be in these outfits, and he'd find like a door he was going to come through, and he'd try to make this huge entrance onstage. And it was nothing faux about it at all. It was totally, completely, authentic—like he was going to be famous. And not only that, he was going to do it better than anybody had ever done it before. He had this courage that I absolutely adored about him. And he was gregarious, too. And funny. He was also fragile and a little boy in a lot of ways, too. He was absolutely driven. He had the moves. He'd do this sidestep thing where he was almost prancing like a horse—and with his hair as white as he could dye it—and he'd come down those stairs like sideways, and when he hit the stage the *intensity* he had was just awesome, awe inspiring, it just lit up the whole place. He really, *really* had something special. Was he physically beautiful? Yes. But that wasn't the bulk of it. I think that he just had that kind of charisma and drive and courage. It's like, he was insecure in life, but never onstage. Onstage, in those moments, he was completely focused. He's always been a very driven individual.

At some point I started dating Nikki. I'd come over to pick up Nikki—they all lived in the Mötley apartment—and Vince would be there. Or I'd call there and he'd answer the phone and start flirting with me, like, "Hey what are you doing? When are we going out?" Dah dah dah. And I'm like, "You've *got* a girlfriend. I'm not going out with you. I'm dating your best friend." Nikki and Vince were really close at that time. I think later they had their battles, but not then. Sometimes I'd come over to pick up Nikki and Vince would be like, "Oh, Nikki's out at the Body Shop watching strippers; why don't we go out and get a bite to eat?" He was always trying to go out with me.

There were a lot of parties at the apartment. I mean, a *lot* of parties. After, after the clubs would close down, we'd end up at their house, everybody getting really drunk, snorting a lot of coke, women everywhere, a lot of people hooking up in the little rooms here or there, coming and going. A couple other bands lived in that apartment building, too. The Heart girls lived across the way. They didn't really fraternize with us, but they were in and out of there once in a while.

And there was a band next door that I honestly can't remember who it was. They never ended up getting famous. But there were always parties going in a couple different apartments; people would kind of roam around between all of them. Their apartment was on the first floor; there was kind of a back window where people would crawl in. The window was on the back alley. When some people came over, they came through the window so they didn't have to walk through all the people out there in the courtyard and the other rooms. It was kind of like the VIP entrance. David Lee Roth always came in that way.

The parties had the normal drinking and drugging, everybody hooking up kind of thing. I remember Tommy liked to run around naked a lot. He was very proud of, you know, his manhood. And there were plenty of girls who were happy to pay him attention, too.

The thing that happened was I was dating Nikki. One night we were all three walking home from the Rainbow and it was a time when I actually had a prescription for quaaludes. I always really liked downers better than uppers back in the day. So quaaludes were great—though they ended up really getting me in a lot of trouble that I probably wouldn't have gotten into, as I review things in the past. But anyway, I guess I lived through it, so hey, it's my history; I own it. But in any case on that particular night, I remember, we were all drinking at the Rainbow. There were some other people at the table with us; Vince actually got sick and threw up under the table. After that, we were just walking home. And Nikki said something to the effect of, "How would you like to have a threesome with me and Vince?" I had dated Nikki maybe two months at that point, but who knows how exclusive he'd been, you know? It *felt* exclusive to me, but who knows *really*? So I said, "Okay, why not? I'll try it."

We got to the apartment and started to hook up. And what happened I guess is that Vince pretty much just didn't let Nikki do anything. Vince just pretty much went for it and, you know, *blocked* Nikki out of the situation. So Nikki got mad and left. And I was like drunk enough and fucked up enough that I was just like, *Whatever.* The truth was, over that couple months when Vince was trying to charm me and go out with me, I kind of had a crush on him anyway. Nikki was very intense, very dark, very mopey. He was like Eeyore, you know, "My life is all fucked up." And Vince was just like this little ray of light every time he came into a room. He was funny, laughing, cracking jokes all the time. That was Vince.

The next morning I had to go out. Nikki was sitting on the living room floor, looking all pouty, and I'm like, *Oh shit.* So I tell Nikki, "Hey, I'm really sorry." And he's like, "It's cool, don't worry about it, things happen or whatever."

A couple of days later, I'm at the Troubadour with Robbin. Vince walks up. He's wearing this T-shirt from the Pleasure Chest on Melrose. It said: "Fuck me now, I have to get on with my career."

It was another quaalude night. Vince and I started talking. One thing led to the next and it's like smash cut to: scene in my apartment/morning. I wake up. I'm with someone. I look over and I see this white blond hair. And I'm like, *Oh shit.*

And then Vince rolls over all cheery. He's like, "Good morning, beautiful."

And I'm, like, *Oh fuck!* 'Cause I literally, I literally didn't remember how he got there. And now I've got to explain this to Nikki.

But then, things started to turn. Vince was so chipper and sweet. We started talking and hanging out and I cooked him breakfast and then we went and bought a dartboard and hung it on the wall and we played darts from the bed and we just like had this whole big long week where he didn't go home—he stayed at my place; we hardly ever got out of bed.

At some point, Nikki started calling. He's like, "Is Vince there? Is Vince there?" And Vince is like making signs, like, *No, no,* you know, but he's grinning like he's really amused. And then Nikki started calling again, saying, "I don't care if he's there or not, but if you could just have him let us know he's not dead or something, that would be great." So finally, I told Vince, "You're going to have deal with this."

And he just said, "Okay, I'm going to go home and tell Nikki that you're my girl and that's it."

And I'm like, "Is that really the smartest move? It might break up your band."

In my opinion, Nikki was always kind of jealous of Vince. Vince just did everything so effortlessly and Nikki worked so hard to grasp everything. It was just two different personalities working toward the same end really, but they were very different. And you know Vince was the lead singer and Nikki was just the bass player and blah blah blah. And I just felt like it was maybe not a good idea. So I said to Vince, "We don't have to go through with any kind of relationship. I mean it's been great, whatever, but we could just call it a day."

But he was like, "No, I'm going to go tell him."

Pretty much from that point on we were together.

On March 12, 1982, the Los Angeles County Department of Health Services issued an official notice of violation to Nikki Sixx (he was the leaseholder), for the "non-removal of trash from the premises" at the Mötley House. Pretty soon after that we were evicted.

Honestly, we could have cared less. We were ready to get the fuck outta Dodge. It was so dirty in there, even *we* thought it was disgusting. Half the time we didn't even know the people who were hanging out there.

Nikki moved into Lita Ford's place in Coldwater Canyon. My roomie Tommy Lee, having finally dropped his former girl, Bullwinkle—after she smashed a window with a fire extinguisher—moved with his girlfriend into a small house with a pool in the backyard. Mick was still living with his girlfriend Linda in Redondo Beach.

After a month or two in her apartment in Hollywood, Beth and I moved to Redondo also. She had very wealthy parents and grandparents. She had a 280Z. I don't know what it was about that model car. Zs have followed me through my life. Leah/Lovey had one, too. She used to drive me to practice and gigs in it. And I actually owned one before that, when I was like seventeen or eighteen, when I was working at the Kasler Corporation. This was after my truck had died. I had the 280Z in blue I think it was. Or maybe it was a 240? 260? I can't remember. I do remember I was making good money at the time. And that I financed it and my dad cosigned on it and stuff. And when I lost my job, when I quit, you know, they repossessed it.

Beth and I loved Redondo. We both did a lot of drugs together. It was just a nonstop party. We married pretty soon after that. I don't remember why, exactly, we decided to get married then. I loved her. I think maybe like I cheated on her and she found out and then to, like, apologize, you know, I said let's get married. I can't really remember exactly the situation. That was three wives ago!

The ceremony was this big deal at the Crystal Cathedral in Orange County. You pass it on the I-5. During Christmastime it's lit up like heaven's gates. Lord knows what their electric bill must be, dude. I don't remember what time of year it was when we got married. I don't remember why we picked the Cathedral, the home base for the international Crystal Cathedral Ministries, which includes a congregation of over ten thousand members and the internationally televised *Hour of Power*, according to the Web site. It's a beautiful place, though; it was the whole fairy-tale wedding. All the guys from Mötley were there. We played a few songs.

Meanwhile, we were getting so fucking well known on the

Strip that we were selling out everywhere we played. The Troubadour, the Whisky, the Country Club. You name it, we were selling it out.

Record stores couldn't keep our album in stock. One place put a painting of me, like this big mural, on their wall outside. We even had some merchandise available through mail order—there was no Web in those days, of course. We sold these rockin' Mötley Crüe leather gloves and T-shirts and other stuff by mail. You called a number and they sent it out.

Right about that time, the British rock magazine *Kerrang!* published the first glossy magazine photo of a Mötley Crüe member—a full-page, full-color picture of... *me.* Though it didn't occur to me at the time, this might have been the first nail in my coffin as far as those other guys were concerned. Nikki and Tommy were the ones who'd always wanted to be famous. They'd formed the band; they needed a singer, so they went out and got me. Now I was getting known as the frontman. I was more famous than them. Nobody said anything to my face, but I knew what they were thinking. If you ask me, a lot of shit between us started right there, with the *Kerrang!* story. You build a wall one brick at a time. I really feel like that was one of the first bricks.

Since nobody at Elektra was gonna put any money into promotion, the only thing to do was go out and play. So that's what we did.

Coffman booked us on our first tour.

In Canada.

I was like, *Canada? Why Canada? What the fuck?* But it was a tour, so I didn't complain. We called it the Crüesing through Canada Tour, but we hardly cruised—a lot of it was a fucking nightmare of mistakes and naïve fuckups.

Before we even got into the country, we were arrested at Edmonton International Airport for trying to walk through customs in our stage gear. I don't know why we were dressed for the stage. It was somebody's idea. I think we wanted to like get off the airplane in Canada like the Beatles coming to America. So we had to be dressed for it. But I don't think any of us had too much experience with flying at this point; maybe we just didn't know what to expect. They confiscated all our chains, studded belts, and wristbands; they also took exception to my trying to carry through some *Playboy* and *Hustler* magazines I bought in the LA airport to read on the plane.

The first night we played, at Scandals Disco in Edmonton, there was a bomb threat made against the band—some people say that might have been generated by management. I don't know. On the day of our second Edmonton show, we arrived at the venue to find the manager of our hotel waiting for us, demanding $260 for some damage we'd caused. He'd brought along two bodyguards to make sure he got paid. What can I say? We'd been bored and someone came up with the idea of throwing our television sets out of our hotel room windows at the same time to see whose would hit the pavement first. Tommy won the bet, but I still think he cheated.

Along the way there was a fight with a group of dudes still dressed up in their ice-hockey gear and wielding hockey sticks—more glam haters. I felt like I was in a scene from *Warriors*. At another show we had cops lined along either side of the stage after an anonymous caller threatened to attack us during the performance. We found out later that Coffman had engineered that fraud as well—it did get good press back home, however. The guy was *way* too good at lying. That should have been a tip-off.

By the time we got to British Columbia, our reputation had preceded us. Nobody wanted to rent us a hotel room. The remaining dozen or so shows ended up getting canceled. I don't really know what was up exactly, but some of it had to do with Coffman. He was struggling financially. He'd apparently re-mortgaged his house three times to keep the band on the road—food, hotel, the whole nine.

Rather than come clean to the band, or ask Elektra for help, Coffman sold 5 percent of his stake in the band to a young guy named Bill Larson, who'd paid with twenty-five thousand dollars he'd stolen from his parents, their entire life savings. The Canada tour had something to do with the deal.

Long story short: Coffman ended up with Larson's twenty-five thousand dollars and whatever was left of our Elektra advance. After we severed ties with him, his wife, Barbara, came home to find him pacing their backyard with a gun in his hand, contemplating suicide. He later divorced her and became a born-again Christian. Having learned the news of Coffman's swindle, the money lost, Larson's father suffered a heart attack; he died six months later. Upon his father's death, Larson himself suffered clinical depression; he eventually filed a lawsuit in hopes of recovering his money. The case was thrown out of court when it was discovered that Coffman had disappeared without a trace. Larson continued to work in the music industry; eventually he became a co-founder of HardRadio. I feel sorry for all these guys, but then on the other hand I don't. They were all vultures, trying to make a buck off people who loved to play music. Sometimes they die. They are eaten by the others in the clan.

In the middle of all this incredible bullshit, in August of 1982, our first single dropped.

"Live Wire" was followed, four days later, by the Electra rerelease of *Too Fast for Love*. It entered the charts at #157.

I remember the first time I heard myself on the radio.

Yes, I do. *Absolutely.* It was right about this time. I was living in Redondo Beach and I was driving to my apartment. It was just a beautiful summer day, like always near the beach. Amazing waves, amazing blue sky, that great cool breeze. And then "Live Wire" came on the radio.

I stopped the car.

I was like, *Oh my god.*

But I didn't... there was nobody... I couldn't... There were no cell phones then. I was all by myself and there was nobody to call and nothing to do. I was just sitting there by myself, you know, thinking, *Holy shit, that's me on the radio.* Yeah. *Yeah!* I was sitting in Beth's orange 240Z. Or maybe it was a 260. I always get those confused. But yeah, man. I heard it come on and it was just greater than anything you could describe. It was a pretty proud moment. It was very surreal.

It's no accident this chapter carries the title it does. It's from a Cheap Trick song, "He's a Whore." 'Cause every musician needs his pimp. They call them managers, agents, what have you. Like I said earlier, it's a necessary evil.

After Coffman left, we needed management... and fast. There was no way Mötley Crüe could run itself. Maybe Nikki thought for a minute we could do it, but there was no way. If we were going to go anywhere, we had to find some suits we could trust.

Because we had an album and a deal, we had a little bit of leverage, but we were still the ones who were putting ourselves out there—we were the ones with our hats in hand, asking to be taken on as clients. (It's kind of weird that you have to beg people to take 10 percent of your income, but that's another fucked-up part of the whole industry.) We set up a showcase at the Santa Monica Civic Auditorium and invited as many potential managers as we could find. The concert was billed as "New Year's Eve-*il*." I don't remember whose brilliant title that was, but we filled the thirty-five-hundred-seat arena with no problem at all. People were being turned away at the door. In the audience was booking agent Doug Thaler. He'd been invited by our good friend Ronnie James Dio. Back in the late sixties, Thaler had played with Ronnie Dio and the Prophets. He almost lost his leg when their tour van was involved in a head-on collision.

As it happened, a guy named Doc McGhee was also coming. He was known as a dude with a pot full of money who wanted to start up his own management company. Doc has since gone down in rock 'n' roll folklore for having discovered Bon Jovi. And although Doc had no previous experience in the music industry, aside from managing Pat Travers, he believed he could turn Mötley Crüe into the biggest rock 'n' roll band in the world. Not only that—he didn't even care whether Elektra was willing to put any money into the venture. *He* was willing to throw in as much money as it took. What a sweet guy, right?

(What we didn't know yet: In 1988 McGhee would be arrested for his involvement in a 1982 conspiracy to smuggle forty thousand pounds of Colombian marijuana. He received a suspended sentence, paid a fifteen-thousand-dollar fine, and was required to start a foundation, which he dubbed Make a Difference.)

McGhee was interested in hiring Thaler to help him run his management company. They traveled together from Florida to hear us play.

Our show was an unbelievable success. Packed to the rafters, people going crazy; fire marshals issued us a one-thousand-dollar fine for using these twenty-foot mortars. McGhee would later say that after he saw that show, taking us on was pretty much a no-brainer.

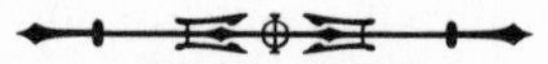

Doug Thaler
Co-manager and Later Manager of Mötley Crüe

I co-managed Mötley Crüe with Doc McGhee from the beginning of January 1983 until mid-August of 1989. Then I managed them myself for the next five and a half years, till the end of 1994. I haven't spoken with Vince in fifteen years. Vince doesn't speak to me anymore.

Basically, I graduated from school in 1967 and I was invited to join Ronnie Dio and the Prophets. That became the Electric Elves. Then it became the Elves, then Elf. I stopped playing for a living in 1972 and became an agent. I signed AC/DC and brought them to the United States. I booked them right through *Highway to Hell*; that was the last thing I booked on them. Same thing with Judas Priest. I started them as a five-hundred-dollar band and booked their tours right through the end of 1979. Pat Travers was a client of mine. Be Bop Deluxe, Thin Lizzy.

After that, I went over into music publishing for a couple years, which was boring as shit; then I joined Contemporary Communications Corporation—they had Ted Nugent, Aerosmith, the Scorpions, Def Leppard. In the summer of '82 I was handling an Aerosmith tour.

Tom Zutaut was Mötley Crüe's A and R man from Elektra; he called me to see if I'd put Mötley Crüe on the bill, at least on the West Coast. I didn't 'cause we had already committed the spot. But right about that time, in the early fall of '82, I went out to California to visit Ronnie Dio and other friends. Ronnie spoke highly of Mötley Crüe, so I went out to see them perform at the Santa Monica Civic Center on December 31,

1982. I went with Pat Travers's manager, Doc McGhee. Doc was new in the business and he wanted me to come in with him.

The show was sold out. They had god-awful merchandise that all sold anyway. It was an amazing, amazing show. They looked phenomenal; they were great onstage. I thought the songs were great; I thought the look was great. There were some amateurish elements—they had, like, propane jets as part of the pyro show, which are totally illegal. I mean, they're good for starting fires, but that's about it. And Nikki had a thing where he wore thigh-high boots and he figured out how much water to mix with isopropyl alcohol and he used a torch and he'd set himself on fire; his legs would be burning. He figured he could take it for about ten seconds. I saw them and said, "Wow, all we gotta do is make a record with these guys." They had all the songs from their first album. And they already had all the songs written for *Shout at the Devil*—they played them in their set. And so I got to hear "Too Young to Fall in Love" and "Looks That Kill." The only thing left for them was making a record with a real producer who makes records that get on the radio.

About the second week of January we sat down with Nikki and Tommy. I said, "Look, here's what I want to do. Basically I don't want you to change much of anything. I think you got great songs; I think you got a great look." I thought they needed to get a real pyrotechnician involved. I told them they needed to make a legit record. I told them, "It'll get on the radio because you got the songs. We'll just take what you do here in Los Angeles and we'll send it all over the world." I knew it would work. And that's basically what we did.

My first impression of Vince? I loved how he sang. It's not that he had such a great voice; it's just that he had a great *sound*. And he had a great *look*. He was only just turning twenty-two. He looked great and he moved great. He was just a great frontman. There wasn't much of anything we had to do with Vince. We took him for voice lessons—really more to try to teach him proper breathing techniques so that he would be able to sing a lot of shows in a week without losing his voice. We had to teach him a few fundamentals. He would do this vocal warm-up. It was shit like Tarzan would do.

I probably spent more physical time on the road with them and in rehearsal halls and things like that than Doc did. Back in those days, neither Doc nor myself really understood addictive behavior syndrome. We didn't really understand alcoholism and drug addiction and stuff like that. People were getting high all over the place. It was the times. We hired a head of security—one of his jobs was to monitor what the band was doing. We knew they were going to get shit; we didn't want them running around strange towns trying to score blow or whatever. So, we just tried to keep as much of a lid on it as possible, and keep everybody together. It really started getting bad in November of '83, the *Shout at the Devil* tour. Of course it wasn't long after that Vince had the, ah, automobile mishap—you know, Razzle was killed. All the guys were like equally wild, equally irresponsible. Equally into drugs and alcohol and debauchery and whatever. Don't get me wrong—there were a lot of fun times, too. But of course managing them was a 24/7 job because you knew somebody was going to be doing something all the time—you just didn't know who it would be and what it would be, but it was almost certain that something was just around the corner. I mean, Vince crashed the car in December of '84 with Razzle. But just before that, Nikki crashed a car in a stupor—that was the summer of 1983 when they were in the studio making *Shout at the Devil*. Luckily nobody but Nikki was in the car and nobody got hurt but Nikki. He injured his shoulder.

With Vince, he did what he did. I wouldn't say there were usually any apologies for it. Vince has a proclivity to do what it is he wants to do. He didn't really think about, say, what are the consequences to other people, what are the consequences to the band, what are the consequences to the band's business, what are the consequences to me—that kind of thing. I mean, he did what he did and he pretty much . . . he did things that he wanted to do. I don't think there was ever any thought of: *If I do this, what are the consequences to the other people in the band? What are the consequences to me going to be?* I don't think he thought things out like that. He just sort of lived in the moment. World be damned, full steam ahead.

I wasn't happy being the one who had to call Vince and tell him he was out of the group. At first I tried to just stall the process. I mean, between myself and their business manager and their attorney, we all just said, "Guys, I understand that you guys are frustrated with Vince's behavior. And that he's done things in the past that have made you frustrated. I understand that even after we called this behavior to his attention, it really doesn't seem to change anything." And we also told them, you know, that "Mötley Crüe is you four guys. It's not three guys." I had just redone this record deal for them. I told them, "The label might not go for this at all. If you throw Vince out of the band, you might not have a record deal anymore."

But the sentiment at the time was clear. Tommy was kind of the leader of that movement. But Mick and Nikki were equally frustrated with Vince's behavior. I asked the guys, "Can't we stall for a few days?" But Nikki had his mind made up. He wanted to drive this thing forward. Before I knew it they had a new singer coming to rehearsal—John Corabi. And yes, being their manager, I was the one who had to call Vince and say, "Vince, these guys don't want you in the band anymore."

I understand why Vince won't talk to me anymore. But I feel like I had a really good relationship with him at one time. I think Vince felt very betrayed by me. I'm in a funny place because, if I had it to do over again, I would've done it a different way. I would've just said, "Guys, you know what? Mötley Crüe is the *four* of you. Period. I'm gonna suspend your contract for now; I'm gonna take a break from working with you. Let me know if you can ever work together again, and I'll come back and manage you. If the three of you want to do something with another singer and call it something besides Mötley Crüe . . ."

Well, you know what they say: woulda, shoulda, coulda.

The truth is, I was frustrated with Vince at that point because Vince wasn't listening to me about *anything*. So I felt like maybe I got a shot if I continue to manage Mötley Crüe—or whatever it's gonna become post-Vince. Because one thing was for sure: Vince was not listening to me anymore. I don't think Vince ever understood my frustration. I don't really know if Vince, now or then, would've given a shit about my frustration. After all, he's the one who always called me "Doc's lackey."

In retrospect, it could have been handled better. But how can you handle something when nobody's listening? Vince wouldn't listen to me. Nikki and the other guys certainly didn't listen to me anymore, either. They went out and hired a singer who couldn't sing Mötley Crüe songs. And they hired him without even making him sing a single Mötley Crüe song as an audition. Corabi sang "Jailhouse Rock" and jammed with them and they hired him.

It wasn't until they started rehearsing for their tour that they found out the real truth: John Corabi couldn't sing Mötley Crüe songs.

Good luck with that, right?

History tells all.

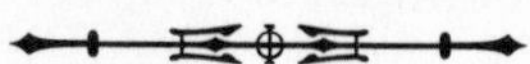

The first official act by McGhee and Thaler, as our new management team, was to book us onto a tour with KISS.

Imagine this:

You're twenty-two, twenty-three. You're in a local band. You've played the Strip; you've played clubs; you've even played a couple of arenas. You've got an album out and some bucks.

And now, suddenly, you are going on tour with KISS, one of the biggest acts around.

Plus…

You get to have your very own tour bus.

It was our first. I will always remember it. There will be a zillion tour buses in the future. Everything will become a blur after a while—trains, planes, luxury chartered jets, double-decker buses, limos, three-wheeled scooters in various third world countries. You hear all about that shit, living like a rock star, touring the world. You've dreamed about it—even if you always say you never wanted to do it, or never thought about doing it, at some point every human being is going to dream, I won't deny it.

And then, suddenly, there you are.

You're living the dream.

You're on a tour bus; you're opening for fuckin' KISS.

Dude!

Thinking back on it now, I can tell you that bus was the biggest piece of shit you can rent. Just stripped and pretty low-end. I mean, some of those buses are like mansions inside, with granite and marble and crystal chandeliers, the whole nine. This was just a big black tour bus with a ratty interior. But it was our first one and we were like, *Oh my god! We have a tour bus.* It was the most exciting thing ever.

The very first show or the second show, I think it was, we played Irvine Meadows. And then the next show was Phoenix. It's not that far of a drive, six, seven hours, something like that? We left after the show. And I wake up on the bus the next day and we're stopped somewhere; I hear all this weird noise. I look out the window and all I see is a wall.

It turned out the bus had broken down in the middle of the night and we were at a truck stop. We'd been there for like twelve hours. I slept like a baby in that little coffin of a space, I guess. And then we ended up spending almost the whole day there, too. So *that* was our first tour bus. It's just funny it was such a hunk of shit.

The other thing I remember about the KISS tour was we had our drum riser. Most of the halls you play in are unionized, you know, and there are all these rules about who can touch stuff where and when. We had the drum riser that me and Tommy built. It was made of giant pieces of wood that were bolted together, you know; it was very hard to assemble and reassemble. This thing, it wasn't built for touring. It was very homemade. Part of the riser had, like, all these branches mounted here and there with all these skulls hanging in them. And these union guys are going, like, "Excuse me, where do we put the skull branches at?" It was very, very funny. Just another surreal thing. Because this was KISS's Creatures of the Night Tour, they had this giant drum riser built in the shape of a tank. I mean it was massive. It was expensive. It looked *good*. And we had all our homemade shit that we'd built in the Mötley House—a homemade drum riser and these skulls with branches and candelabras. Here we were and all our big crazy ideas were actually being treated with respect; all that playing with pyro gel in the living room of the Mötley House was paying off.

One thing that wasn't rinky-dink was our playing. We were fucking playing our asses off. I mean, we weren't blowing KISS away, but we were definitely, like, competition. People were loving us.

Which apparently pissed the fuck out of Gene Simmons. He did not like it one bit that these nobodies were hogging the spotlight. At least that's what I heard. He never hung out with us. There was maybe this little, like, "Hi, how you doing?" But that was basically it. They didn't stand around and watch us play. We were basically, you know, almost still a club band. But we were just doing really good. Every show there were a lot of people there to see us. Most times, people don't give a shit about the opening act. They come late because all they want to see is the headliner. Which was still the same with the KISS tour, but there were a lot of people there to see us, way more than it would usually be.

We only did like five, six shows before we were kicked off of the tour. It ended in San Francisco, I think it was. McGhee and

Thaler said it was because we were upstaging the headliners. Gene Simmons said he booted us off for bad behavior. That was probably more accurate. I found out later that Tommy and Nikki had been discovered having sex with Eric Carr's girlfriend while he was onstage. Ironically enough, years later, Gene Simmons would reportedly call up Nikki wanting to do a deal for film rights to *The Dirt*.

Our first album took three days to record.

Our second, *Shout at the Devil*, took more than nine months.

The setting this time was the historic Cherokee Studios, on Fairfax Avenue in Hollywood. It was a far cry from our first studio on Pico. This one boasted a rich heritage of recording artists and platinum albums, from Ella Fitzgerald and Frank Sinatra to David Bowie, Elton John, and Rod Stewart. The producer was a guy named Tom Werman. I had no idea who he was.

As you could imagine, it was hard telling where the recording stopped and the partying began. Girls came and went constantly; it was a fuckfest. All of us had girlfriends, or in my case I was married of course. The burrito trick was often employed. Ray Manzarek, the Doors' keyboardist, was in the adjoining studio recording his *Carmina Burana* album; he spent a lot of time doing our cocaine and fucking our chicks and regaling us with stories about Jim Morrison.

There was the night that Nikki, Tommy, and his drum tech Clyde "the Spide" Duncan were hassled by some cops and then took turns pissing into the window of their patrol car before running off. The night that Tommy threw a brick through the control room window. The night Nikki and I lay on our backs on the floor and chanted into microphones above our heads while a gong, suspended on a rope and spinning in circles, made a shimmering sound overhead. The night Nikki managed to convince the engineer that if he listened closely to the half-track played backwards he would hear the words "Jesus is Satan" in the mix.

Satan was a big topic at this time. What a bunch of BS. There are some stories about guitar picks flying upward and sticking into the ceiling. Nikki was rumored to be messing around with the occult and devil worship with Lita. I don't know if that was true, but I do know that Nikki was talking a lot about his grand vision of the album and tour looking like a cross between a Nazi rally and a Black Mass service.

It's probably significant to note here that during this time, while my wife, Beth, was pregnant with our first (my second) child, I had begun to dabble with heroin. Nikki was still in a lot of pain from his shoulder injury; he started doing heroin, too, partially for the high and partially for the pain—as you might know, heroin is the most powerful known analgesic. Of course, it causes a whole other set of difficult problems for some people, as well.

Pretty soon, it got to the point that we were smoking heroin every day. We never shot; we chased the dragon, which means we used a piece of tinfoil and a lighter and a tube of some sort to chase the smoke as it rose. My shooting days had ended with Lovey. The heroin high is dreamy, numb, and comfortable, a little bit queasy for some. It kind of became a routine. We'd go to the studio, smoke up, record some music. You don't get the heavy nod with smoking so much, unless you really smoke a lot. Even so, it's probably an understatement to say that heroin changed the course of things quite a bit. Nikki was addicted to heroin for several years. For some reason I never got addicted. I remember being a little sick one time, but that was it. I could take it or leave it. Like I've said, alcohol has always been my drug of choice. That and pussy. I never even smoked a cigarette.

In the middle of recording the album, we were signed to play this huge, three-day festival on the outskirts of Los Angeles, in San Bernardino. The vision of Apple Computers' then–head honcho, Steve Wozniak, it was held in a regional park and broadcast live on cable. Official attendance was listed at 370,000. It was fuckin' huge.

We were slated for day two, Sunday, May 29, 1983; it was billed as Heavy Metal Day. We were way down on the bill, but we were there, on the same fucking stage as Ozzy, Judas Priest, the Scorpions, and headliners Van Halen, who were being paid an unbelievable $1.5 million to perform. I remember being back in high school in my truck with James, listening to Van Halen, writing down the words to songs. James's whole thing was Van Halen—that's why he had recruited me in the first place, 'cause I reminded him of David Lee Roth…the big-deal rock 'n' roller who would later take me under his wing.

Now we were playing on the same bill as all these legends.

Holy fuckin' shit.

It was way too fantastic to believe.

To get to the gig, they had to fly us in by helicopter. There were so many people, it was the only way to get in and out effectively. Of course, it was the first helicopter ride for all of us. It was amazing—like the first tour bus, you know, but a million times better. Like the difference between smoking pot and doing a shot of cocaine. Here you are, you're young, you're in this band, and you look down and there's just more people than you've ever seen in one place at one time, and they're all like tiny ants around this tiny dollhouse stage, and then the closer you get, the more massive everything becomes, and it spreads out before you, as far as your eye can see. You can't fuckin' believe it, you're going to be playing with your idols.

All of us brought our wives and girlfriends. Or come to think of it, Beth didn't go. That's right. During this time, when we were making *Shout at the Devil*, that's when I started kind of, you know, falling out with Beth. She would probably say it had something to do with me doing heroin and cocaine, or fucking women or whatever. But I remember I actually chose to stay at the studios rather than go home 'cause she was developing, like, this hand-washing obsession, like some kind of germ-phobia. Later, by the time our daughter was born—Elizabeth Ashley Wharton—on April 13, 1985, contradictory to earlier published reports all over the Web, Beth had really become, you know, like totally *neurotic*. None of my friends were allowed to come over because they had *germs*. It was fuckin' crazy. Stuff like that. I couldn't take it. I'd rather be getting germs at the studio.

But none of that mattered yet as we set down on the helipad in our private chopper. I remember the prop wash blowing my hair into my face as they ushered us to our, like, compound. Every band had their own area. Like Mötley had their section and Judas Priest had their section. Nobody really visited anybody else's compound. It wasn't like all the rock stars were at this big table and we hung out. It was in this big field, you know. It was basically trailers; big trailers were the dressing rooms. We were partying pretty hard. Later I saw this interview of myself after we went onstage. It was with MTV. I was just fucking coked out of my mind. You could tell. That and Jack Daniel's or beer or whatever. You had to drink. It was really hot out there that day. It was funny 'cause I was talking fast. I wasn't incoherent or anything. It was just comical. At this point I was just doing it casually. There would be a point later on where I would have coke hidden around the house and I would go around and do it secretly, you know. Or I thought it was secretly. I thought my wife didn't know, but now I'm pretty sure she did.

We played second, after Quiet Riot. We kicked off about twelve thirty in the afternoon, which was pretty much on time, a miracle considering that Tommy Lee passed out just before going onstage and required oxygen to revive him. We thought of the concert as a great opportunity to test some of the new material we'd been recording. We got a huge response from the crowd. By the end of "Shout at the Devil," everybody was singing along, which was just incredible, being that it was the first time anybody heard it outside of the band.

After leaving the stage, we headed back to our dressing room. When we arrived, Mick's girlfriend punched him in the face for no apparent reason. Sometime around then, I started making it with Zutaut's date, about which much has been said. I have this to say: She was blond. She was hot. She had big boobs. She was wearing a little bikini. I fucked her... as I have thousands of others. Zutaut didn't give a shit. She wouldn't have even been there with him if it wasn't for his association with Mötley Crüe. Everybody knows that. I say the issue is dead.

By the end of the third day, there were 130 arrests at the Us festival and one murder, reportedly a drug deal gone awry. Our performance there was probably the most important of our career. Five months later, *Shout at the Devil* would sell two hundred thousand copies in its first two weeks, eventually reaching #17 on the charts. It would go on to sell over 3 million.

We could never have imagined what would happen next.

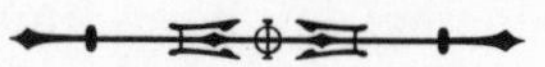

Doc McGhee
Co-manager of Mötley Crüe, '83–'89

Vince was an aggressive, over-the-top frontman. That band was just so aggressive. The abuse factor was running rampant. They thought they were above the law. They were in so many situations that they just skated out of. When you're the biggest band in the world, there are no limits. They got whatever they wanted. And they did whatever they wanted. It was torture, because we'd be thrown out of every fucking hotel in the world. It was a daily thing. And, you know, they weren't vicious—they aren't vicious people. They're fun-loving guys. But they just took no prisoners, you know what I mean? It was just... nuts.

For years, we were enablers as well. I wasn't putting the drugs up their noses personally. I wasn't pouring bottles of liquor down their throats. We didn't encourage abuse, but honestly, we certainly didn't discourage most of the antics that were going on. The weird thing was that after the Razzle crash there was no perceptible change in Vince. He didn't let on at all that being involved in that whole thing affected him. Same with Nikki. When he ODed on heroin, what does he do? He checks himself out of the hospital and goes to get high. It was our job—Doug Thaler's and mine—to be their conscience. That's all we did. That was our *job*. "Let's go apologize every day for them." When Nikki died—for that period of time where we thought he was dead—I called Doug and I said, "I'm out. I quit." And Doug said, "Yeah, me, too." He said, "That's enough; we're not going to watch these guys just kill themselves." So we canceled a European tour and said, "We quit." We said, "If you guys want help, we'll get you help. But we're not going to sit here and watch you guys die."

The other drug was pussy. The shit we used to go through on behalf of pussy. Vince was by far the worst. Vince just had this thing that he had to be with some girl. I mean, it didn't matter who she was, they all looked exactly the same, so he couldn't get confused. You could just spot them—Vince's type. He couldn't go to sleep without somebody with him. It was just one of his things.

When the band was trying to get sober at some point there was a lot of stuff that came out during their actual sessions. I don't think those are things I can talk about. But I think, you know, I think Vince... just... you know... he loved chicks anyways. So, it wasn't, that wasn't, you know, the hardest thing to figure out. But, but the amount of attention he had to have from them and the way he demanded things was a little obsessive. Girls would show up on like a daily basis. It would be like, "Tiffany's backstage at the door with her suitcase." So I'd walk out there and go, "Yeah, Tiffany? What's up?" And she'd be, "Well, Vince told me to come. He said he loved me. We're going to get married." This is like all the time. This was *all* the time. And then I'd walk to the dressing room and go, "Hey, Vince, Tiffany's out there; she's . . ." And he has no idea who I'm talking about. It doesn't even ring a bell. It was kind of like a running joke. And I'm the one telling the proverbial Tiffany that she has to go home. We'd let her just go to the show; then we'd get her a ride home or something, put her on the Greyhound bus. Mitch Fisher at the time was their road manager; he had to do all that.

The eighties were an aggressive time. It was very free, but you have to remember, it was all about fun. It wasn't like the sixties: That movement had substance. The eighties weren't about changing the world, Vietnam, all that stuff. It was about anarchy and having a great time. That's what it all was about. There wasn't any lesson to be had out of the eighties other than having a great time. And that's really what it was about. Mötley Crüe served as the poster boys of that general eighties zeitgeist.

Early eighties, all anybody had to worry about was a few STDs. There was no AIDS yet. You'd worry about catching the clap, or crabs or something. But other than that, it wasn't too bad. Back then, the worst thing was herpes; *everybody* was worried about herpes. But in the early eighties sex wasn't something that could kill you. It was like if somebody was having problems, it was penicillin time. Probably once a week somebody got some shots or got something. They'd be like, "Doc, I'm having a problem." And they'd whip out their dick and be like, "Dude, check this out." And I'd be, "Oh my god, that's disgusting." Which of course made them laugh like loons. Lemme tell you something, I've been doing this a long time with the biggest bands in the world. There's no one like these guys.

There are a million stories that we lived through. The bullet train ride where me and Nikki got arrested, which you don't need to talk about. The fires in the hotels in Switzerland. The guns they used to carry. They used to carry starter guns through Europe. Handguns. They look just like .38 pistols, except they only shoot blanks. They even had shoulder holsters. When you shot it off, the round sounded like a real bullet. You know, the kind of thing they use for track and field. They'd have the bus slow down and open the door and shoot people on bicycles and shit. The people would crash, thinking they had just been shot for real. The guys were nuts. They'd have shoot-outs in hotel lobbies, pretending to be in a movie. SWAT teams would come. It was crazy time.

A *zillion* stories. It's like you couldn't even . . . if you stayed here for literally a week—I bet you I can stay here for a week just going chronologically through the crazy shit they did all over the world . . . *that they don't even remember.*

With Mötley Crüe, it was low IQ, high rpm. They just went out there and turned it on. There was no dimmer switch. It was awesome.

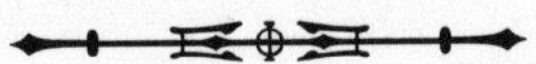

Chapter 6

ANOTHER BAD DAY

December in California has always been one of my favorite times of year. The air is crisp; the sunsets are killer. While the rest of the country is wearing a winter coat, we're still in shorts and flip-flops, my favorite mode of dress. Say what you want about the change of seasons; I'll take the beach.

By December of 1984, I was twenty-three years old. I had two children (little Neil was living a lot of the time with my parents; Elle was a toddler) and one wife (Beth and I were having a lot of problems but still together). Our place was a two-bedroom apartment in a ten-story high-rise, right on the beach. I think we were on the fifth floor. It was right on the ocean; the sand was below us. It was really nice. Parked outside was my newly acquired 1972 Ford De Tomaso Pantera, the first exotic car I ever bought with my Mötley Crüe earnings. Over the next few years, the inventory would reach something like thirty different rides, each one more chill than the next.

On December 6—I'm pretty sure it was December 6—I decided to have a party. I invited some of the neighbors from the building, including the newsman who lived next door. Tommy came, of course—he was now a semi-permanent fixture at my place; he'd recently split with Candice after being married only a few weeks or months, I can't remember which. The guys from the Finnish band Hanoi Rocks—they're credited with being one of the pioneer hair metal groups—also showed up. Their drummer was known as Razzle. His real name was Nicholas Dingley. He was a good buddy of mine. I didn't expect to see them, as they were midway through their first American tour, a monthlong grind to promote their fifth album, *Two Steps from the Move.* I think we met actually in Europe, on the Iron Maiden tour—more about which later. I think they played some of the shows or something, too. I can't remember. But we made friends with them and they were in our town, in LA. Their frontman, Michael Monroe, had fractured his ankle, so the band had to take time off while he healed enough to go back out. Razzle called me, you know, and I'm like, "Hey, I'm having people over if you want to come out." And that would have been enough for Razzle. He was never one to miss out on a party.

This was a point in time when I actually thought I was a drug dealer. No shit. I was kind of semi-trying to be a coke dealer. I *wanted* to be a coke dealer. I'd bought like a pound of coke. I had a shitload of fucking blow. It was funny 'cause my next-door neighbor, this TV news guy, was this real straightlaced guy when I met him. About two months after he met me, he was a fuckin' mess. We were doing blow together all the time. And then he has to go in and anchor the shows and shit and he's just like *wired*, you know? His bosses actually told him at one point that if they heard he was hanging out with me anymore he'd be fired immediately.

The thing about me being a coke dealer was this: I didn't actually sell much. I was a lousy dealer. I just ended up doing all of it, sharing it with my friends. I didn't really know *how* to sell it, you know. What was I going to do, go out and work the curb with the homies? What happened was the opportunity arose one night. We were fucked up and somebody said, "Dude, let's get a pound!" And it seemed like an incredibly good idea at that moment. Because the thing with coke is this: It always runs out. So it's like a dream when you're doing it a lot to always have enough, to never run out, you know? That's every addict's dream at some point. Buying a huge stash. Hunkering down and getting high with nobody to bother you (remember Lovey's bathroom?). So what the fuck, I went out and did it. I forget how much it cost. It was cheaper than buying it in small quantities. Kind of like the same principle as Costco. I remember it was a connection through Mick. Mick always had all these weird relatives and connections. Mick knew somebody who was a drug dealer and they got me the drugs. So I had the blow for a while. It lasted a long time.

In *The Dirt* it says that this party of mine was specifically held to celebrate the upcoming recording of our next album, *Theatre of Pain*. I don't know about that. I remember it was just a get-together, a holiday party. People make more out of shit than they have to. You don't need a reason for a party. It's just a party. We had a million of them. Although since I'd been with Beth, I hadn't really hosted many parties—she had the whole germ thing, plus we had the new baby, plus Beth was generally pissed that I was never there. But I'd been on tour for a while, so maybe we were trying to make it work. Maybe she said okay to the party because she was trying to get along with me, too. So, for the record, it wasn't an album party, and it wasn't, like, a secret drug party or anything. It was just a normal party, hanging out at the apartment and on the beach and all that stuff. Kind of a celebration.

We'd come a long way since New Year's Eve-il, 1982. The phenomenal success of *Shout at the Devil* meant we had finally made it. We were playing sold-out shows, our songs were constantly on the radio, and we had more women and drugs, obviously, than we knew what to do with. We'd made our debut live appearance on MTV during their *Halloween Horror Special*; that same night, MTV aired the video for "Looks That Kill" for the first time. They also ran a Mötley Crüe Halloween contest, and the winners—along with twenty-five of their friends—were flown in especially for the show and took up the entire front row. It was a whole Mötley-based celebration.

Next came a twenty-three-date tour of the U.S., traveling between shows in Doc McGhee's eight-seater plane—one hell of a big step up from a tour bus, I think you'll agree. (Though all of us briefly thought we were dead one time when the aircraft suddenly went into a nosedive due to an electrical malfunction. The pilot managed to bring the plane out of the dive and make an emergency landing; the only damage sustained was the band's stage makeup and facial cleansers, which exploded inside our luggage... due to the sudden drop in cabin pressure.)

With the release of *Shout*, we had moved on from the glam/punk image—and not just because every other band seemed to be copping our style. Nothing we did had to do with others. It was about ourselves: We just wanted to take things to the next level. We settled on a look something like *Mad Max* meets *Escape from New York*—the band's two favorite movies when we were living together at the Mötley House. We had a futuristic stage set specially made for the tour, with a painted backdrop of a city skyline identical to that from *Escape*, which is hands-down the best flick Kurt Russell ever made. Tommy's drum riser was constructed to look like rubble from an exploded freeway; Nikki's and Mick's amps were decorated with mean-looking Styrofoam spikes. Before each show, one of our roadies would walk onto the smoke-filled stage wearing a horror mask and miming to a backing tape of someone reciting

Edgar Allan Poe's 1843 poem "The Conqueror Worm," which contains the line: "That motley drama—oh, be sure / It shall not be forgot."

Okay, so maybe that was kind of out there. But you get the picture. We were doing whatever we wanted to do creatively and the fans were eating it up. On the basis of that, nobody could tell us no. The proof was in the sales figures. Deliver the numbers; the suits will make sure you have enough rope to hang yourselves.

In January of 1984, during our first-ever show at the famous Madison Square Garden in New York City, we were presented with our platinum albums for *Shout*. We'd now sold over 1 million copies.

Ozzy Osbourne was a fuckin' god to us. So when our management booked us onto the first leg of Ozzy's *Bark at the Moon* tour, in March of 1984, we were incredibly psyched. This was almost as good as headlining our own arena tour.

During our first sound check, Ozzy was the first guy to come over and say, "Hi. Welcome to the tour." He took an instant liking to us; from then on, he hardly spent a night on his own tour bus, preferring to travel with us. Ozzy was rich and Ozzy had lots of drugs. And he was kind of lonely, I think. He took his assistant with him everywhere he went. He always wanted people to party with him, so he was very generous.

When you're with Ozzy, all kinds of mayhem ensues. Ozzy, Tommy, and I nearly get arrested for urinating on a police car after the three of us got wasted on sake. Ozzy takes a dump in Tommy's bathroom and wipes his shit all over the walls. Ozzy steals a car with keys in the ignition and we go joyriding; then he smashes the windows and trashes the upholstery. Ozzy strips off his pants, sticks a dollar bill in the crack of his ass, strolls into a bar, and starts offering the bill to anyone who'll pluck it out of there. Ozzy grabs a woman's shopping bag and takes off running, then returns a few minutes later wearing a dress he's found in the purloined bag. Ozzy snorting a line of ants off the pavement. Ozzy licking a puddle of Nikki's piss off the pavement...

All of which, of course, prompts...

(Cue up the shark theme from *Jaws*.)

The arrival of Sharon Osbourne.

Big Momma Is Watching.

Once Sharon got there, all fun screeched to a halt. (Literally.) At the next concert, we were only allowed one case of beer backstage; bringing girls back was verboten. We couldn't do this and we couldn't do that. There was a whole set of rules we had to follow. We had these T-shirts made up—I wish I still had it 'cause it was a great T-shirt. It said: "No Fun Tour '84." It had a smiley face with bullet holes in it. On the back it had the big circle with the line through the words "sex," "drugs," "booze," and "pussy." We had everybody wearing them. Even Ozzy's people were wearing them. And Sharon was fucking pissed. It just really sickens me today to watch everybody fawning all over Sharon Osbourne. She's a talent judge on TV and she has her own show and this and that. This is the most evil, shittiest woman I've ever met in my life. She would fucking have you killed if it was to her advantage. She's just...it's just...if people really *knew*.

I guess Sharon was gone by the time our last night on the tour came around. Ozzy ordered the crew to drop sixteen pounds of glittery flour from the lighting rigs onto our heads while we were playing. As we left the stage, Ozzy and his merry band of pranksters were waiting in the wings with custard pies.

Not wanting to be outdone, while Ozzy was playing—dressed in fishnets and garters—I went out there in a full suit of armor that we'd found lying around backstage. I was holding a chalice in both hands, like a Knight of the Round Table presenting King Arthur with a drink to quench his thirst...

Only the chalice was filled with flour. As Ozzy came toward me, grinning like a loon, I heaved the contents in his direction.

And then I mooned the audience.

Did you know you can't be a monster of rock unless you're pelted with animal body parts and bottles of piss?

We found that out in August of 1984, at the legendary Donington Monsters of Rock Festival, held at the Castle Donington racetrack in England. For a rock 'n' roller like me, it seems like Europe and especially England are maybe the birthplaces of rock 'n' roll. I know, I know... rock 'n' roll was born in the good old US of A. But it seems like it was grabbed up from there by the Europeans, you know? And then reexported to the states in the form of the Beatles and the Stones. We all love Elvis. I love Elvis—I'm covering one of his songs on my album. But somehow, being at Donington felt like I was making a pilgrimage to the Stonehenge of rock 'n' roll.

AC/DC were headlining that day. We were at the bottom of the bill—behind our old friends Y&T (argh!)—and went onstage at noon. Though the crowd would grow as the day went by, there was still something like sixty thousand people in the audience. The English fans tend to be a bit more wild and crazy than Americans; think drunk soccer fans at a concert. They pelted the stage with some weird shit—unidentified pieces of animal flesh and whatnot; the eyeball of a cow was later found lodged in Tommy's drum riser. Then there's the Donington Piss Baptism—the fans drink their beer and then piss into the empty bottles, then throw the bottles up onstage. Usually the first act received the piss baptism. I don't know when we'd first heard about it—maybe from the members of Y&T. And we were like, *Fuck, this is going to suck.*

But for some reason, the piss bottles were never launched. Animal parts yes, piss bottles no. Which supposedly meant that they liked us, I guess. They seemed to. The reaction was awesome. In a moment of exuberance, Nikki threw his bass guitar into the audience. It hit this guy in the head and smashed his glasses. A few members of the audience took the bass to the side of the stage and began ritualistically smashing it to pieces...whereupon enthusiastic fans fought over the bits—a string or a peg here, a piece of fretboard there—each wanting to take home some of Mötley Crüe as a souvenir.

After Donington, we gigged around Europe. I was drinking heavily. In Stockholm, Sweden, I showed my affection to Eddie Van Halen by playfully biting his hand. His then-wife, the actress and later diet spokeswoman Valerie Bertinelli, gave me a ton of shit. In Paris, staying at the megabucks Ritz Hotel, where Princess Diana spent her last night on earth, I accidentally broke the glass panel in the front door to the place. Luckily they didn't hold me responsible.

In Nuremburg, Germany—which turned out to be the last Van Halen performance with David Lee Roth in the band—we were partying in Ronnie James Dio's keyboardist Claude Schnell's hotel room when Schnell unwisely decided to leave the room. In his absence, we threw all the furniture, including the bed, chairs, desk, TV, and dresser, out the window. Some of the furnishings landed on top of two brand-new Mercedes-Benzes parked below. Schnell returned to find his room swarming with irate German cops. He, Dio, and the rest of the band were thrown out.

In October of 1984, as we joined Iron Maiden's *Powerslave* tour for its European leg, *TFFL* achieved gold status, having sold five hundred thousand copies of the Elektra version in the U.S.

Though we were pumped to be with Iron Maiden, the experience wasn't like the one with Ozzy. We didn't really socialize at all with the band. They didn't really say two words to us, except the drummer, Nicko McBrain. He was probably the most, you know, outgoing of the bunch. He'd say hi a lot. If we happened to be in the same hotel, he'd be the one down at the bar.

I was pretty burned out by this stage. My voice was pretty ragged. There was a bullshit report somewhere about cortisone shots and all this. Back in those days, you'd lose your voice once in a while. I mean it happens, you know? I'd been singing (and partying) nonstop for like five years. The treatment for losing your voice can sometimes be a cortisone shot. That's it. It's just a shot in the arm or the butt. It's not even a big needle. It's just a regular needle, the same kind you get for a normal vaccination or whatever. Like the same kind of needle the doctor would use when he gave us our weekly shot of penicillin. It was preventative, you know? We'd all line up in the shower. The doctor would come in before a show, shoot us all up. Or sometimes, in case our wives or girlfriends happened to be coming in, you'd request one.

As for the cortisone... it just takes the swelling down in the vocal cords. In theory. It helps a little bit, but it doesn't help a lot. It's a temporary fix. And we know now that it's better to stay away from cortisone. Cortisone is bad for you. You can't do it all the time. It's a steroid and it's just... it's bad for you. If you take it, you gain a lot of water weight; there are a lot of bad side effects.

The only *real* fix for a sore throat is not talking or singing for a couple days. Luckily, it's been years since I've had any throat problems. Today I play five days a week, *period*. Some conditions are harder than others. Like it's harder to sing in the winter because the heaters dry out the air. And then you're always going inside and going outside, going from the warm air into the cold. In the summertime it's better, but you know, as a singer, if you get a little bit sick it goes right to your throat. That's just what happens. And you know you still got to sing no matter what. There have been days I wanted to cancel, but I didn't. You have to do it. I've never canceled a tour, or canceled a show because of a bad throat. Never. I've been lucky. Some singers develop those polyps on their vocal cords.

(One thing that always irks me: people who tell me to drink tea and honey for my voice. That's an old wives' tale—think about it. When you drink something it has *nothing* to do with your vocal cords. It actually bypasses your vocal cords; it's a whole different tube, you know? Drinking is the esophagus, not the windpipe. The voice box is in the windpipe.)

We did more than twenty shows with Iron Maiden. We went from Germany to Belgium, France, Denmark, Sweden, Finland, Italy. After the final show, in Basel, Switzerland, Tommy and I went back to our hotel room and decided to try out the flare guns we'd bought earlier that day. One of the guns went off. There was this blinding flash of orange light. We both dove for cover as the fireball flew around the room before coming to rest in the middle of Tommy's bed and setting it ablaze.

When we went next door to tell Doc what had happened, we left our keys in the room—we couldn't get back in. With smoke billowing from under the door—and the sprinkler system already in high gear—we had to summon the hotel staff. The management was not pleased; somehow we convinced them it was an accident. The next day, on the way out, we broke the mirrors in the elevators for good measure.

By the time I got back to Redondo, I was toast. Since we'd hooked up with Thaler and McGhee we'd been working basically two years straight. All of us needed rest pretty badly, but I'm not sure I was getting much, especially since one of my first acts upon returning had been buying that pound of blow.

The party at our place at the beach went strong for a couple days. Day became night became day. We were drinking Jack Daniel's and beer and a mix of brandy and Kahlúa and doing quaaludes and smoking pot and, of course, we had the seemingly never-dwindling pile of coke.

On day three, December 8, 1984, Mick showed up. That was a surprising development because he never partied with us. I guess he was fighting again with his girlfriend. He was a frail guy. It seems like his women were always taking advantage of him and giving him shit. Sometime that afternoon, Mick waded out into the cold waters of the blue Pacific, drink in hand, intent upon drowning himself, I guess.

Later, having passed out for a few hours, I woke up in my bed. Looking out my fifth-story window, I spotted this black-clad shape on the beach. It looked like a dead seal, only it seemed to be dressed in a leather jacket. I grabbed some people and went downstairs to check it out. It was Mick all right. He was all sandy and wet, still wearing his leather pants and jacket and motorcycle boots.

"Just leave me alone," was all he could muster.

It was afternoon by then; the sun was out; I figured he was far enough back from the ocean that the high tide wouldn't get him. I followed his wishes, went back to the party.

Toward dusk, the booze finally ran out. There was a liquor store just four blocks up the road. I could have walked there, but I'd been partying for three straight days, you know—walking there was out of the question, too much reality to deal with, if you know what I mean. I'd just bought myself a new car, a vintage '72 Ford De Tomaso Pantera. It had a bright red finish with a sleek black leather interior; it was a fast and beautiful car. One thing I didn't know at the time I bought it—a time before the Internet made researching things easy—Panteras were known to have a lot of problems. Frustrated with *his* Pantera, Elvis Presley blasted it full of holes with a handgun.

But I'd had no problems with mine up to then. It was my first real splurge of a purchase. I was just so proud of it. Razzle thought it was cool, too. He wanted to check it out. So I was like, "C'mon, bro, let's go make a liquor run." I didn't see any problem. We'd drive the four blocks to the store, get some supplies, be back home in a flash. I'd been driving drunk for about as long as I'd been driving. It had never been a problem before. The coke kind of evened things out. When you were doing a lot of blow, the alcohol didn't really affect you. We'd be traveling eight blocks, total. We told everybody we'd be right back.

Razzle was a drummer. He was a fun guy, kind of a hot dog—he put his own name on the front of his drum kit rather than his band's. When asked about this, he said once that he probably wouldn't be with Hanoi Rocks forever. He was setting his sights on the long term; his dream was to play for a stadium rock band like Heart or Iron Maiden. I kind of admired that about him. He was honest enough to tell the truth. (And he was real: He didn't think about the fact that he could have just bought a new drumhead. They weren't that expensive!) He had aspirations.

Another thing about Razzle: He wasn't actually Finnish. He was from England. A place with the fanciful name of Royal Leamington Spa. Adopted at a young age, he'd grown up on the Isle of Wight. He was tall, with dark hair. He was *into* glam—after he joined HR, those guys went more in that direction. What can I say...the guy looked great in eyeliner. Together, we could put a big dent in a room full of groupies with no sweat.

Razzle was just a really nice guy—the guy I vibed with the most of the band. He was a lot of fun, you know, and they were really a great group. They were fun to watch and stuff; they were cool. I mean, when I was on the road, I would often want to stay and watch other bands we were playing with. I was a *fan* of rock 'n' roll at the same time I was part of it. When we opened for AC/DC, I watched them every night. Every single night. Or like when Whitesnake opened for Mötley, I actually would sing. I would help them sing the backgrounds. No, I wouldn't go onstage. I'd be in the back. On a microphone like where the soundboard was. Or when we played with the Scorpions. I watched them all the time. The same was true when we were on tour with Razzle and Hanoi Rocks.

According to official police reports, the accident happened at 6:38 P.M. I don't know who came up with that time. I don't think I was wearing a watch.

We got to the bottle store no problem. We shopped—picked up a couple of hundred dollars' worth of booze. Then we set off back to my house. The Pantera didn't have any backseats, so Razzle was sitting beside me in the passenger seat holding the bags of booze in his lap. We were driving along, chatting about this and that, two long-haired guys out on a booze run, me in my customary Hawaiian shirt and shorts, Razzle in his high-tops, leather jeans, and frilly shirt.

Because it was December, it was already dark out. It gets really pitch-black in the winters by the ocean, partly because of the marine layer, a wet fog that leaves the streets slick during most evenings. I wasn't far from home. As I rounded this curve leading to a hill, I downshifted; the car had so much power, the tires broke their grip on the wet pavement. According to a police report, I swerved to avoid a parked fire truck. My blood alcohol level would later test at nearly twice the legal limit.

The next thing I knew, the Pantera had lost its grip on the asphalt and was sliding sideways. I tried to turn back into the skid;

meanwhile the car drifted into the oncoming lane. The next thing I knew a pair of headlights appeared at the crest of the hill and was bearing down on us—a white Volkswagen driven by an eighteen-year-old girl. The police would later say I was doing 65 mph in a 25 mph zone when the tires came unglued. I don't know how they could know that. The VW struck the passenger side of the Pantera.

When I came to, I was still in the car. Razzle was actually in my lap, you know; the impact had sort of thrown him into my seat. I was holding him. There were broken booze bottles everywhere. Later I'd hear the cop saying something about how bad we reeked. Well, of course we reeked—Razzle had been holding a party's worth of liquor in his lap. At this point I was really woozy. I became aware of people, you know, people trying to help us get out, but it was weird, it was surreal. There was no sound at all, like there were technical difficulties. And people were trying to get us out. I remember myself saying, "Razzle, there's help here." And then I was pulled out of the car and he was pulled out of the car. And he was put right onto the stretcher and taken away.

Like a lot of accidents when people are drinking, I was totally uninjured. Well, I had a slight concussion and maybe a broken rib. And I had a couple of cuts, but that was it. I remember they took me out of the car and I was sitting on the curb, just waiting, kind of dazed, not really knowing what was going on. I could see the car. My new *Pantera*. It was just mangled, you know? I wasn't really thinking of anything. It was like I was out of my body. I was observing everything. Like it was a movie. It was very strange. I remember that.

Then I guess Beth showed up. Beth and Tommy. They came running onto the scene, 'cause it was only a block or so away. They said they'd heard the sirens and they'd known it was me.

I remember the cops gave me the Breathalyzer test. I guess I was too dazed to refuse. I don't remember riding in the squad car or being put in the squad car. But I remember being in the police station. But I wasn't in jail or even in a cell. I was in an office.

Meanwhile Razzle was taken to South Bay Hospital. Tommy drove after the ambulance, taking along his wife, Candice, as well as Beth and members of Hanoi Rocks. After a long, tense time in the ER waiting room, a doctor came out and advised them that Razzle had died at 7:12 P.M., the result of severe head injuries.

The passengers in the Volkswagen were in critical condition. The driver, eighteen-year-old Lisa Hogan, was rushed to Little Company of Mary Hospital in Torrance—she would remain in a coma until the end of the month, with a broken arm and two broken legs. Her head injury would leave her with damaging psychomotor seizures. Hogan's twenty-year-old boyfriend, Daniel Smithers, was taken to South Bay Hospital, suffering a broken leg and head injuries. He would later have to undergo rehabilitative therapy to learn how to speak again as a result of brain damage. Ironically, Smithers had previously worked as a counselor at the Palmer Drug Abuse Program on Van Nuys Boulevard, where I would later undergo treatment. The driver of a third car involved, twenty-five-year-old Karimi Khaliabad of Torrance, was uninjured.

(Another irony I have since discovered is that the date of the accident, December 8, 1984, was the first day of National Drunk Driving Awareness Week. The final five Hanoi Rocks shows (in California and Arizona) of the band's thirty-city U.S. tour were canceled, including what was to be their Los Angeles debut the following Friday night. Hanoi Rocks returned to Finland and played two contracted gigs in the capital, which they dedicated to Razzle's memory. Tommy offered to play drums at the shows, but former Clash drummer Terry Chimes took the drum stool instead for the televised special. There was no animosity between me and the surviving members of Hanoi Rocks. Their lead singer even offered to stand in for me if I was jailed for any considerable period of time...well, maybe there was a little animosity.)

Down at the station, it never even dawned on me that Razzle could be dead. I just assumed somehow he was in another room giving his statement. I kept asking, you know, "How's my friend? How's he doing?" The cops didn't answer me for a long time. Nobody would tell me anything. Everybody kept saying, "We don't know.... We're not sure.... I'll go find out."

And then, it must've been like a lieutenant or something, a plainclothes guy, an officer. He's the one who told me. He said, "Your friend passed away." And I... it still didn't register. It just didn't hit me. It didn't; I couldn't... I really didn't understand what that meant. I had a concussion; I was having trouble processing everything. Three days being up probably didn't help, either. I started thinking to myself, you know, *If only I'd gone to the liquor store alone, or walked, or sent someone else for the booze. If only the car had skidded at a different angle so that I'd be the one lying on a slab in the morgue.* And I still didn't know what had happened to the people in the other car. What if more people had died as a result of their injuries?

The cops released me just as the sun was coming up the next day. My ribs hurt so much that I could hardly breathe, let alone walk, but the pain was nothing compared to the hurt I felt over Razzle. He was fucking dead. That was so fucking final.

Twelve hours earlier—with the possible exception of my fucked-up marriage—my life had been going so great. Now everything had changed. I was still the same person, but even I knew things were never going to be the same again.

I got home and Beth and Tommy and Mick and all them were there. Tommy said I should try to get some sleep, but that was the last thing I wanted. I was frightened to close my eyes—I was afraid that I'd relive the crash over and over again. All that day the phone never stopped ringing. Family and friends calling to offer support, reporters calling to get the story. And then the phone suddenly stopped ringing and we just sat there in eerie silence for what seemed like an eternity.

And then it rang again.

This time it was Doc McGhee, telling me the police had decided to charge me with vehicular manslaughter. I didn't want the cops coming to my home to arrest me, so I went down to the station and turned myself in.

I was obviously afraid.

The preliminary hearing was held at the Torrance Courthouse in California's South Bay Judicial District; the parents of the two injured kids were in court. I will never forget the way they stared at me.

I was released on twenty-five hundred dollars bail. While I was awaiting trial, the first thing I had to do was to seek treatment for my drinking problem. As far as I was concerned, I didn't have a drinking problem. I wasn't a wino lying in the gutter, was I? I was never the kind of person who started drinking when I woke up. I had a house, and friends, and a career.

Alcohol, for me, has always had a couple of purposes. First, it's a good way to just not feel anymore, you know? To just obliterate anything that's bothering you or whatever. Plus, it's like a social thing. For me, I've always been a pretty shy person; it makes me less shy. Like nowadays, when I'm not drinking very often, it's hard for me to go to parties. I feel uncomfortable around people.

But as long as I had that drink in my hand it was, like, safety. I didn't have to be drunk. I just had to have it; I just wanted to know it was in my hand. I'd have a couple of drinks to loosen up, and then sometimes you just have too many drinks. And then, you know, you're screwed. I guess that's really it. I know with drugs, too, it's like there's a line. Below the line, you're good. You're fine as long as you stay below that line. Above that line, it gets bad real quick. But somehow it's really hard for me to walk that line, you know? You try to be moderate in your intake—but then you always end up going *over* the line. That was my problem. It was like I never knew where that line was. I couldn't see it because once I crossed it, it was already too late. I would tell myself, *I'm only going to have a few drinks; if I start feeling buzzed I'm not going to drink.* But that never worked. Toward the end, I mean, like toward 2007, 2008, before I got sober most recently, I never even got buzzed when I drank. I went from completely sober to blackout. One minute I'm hanging out with friends; then the next thing you know, I'm waking up the next day, not remembering anything. There was no gray area. It was white and black. That was it. That was the hard part.

Back then I had none of this insight. But I had to follow what the court said. I was facing serious charges; I'd killed a man. The lawyers said I could do up to seven years if I didn't play the game as directed. Doc said he'd booked me into this nice facility on Van Nuys Boulevard that was practically a country club, with tennis courts, a golf course, even a lake for boating. The story of the accident was on the front page of every newspaper; editorials urged authorities to make me an example, to give me a life sentence in order to discourage other drunk drivers for whom I, with my outlaw, party-hard image, was a role model.

The truth was, I didn't want to show my face anywhere. Everywhere I looked I saw a pointing, waggling finger. I was deeply ashamed. The thought of escaping the nightmare that had become my life began to sound very appealing. I agreed to go along.

Of course, there was no country club; that lying sack of shit was just doing his thing like he always did—telling me what I wanted to hear. He pulled up outside a grim-looking hospital. There were bars on all the windows. I wanted to run, but I had no choice.

I spent the next thirty days in detox, undergoing intense therapy, which was basically reliving the accident over and over again while frowning therapists jotted down their observations. My folks and Beth came to see me, but no one from the band. Not even Tommy. Nikki called once, when I first arrived. I never heard from Mick.

One of the main things I learned in rehab—the first of many, many visits—was who my real friends were, you know? Beth was very supportive. But Nikki, Tommy, and Mick were like: *Fuck you. How could you do this to us?* I was like, *What do you mean, how could I do it to you?* These guys were all doing just as much drinking and drugs as I was doing every single day. I was just the unlucky one. They didn't have an accident—but they easily could have. Every one of them drove fucked up. It could've happened to anybody. Look at Nikki. He actually died from an *overdose* and was brought back to life. What happened to me could have happened to any one of the band members. But all they could think of was themselves.

At some point, I had to meet with my lawyer in the district attorney's office. The families of the victims were there, too. It was tough. It's hard to remember.... I mean, I kind of remember. It's very hard to think about it, you know, because, I mean... these people were injured for the rest of their lives. Like, when I saw them, you could tell they were very fucked up. That was probably more emotional than going to jail. Not probably; definitely.

As I said in *The Dirt*, in order to avoid a trial, my lawyer advised me to plead guilty to vehicular manslaughter and strike a compromise. He figured that since the people drinking at my apartment were mostly in Mötley Crüe and Hanoi Rocks, the party could be explained as a business meeting and we would be able to pay damages to the families through the band's liability insurance, because there was no way I could afford them on my own. This was why the families of the victims agreed to what everyone saw as such a light sentence: thirty days in jail, $2.6 million in restitution, and two hundred hours of community service, which I'd already been chipping away at on the road, doing high school talks and radio interviews around the country on the evils of drinking and driving. A newspaper headline touting the settlement read: "Drunk Killer Vince Neil Sentenced to Touring World with Rock Band."

My lawyer managed to keep me out of jail for more than a year.

In August of 1985, *Theatre of Pain* hit #6 on the charts, the highest of any of our albums. By November, "Home Sweet Home" became MTV's most-requested video. Also in November, a U.S. Senate committee condemned Mötley for our lyrics, which they said degraded women and glorified violence. In response we designed a giant, spread-legged woman as a backdrop for our show. Naturally, we entered the stage through her pussy. In May of 1986, Tommy married his first television actress, Heather Locklear, of *Melrose Place* and *Dynasty.* Nikki, we would later learn, was struggling with a full-blown heroin addiction. I toured America and the world with Crüe on a big private jet, socked away some money (most of which went to my lawyer), did my community service, and somehow managed to stay sober, even as the rest of the band debauched their way through the days and nights. (Part of that time I was assisted in my efforts by a pair of thugs hired by Doc McGhee to oversee my sobriety.) I will say that at this time I redoubled my efforts with the ladies. Unable to drink or drug, I had to pass my time doing something. I fucked my way across the world with a vengeance.

Literally one day after moving Beth and Little Beth into a new $1.5 million mansion in a gated community in Northridge, CA—I wanted to make sure they were safe and well taken care of—I took a cab to the nearest police station and turned myself in.

The date was June 15, 1986. They brought me to a quiet rinky-dink jail in Torrance to serve my thirty-day sentence. The Gardena City jail.

The first thing that happened when I got to jail was I was made a trustee—a privileged position. My job was to bring food to the other prisoners, clean cells, wash squad cars and other vehicles. People got a kick out of being served by a rock star. The sergeant on the night shift was a hard-ass, but everyone else was constantly asking for photos and autographs. You gotta understand that a jail is not like a prison. A prison is made for long-term stays, so they have recreation, classes, things to do inside. A jail is usually just a holding tank. Cinder-block walls. Not much in the way of activities. As luck would have it, being a trustee qualified me for extra privileges: TV and visitors. On the weekends the guards would bring in burgers and six-packs of beer. In the real world my sobriety had been monitored by the courts. I'd actually managed to stay sober for over a year. Here in jail, I was chugging down brews.

One afternoon, a blond fan found her way to the jail. The sergeant on duty gave me permission to bring her back to my cell for an hour. I don't know how many prisoners get to have the experience of fucking a beautiful girl, in Daisy Duke shorts and a Lycra halter top, on the metal bunk in their cell.

I will tell you this. It was kinky. I'm not sure I *ever* saw a girl that turned on.

With the standard time off for good behavior, I walked out the doors of the jail after eighteen days. That's what Razzle's life, and the permanent health of those other two kids, was worth, according to the judicial system.

Thinking back on it today, I have a lot of different thoughts.

When it first happened I kind of shut it out of my mind, you know; I didn't really comprehend exactly what I had done. I mean, I knew somebody died. I knew two people got seriously injured…

but it was weird, psychologically, I just kind of tried to, not forget about it, but just maybe I tried to minimize it. Like on the computer, when you click on the little symbol and you minimize the screen. It doesn't make it go away entirely, but it's off your main screen, if you know what I mean.

But then it was very strange, because as time went on I really had hard times dealing with it. And I think that's because I really didn't get punished, you know? It was kind of hard to deal with the fact that I caused so much damage in a lot of people's lives and basically all I got was a slap on the wrist. I mean, I paid a big restitution, $2.6 million. I paid a lot of money. But it's only money, you know?

I went to jail for thirty days, but I only served fifteen. And while I was there I drank and got laid and got a nice suntan. Putting me in jail didn't, it didn't do anything.

The only people that punished me over the whole thing were the band members. They treated me like shit by not supporting me. And the truth is, they did it out of their own selfishness—not because they thought it might teach me a lesson or anything. They were just being themselves, just assholes. They couldn't be bothered to go out of their way for somebody else.

I think if the court had punished me more, in the long run, it would've saved me from the demons that I still have. You know maybe if I was punished harder I would maybe have stopped drinking like twenty years sooner. I mean this is how fucked up this was. I was looking at going to jail for seven years, losing my whole career. And the court tells me, you know, that to stay out of jail I can't drink, I have to stay sober and be in a program, all that. So my reaction is that I'm pissed off, right? Instead of being motivated to stay out of jail by doing something so easy—not drinking—I'm pissed off that the court is telling me what to do. I hate when people tell me what to do. I hate it so much it sometimes clouds the big picture.

To try and make things better, my manager, Doc McGhee, promised me that if I didn't drink, he would buy me a Rolex watch.

And *that* would be my motivation for not drinking.

Not because I just killed somebody and hurt two people. Not because I was facing jail and might lose everything, including my future. But because my fucking lecherous, co-dependent, enabling manager offered me a fucking Rolex watch.

I took the deal.

On the day I left my new Northridge house to head to jail, I removed said diamond Rolex and placed it carefully in the drawer of the bedside table, on my side of the bed.

I figured I'd get it when I got back.

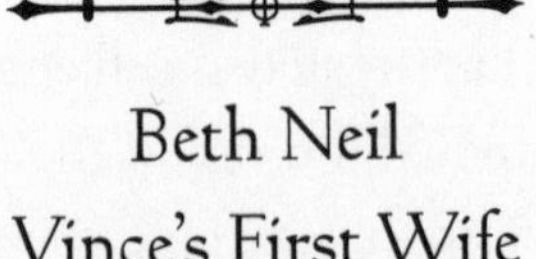

Beth Neil
Vince's First Wife

We got married on January 3, 1983, about two years after we started dating.

During that time, things started to escalate for them professionally. They had a lot of opportunities; they started going on tour; our life started to change. I went with him sometimes, but it was really kind of a *thing*—at certain points Vince was the only guy who had a significant other. Some came and went, but it was kind of like there's a girlfriend time and there's non-girlfriend time. Which was fine. I mean I sort of made a conscious decision, you know: If he wants to be a rock star more than anything in the world, I can't nag him and fly around and follow him around and do the things that some of the other girls did from time to time. I had to just let him live his dream and make the point that as long as our relationship is good between us, at home, in our little world,

I'm not going to get bent out of shape about jealousy and stuff. I really wanted him to live his dream.

You have to understand how much things changed. It went from nobody caring about Mötley Crüe to like a *lot* of people caring, a lot of people showing up for shows. I mean, I saw him first on probably their third or fourth gig. Now it was like famous people were calling and hanging out with the guys, blah blah blah.

Over time, what happened was, whenever he would go away on tour, I'd go out partying with like Lita Ford, who Tommy was seeing. We'd go backstage to concerts, we'd fly out to concerts, we were sort of living the life when the guys were gone, we wanted to have fun, too. Vince didn't like it. He'd go have fun and it's two in the morning and he calls me and I'm not home. And then he's all freaked out. He's like, "Where are you? What are you doing?" It wasn't like big fights; it was just like little, little things like that.

So he started talking a lot about "I want to have a baby; let's have a baby." And he even named her before she was ever even conceived. He said, "I want to have a little baby; I want to name her Little Beth." He had her all picked out. "She's going to have this kind of hair and these kind of eyes" and blah blah blah. He'd talk about it. It was pillow talk or whatever. Finally it happened. I was pregnant.

I remember it was August; Vince was getting ready to go over to Europe for a European tour. That's when I found out I was pregnant; I didn't go on the tour because I was like two and a half months pregnant. So he went off to do the tour; that's when they met Hanoi Rocks.

While they were gone, you have to think of the time period. Right about that time, the whole HIV thing got really, really big. Before, I never cared if he was getting a blow job from some girl in Amsterdam, or if he took some groupie home drunk and screwed in Berlin. I mean, what did that have to do with my life, you know? I wasn't going to go call him at two in the morning asking, "Where are you? What are you doing? Did you sleep with anybody?" I just wasn't going to do it.

I knew he was going to. It may sound like rationalization, but it really was a conscious decision. It's like what he does when he's there I'm not going to try and govern, I'm not going to get torn up about. I'm just going to know that he's exploring his life as a twenty-one-, twenty-two-year-old man, as a rock star, and he'll be able to value this and put it in perspective. He knows what we have and he knows what that is. And I'm just not going to worry about it. The thing was, I knew they were all trying to craft this wild party persona. I knew that if it came down to choosing between me and the band he was going to choose the band first. So I just wanted to preserve what we had. If that meant that I had to look the other way to a certain extent, then that was okay; I'd look the other way. The good times we had were justification enough.

Then, when I became pregnant, my attitude shifted. I told him, "You cannot sleep around anymore." And he goes, "What are you talking about? I don't sleep around." I look at him. I'm like, "Vince, I'm pregnant. You can't come home with all kinds of diseases." Plus, they were all really starting to get into drugs at that point, coke and heroin. And the whole HIV thing was just blowing up at that moment. I'm like, "Vince, come on. I know you've slept around, I've never said a word about it, I've always looked the other way, but I'm pregnant now. You can't come home off a tour and sleep with me and hurt our baby. You have to be careful now. You have to not share needles." Like there were times when they'd have a tattoo guy come backstage at the show and he'd give everyone tattoos with the same needle.

I guess that's why I got the rap as a germaphobe. Call me names if you want, but I'm not sure anybody in their right mind would disagree.

When they came home from the European tour, I was five months pregnant. We were living in Redondo, in a building on the beach. We were on the fourth floor. It was a cool place, with a sliding glass door across the front. You could see the beach. Vince had spent a couple months in Europe and he had made really good friends with Razzle.

He'd been home for a day or two and Razzle and the guys were in town. I cooked a lot and stuff; he wanted to have the guys over to the beach.

It was pretty early in the evening and Tommy was there. It was like six o'clock; they wanted to go do a beer run. Vince had the Pantera. I don't remember the coke thing. As far as the coke goes, I think he's mixing that up with a different time period. When we first lived in the apartment, before I was pregnant, we did do a lot of coke. There were times when we stayed up a couple of days straight. There was a time when he thought the best way not to spend money on coke would be to buy a whole bunch and to deal it. There was this girl and her boyfriend who we knew; they dealt coke and we bought a lot of coke from them at one point.

Now, what he'd been doing in Europe when he was away from me I have no idea. But I can tell you when those boys came over it was not a three-day party. They had come over at two in the afternoon. We were just going to show them the beach. I wasn't partying of course because I was pregnant. Nobody was *that* fucked up. This wasn't the Mötley House; this was a married guy and his pregnant wife having a cookout. Honestly I would tell you, but Vince wasn't... I wouldn't... I was very protective of him. I wouldn't let him go drive if he was really messed up or something. He said, "Razzle and I are going to go get a beer." They maybe had like four beers in a couple hours or something that I was aware of. And I looked at him right in the eyes, 'cause he used to get a look in his eyes, when he was wasted. Kind of a blank, belligerent stare. And I kind of looked at him and thought, *Nah, he's okay; he can go; he's not too fucked up to drive.* Because I could've easily driven, you know? And I said, "Okay, all right. See you in a bit."

And then they left... and I just started feeling really sick.

I'm like, *Something's wrong.* I turn to Tommy and I go, "I'm afraid something's wrong."

And Tommy's like, "Nothing's wrong; relax. They're fine; don't worry about it." But I kept getting more and more nervous. Finally, I'm like, "Tommy, you have to take me to find Vince." It hadn't been very long, maybe twenty minutes. But the store was only four blocks away. And I just had this terrible feeling. "I'm afraid, Tommy," I said. And he's like, "No, he's fine, don't worry about it, they're probably just at the beach, he's probably just showing Razzle around." But I made Tommy take me anyway. I'm like: "Take me in the car, we're going to go find him."

We only went a couple of blocks before we got stuck in traffic. I jumped out of the car and ran toward the flickering lights of the police cars. It was dark. It was winter; it gets dark like five thirty. I remember seeing Razzle's tennis shoe in the roadway; they were putting him in the ambulance. Vince was sitting on the curb.

What happened basically was, on the way home from the liquor store—a small mom-and-pop shop a block from the beach—there's this blind hill. The road is slanted, and you're kind of coming up a blind hill and there's a stop sign there. And so what Vince did was he came that block down toward the beach, made the left-hand turn, accelerated in the Pantera, which is a mid-engine car. There was water that was draining across the street from where they were building a condominium; it wasn't raining. The car's back end went out, and he went into the oncoming lane. Then the Volkswagen and another car came over the hill not knowing that there was anybody in the lane. And then, you know, the accident happened.

When Vince got out of jail, he was still wearing the clothes covered in Razzle's blood. He was in shock. He turned to me and he said, "His head was in my lap. He died in my lap." He was freaked out and heartbroken. He literally went into like hibernation. He wouldn't answer the phone, he didn't want to talk to anybody. Like everybody's calling him. It's a *big* story. Everybody on TV is talking about him. And literally, if he could've run away and hid he would've. I mean he did hide to the best of his ability—he just stayed home.

The whole argument for getting him out of going to jail for very long had to do with money. "If Vince is going to pay restitution to the victims, you're going to have to let him go on tour and make money—he does no good to anybody in jail, right?" So that was his whole like little chip to get off—that was his Get-out-of-Jail-Free card. Like they would all agree to let him off and without any serious punishment so he could go out and make this money so that he could pay off all the victims and their families for their wrongful deaths and lawsuits and things. And so that's why he didn't get severely punished. That was the deal his lawyers made. First we went to the superlawyer Robert Shapiro. But he was like, "Listen, I have a big name; if I'm attached they're just going to see that it's a celebrity lawyer case, so let's give him somebody that just looks like a regular everyday guy who practices law." And he was a good lawyer, a really nice guy, and he went in and pleaded the case and they all signed off on it. They could've done a lot more to him, but really in the end all anybody wanted from him was the money,

Jail or not, he was punished for what he did. You can't say he wasn't. You could see a change in him after that. He kind of spiraled out of control a little bit. In the beginning, he just liked to party. But later, it was more like he was medicating pain. Things took on a different cast. Razzle's death really changed Vince's life. I'm not sure he knew that or that he knows it, but it did. Before Razzle died, Vince was a happy drunk. After that, he turned dark. I don't think he's ever recovered.

Chapter 7
AC/DC

At first it seemed as though things were improving between Beth and me. But as with the girl in the old song by The Sweet, sometimes luck, like sexual preference, runs in both directions. That would be the story of my life over the next few years, high highs and low lows. Somehow, I was never prepared for either.

The first week I was in jail, Beth came to visit every day and whenever I could use the phone I would call. It was a communal telephone that everybody had to share, but sometimes the guards would let me use their phone to call out.

The second week she didn't come at all. I left messages at different times of the day; I couldn't get hold of her. I didn't know what was going on. I had no idea.

After eighteen days, I was released at 12:01 A.M. of the next day. I assumed Beth was coming to pick me up. I left messages, you know: "Please pick me up; I get out at midnight." But there was nobody there to pick me up.

I got this really bad feeling. I'm not sure if I have ever felt more alone. My friends and exes and people who work for me would probably tell you that one thing they all have noticed is that I don't like being alone and that's why I constantly have to have a woman by my side. It's true I don't like being by myself. As I was standing out there in the dark, it hit me that everything I had, everything I'd achieved, all the outward trappings... all of it didn't amount to shit. I had nobody who cared about me. A gaping hole opened up in my midsection. It was like I was little and my mom had forgotten to pick me up from school. Only it was worse because I was a grown man. I had nothing to show for it.

I wanted to scream, to cry, to get totally wasted and beat the fuck out of somebody. Instead I went back into the jail. I was like, "Can I please use your phone?"

I called this guy; he was my sponsor for AA. His name was—what was his fuckin' name? His... name... was... Keith! That's right; his name was Keith. He was a great guy. He came to pick me up. I didn't even remember where the house was 'cause I had literally only slept there one night; all the houses looked the same. After an hour or so of driving around we finally hit upon a house that looked vaguely familiar. I'm like, *I think this is my house!*

Nobody was there. The pool and backyard looked vaguely familiar, but the curtains were closed, so I couldn't look through the windows to check the furniture.

I broke a glass pane in the back door, unlocked the dead bolt, went in.

It was my house, all right... but the place was empty. Everything was gone. I was like, *What the fuck happened?* There was no bed. There was nothing. Beth had taken every stick of furniture. She'd even taken the fucking ice trays from the refrigerator. My new car, a Camaro Z28, was still in the garage, but she'd taken the keys.

The only other thing she left was the twelve-thousand-dollar diamond-bezelled gold Rolex watch that Doc McGhee had given me for staying sober.

It was lying on the bare expanse of carpet in the bedroom, right where my bedside table used to be.

I immediately got on the phone and called her parents, her friends, and anyone else I thought might know where she was, but they all claimed they hadn't heard from her and didn't know where she was. Frankly, I didn't give a fuck about her, or the furniture; I just wanted to find her so that I could at least stay in touch with my daughter.

Oh yeah, and I wanted my fuckin' car keys back.

I struck out on both counts. I remember it cost like six hundred bucks or something to get a new set of keys. It was a couple of months before I heard from Beth. Little Beth was like three. I'd been the one who insisted on naming her after her mother; I wanted a tiny version of her to adore. I hated not seeing her. Finally Beth called and she was like, "We're done; I left you; I'm gone." And I was like, *No shit, I think I figured that out.*

I don't really remember her reasons she gave for leaving, but she had her reasons. To these women, if you talk to them, they'll tell you I'm a handful. There's a lot of shit in my life. You know especially when I was drinking and doing drugs. It was... it was obviously not... I know it was not fun for them. Lia, my current wife, didn't have to go through it because I don't do drugs anymore. My wife before that, Heidi, she didn't have to go through the drug thing, either; I did drink a lot at that time. But the first two, Beth and Sharise, absolutely. Especially Sharise, my second wife, Skylar's mom... the one I'm about to meet in the story line.

But one thing I can say: All of these women knew what they were getting into when they hooked up with me. There were plenty along the way who decided they didn't want to be a part of this. They're the ones who moved on.

I didn't see Beth again until about ten years later, when she and

Little Beth came to a Crüe concert in Florida. The two of them ended up moving around a lot over the years; they are very close. Little Beth now goes by the name Elle. A few years ago she turned down an acceptance to Juilliard because she decided she didn't want to spend her life...singing opera. She sang soprano and mezzo-soprano—I guess she gets her high vocal range honestly. For a while she was trying to be a country singer. She visited me last Thanksgiving. She's trying to get on track as a writer—that's a plug, because she's a beautiful and intelligent blue-eyed *brunette.* I love listening to her talk. She's very smart and knows what she wants. And she seems to love me, even though I wasn't there during her life. I love her so much I can't start to describe it.

Back to the past: June 1986.

I was out of jail. I was a free man again. I had about eighteen months of court-mandated sobriety behind me—I was not squeaky clean but a lot cleaner than I'd been since I was probably fourteen years old.

It was time to live a little.

I ordered a house full of furniture and got a couple of my buddies to move in with me. It was cool; I had no wife to tell me what to do anymore. Why not enjoy it?

Around this time, the band was sort of on a hiatus. While I'd cleaned up, the rest of the guys had continued their downhill slides. Following his grandmother's funeral, Nikki resolved (once again) to kick drugs so he could write for the next Mötley album, which we were due to record. Tommy was recovering from torn ligaments on both sides of his ankle—he'd wiped out on his dirt bike doing a wheelie in front of his house. He couldn't play the drums until he was healed. Mick was in his own private world, as usual. With nothing else to do, I started spending a lot of my time at the Tropicana, a strip club in LA that featured female mud wrestling.

The Tropicana was on Western Avenue and Santa Monica Boulevard, which is kind of a shitty part of town. Did you see the movie *Stripes?* Remember in *Stripes* when they had the mud wrestling? That was actually in the Tropicana. Yeah. I actually knew some of those girls who were in the movie. They worked at the Tropicana. It was just a fun place to go to. For rock guys like me, strip clubs are different than for regular guys because you usually can fuck the girls at strip clubs; a strip club is basically a place to go for the specific purpose of getting laid. You get them when they get off work and then you take them home.

I didn't only go to the Tropicana. I went to a lot of different places in those days. There were strip clubs, nightclubs, bars. On Friday nights I'd go to the Tropicana. On Thursday nights I'd be at Carlos'n Charlie's. On Wednesdays I'd be at the Rainbow. It kind of depended on the day. Carlos'n Charlie's was cool; it was right across from the Roxbury. The last time I went there I was sitting at my table with a bunch of girls and my security guard and all of a sudden a gunfight broke out inside the place. It was fucking scary. I was on the floor crawling to the door.

The Tropicana sort of became my hangout because I dated a couple of the waitresses there. And probably three or four different girls who wrestled there, too. Let's face it. The Tropicana was like my mini-mart for pussy.

After I'd been going there for a while, I decided to build my own mud pit. I put it behind the house, next to the pool.

I would have the girls come over and wrestle. It's not that I loved wrestling so much, but it was more fun than the strip clubs. And the girls were a lot cooler and a lot of fun. After closing time or whatever, we'd bring a dozen or so girls back to my place and stage our own private female mud-wrestling contests while me and my buddies sat around in bathrobes drinking cocktails. I also invited all the local drug dealers to come and hang out, because where there were drugs there were chicks. They sure were fun times. At one of the parties some guy in a suit, who I'd never seen before that night, handed me a rock of cocaine the size of a fucking golf ball as a way of thanking me for my hospitality. I was like, "Thanks, dude! Come again." And he did. In fact, he practically moved in. His name was... call him Whitey. The house already had beer on tap in the bar. Now we had a resident drug dealer. Speaking of which, even though I was doing drugs on a pretty regular basis, I kept going to Narcotics Anonymous and Cocaine Anonymous meetings. That's where the hot chicks were! Especially the cocaine chicks. They're just good-looking girls trying to get off doing blow. Believe me I know the routine (see Lovey above). It's a great place to go meet girls.

Sharise Ruddell was one of the dozen or so girls I'd regularly bring over from the Tropicana to entertain the guys. And yes, I know, every account of Sharise begins with the fact that she was a mud wrestler. But she didn't do it for long, and she has since become a very successful businesswoman with a thriving clothing line.... I think you'll be hearing from her later. But she could wrestle her ass off, and that's why I first noticed her.

Sharise stood out from the other girls. She was an Amazon, with blond hair, a fabulous rack, and a killer body that looked great covered in mud. An incredible specimen of womanhood, she fought dirty and she won every time. Later, when we were recording *Girls, Girls, Girls*, I suggested we pose for a band photo at the Tropicana and have Sharise and some of the other girls dancing onstage in the background. She'd once dated Bret Michaels of Poison (the only other major rock star who deigned to be interviewed for this book); pictures of Sharise and Michaels posing together in a swimming pool can be seen on the inside sleeve of Poison's *Open Up and Say...Ahh!* There aren't many women who can say they've had their picture on the inner sleeves of albums from two different bands. That is the case with Sharise. She was a stunner.

I don't remember exactly what brought us together. She'd come over to the house with the other girls, but she was a cut above, you know? We just hit it off. She was hot looking, and fun, and it seemed to work. When we started going out, she stopped dancing. Instead, she developed a shopping habit.

And instead of wrestling with the other chicks she fought with me all the time.

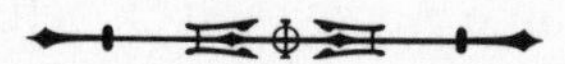

Sharise Ruddell Neil
Vince's Second Wife

My mom was the homecoming queen and my dad was kind of the Fonz, captain of the car club. He had the convertible '57 Chevy; he had the old 'Vette with the cutouts in the side. He had a bunch of hot rods. My dad lived in Norwalk. My mom went to a Christian college nearby. It's in the Valley, near Knott's Berry Farm. They call it the Inland Empire. They met and by twenty, twenty-two years old they were having me, the eldest of four, two boys, two girls. My dad owns a construction company; my mother was a florist. Just a normal girl. That was me.

I grew up in Huntington Beach. My parents put us all in Christian school. We lived in this little bubble. I was the leader of my pack of siblings. Anybody messed with my siblings, they messed with me. You got completely punked if you ever said anything to any one of my siblings. Growing up a tiny girl, I had to develop like a Napoleon complex. If you stepped to me, I stepped back twice as hard.

In junior high I got in trouble for reading *Surfer* magazine in Bible class. The slits in my skirts were way too high. They were supposed to be two inches and they were eight inches. Then my parents put me in public school. I was the only girl on my high school surf team. I was that girl. But my parents still made me go to Sunday school every Sunday as long as I lived under their roof. I graduated high school at seventeen. I was out of the house the next day.

I was not a rocker by any means. I was kind of a punker, like a surf punk. I didn't even follow rock 'n' roll. I did love Van Halen and Led Zeppelin, but that was the extent of it. I was really more like Prince, TSOL, Siouxsie and the Banshees. That was where my musical tastes were. When I met Vince I didn't even know who he was.

After high school I moved to Huntington Beach. I had a boyfriend there and I knew everyone. I lived on Main Street by the pier. All the pro surfers were my friends. I hung out in the surf shops. I lived in my bikini. And no shoes. That's who I was back then. The quintessential surf chick. I helped out at the surf contests with my pro-surfer boyfriend. I was completely immersed in that culture. I loved it. Of course I had to have a job. I worked at night. My first job was as a telephone solicitor. I'd actually pretend to call people. I'd just dial TIME because I hated to talk to people. Then by the time I became nineteen or twenty I'd had enough. I had to get a real job. I became an office manager for a life insurance company; I became a nine-to-fiver.

About the mud wrestling at the Tropicana: For the record, I actually started as a round girl. And I was never a stripper. Never! I was the girl who walks around the ring in her bikini between rounds, holding the card. How it happened was this girl I met brought me to the Tropicana and I watched. And literally all the girls were just wearing their bikinis, which I lived in anyway for free—all day long people saw me in my bikini. And so it didn't seem like that big of a deal to me to wear one and get paid. And then I saw the girls wrestling and I thought, *That's not so hard. I can fake wrestle another girl in my bikini in the mud for that much money.* I watched my friend do it and I was like, "I can do that. Why not?"

The Tropicana was a two-story club, really pretty inside. It was in Hollywood. All the waitresses and the wrestlers were like the most beautiful girls, models and actresses. They did this at night and then they would go on their auditions and stuff during the day. The mud pit was kind of in the middle of the club. They had all the chairs around. It was just a square that had kind of a tarp formed around it, and then the mud was in the middle. But it was not mud, exactly. It was like a mixture of foam and this cement-colored grossness. It smelled awful. It was not cute at all. And it was cold. It was not heated. You'd get bachelor parties and stuff; there was a big bar and there were really pretty waitresses. The first couple of times I wrestled, I had to do some drinking... but I don't want to get too much into this. I literally worked at the Tropicana for three months. I mostly round-girled, you know, where you carry the card for each round.

Vince came in there one night. He was a regular. All the girls knew him. Everybody was friends with Vince. And that is actually how I met him. He had a party at his house; the girls invited me. It was a pool party in the summertime. Some of the girls said, "Hey, we're going to Vince Neil's house." And I was like, "Who's that?" And they were like, "He's the singer for Mötley Crüe. It should be fun, you should come." So I went. And I literally walked into this, like, 1980s family house in Northridge that he was living in. It was suburbia. Like endless mom and pop, a tract home in a neighborhood of families.

I walked in, everything was beige. I thought I was going to walk into a rock star's home—black lacquer, leather couches, a disco ball on the ceiling or something. But it was a completely normal little cute house. I didn't even know who Vince was. I walked into the back and I was like, "Which one is he?" I didn't even know. Because everybody just looked normal. There was not a lot of drugs; there was nobody getting wasted. It wasn't a kegger; it was just like nice people sitting around the pool chilling out. Finally, somebody introduced me to him. I was like, "Oh, nice to meet you." And that was it. Normal day, margaritas by the pool, and then I went home to Huntington Beach with my friends. The next time I met him, he had a Halloween party.

Up to that point, I thought he was nice. But he was not my type. He had long hair. I don't even think he was drinking then. I think he was sober. He was just a nice, pleasant guy. Then one night I'm working, I was round-girling at the Tropicana, and he came in, and after my shift I was walking to my car and he runs after me. He's like, "Excuse me, excuse me." And I was like, "Oh, hi." And he was like, "Didn't you come to my party? Isn't your name Sharise? I'd really like to take you out to dinner."

I was petrified. I was like, *Ohmygod! How do I get out of this? Because this guy is not my type at all.* I'm into surfer guys, you know, totally built, baggy trunks, tan—that's my type. And this guy was wearing laced-up snake pants with leopard shoes and a skintight T-shirt cut down the middle that he had clearly cut himself, and tons of gold, chunky gold jewelry. And he had long hair and I was just like, *Oh my god, how do I get out of this without being rude?* So I said I had to work. And he's like, "What about the next night?" So I went ahead and gave him my phone number, thinking I'd blow him off when he called. All I knew about him at that point was that his band looked like girls, that they had ratty hair and he was the one with the white hair who'd somehow been in jail. People said he was cute, but not to me. But then he called and he said that he'd like to take me to dinner at L'Orangerie and he was going to send a limo for me. It was one of those offers you couldn't refuse.

I went and I ended up having a really nice time. He was very interesting, very well mannered. Worldly. He was so complimentary. He just knocked my socks off, what a gentleman he was.

Afterwards we went to the Comedy Club and his manager was there, so we sat at their table and really had a nice time. Vince started to drink; he got a little sloppy. On the way home he tried to give me all the jewelry on his body. He was like, "Here, take my bracelet; take my necklace. I want you to have it. Here, you want my ring? What do you want? I'll give you anything you want." I had never met anybody like him. Of course I didn't take anything. But, you know, he was so *not* what I was expecting. He was just very sweet and charming. I had a really nice time.

Of course, what I didn't know is I didn't meet Vince; I met his rep.

It's like the comedian Chris Rock says: The first time a woman meets a man, she doesn't meet him, exactly. She's meeting his rep. His surrogate. That's who I met first, the nice Vince. That's the Vince I fell in love with.

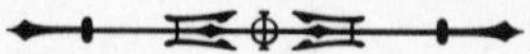

In September 1986, we signed a six-plus album deal with Elektra. I don't know how much money we got, but it was a lot. Suddenly I was rich.

They brought back Tom Werman to produce the album that would eventually be called *Girls, Girls, Girls*... a more apt title for that time period would have been difficult to come by.

In between bouts of partying and fucking, we recorded the album. The whole process took about eight months. While we were in the studio I got a call offering me the role of the prince in a rock musical version of *Cinderella*. I was excited about the idea and even met with the producer. But in the end I had to decline; the musical would be running while Mötley was on tour. It was fun to think about, tickled the fancy of my inner entertainer, I suppose.

At this time, Nikki was still shooting heroin—as well as freebasing coke. He had a new girlfriend, the former Prince protégée Vanity, who used to be amazing looking but was now a stone freebase addict. She would eventually lose a kidney to her addiction. Nikki's weight had dropped from 204 to 160 pounds in less than a year. He probably thought he was "elegantly wasted," but he just looked awful. I mean, his fucking legs were like matchsticks.

Mick came up with the album's title track, "Girls, Girls, Girls." If you've ever wondered why the solo at the end of the song ends so abruptly, it's because Mick was so wasted that he fell off his stool while recording it. As to the cover look, by now our image was dovetailing from the Road Warrior vibe to a sort of motorcycle-outlaw theme…a prelude to today's *Tattoos & Tequila*, I guess. Nikki came up with the design for the *Girls* album sleeve, which featured a new Mötley Crüe logo designed by Chris Polentz over a photo of us posing on our Harleys. At that time, we were all about our motorcycles, hard likker, black leather, and pussy, pussy, pussy—maybe that would have been a better title?

For you aficionados, it might be interesting to note that the opening revving sound on the album was recorded in the courtyard of Conway Studios with my new Harley; for the outro sample, Werman took the bike for a spin through Franklin Canyon and recorded the bike shifting through the gears. I helped contribute to the opening track, "Wild Side," which was Nikki's alternate take on the Lord's Prayer. *Girls* also features another first for us: gospel singers performing backup vocals. (The more money you make, the more the company lets you spend on recording frills.) They also spent the money to use street noises recorded in downtown Los Angeles to aid the whole sonic flavor of the thing. Ted Nugent band member Dave Amato contributed backup vocals, as did Pat Torpey, who previously drummed for Robert Plant and Belinda Carlisle and later would drum for Mr. Big. The final track on the album is a live version of Elvis Presley's hit "Jailhouse Rock," recorded at Long Beach Arena, California, on the previous *Theatre of Pain* U.S. tour.

In May 1987, the title track of the new album was released as the first single. The song peaked at #12 on the U.S. charts—the highest placing yet for a Crüe single.

The album followed soon after—it entered the *Billboard* 200 at #5, the highest positioning of a metal album since Led Zeppelin's *The Song Remains the Same* almost a decade earlier. It went on to reach #2—Whitney Houston's second album, *Whitney*, beat us out. According to the story, or the mythology, depending which you believe, there was a bunch of intrigue and hanky-panky involving

CBS honcho Clive Davis, who supposedly bribed buyers with a trip to keep Whitney on top. Who knows? What I do know is we all felt like *Girls* should have been our first #1 album.

In preparation for the upcoming tour, I sold my house and rented a small apartment in Hollywood, putting most of my possessions in storage. If it is true that Mötley Crüe has always been known as a sex, drugs, and rock 'n' roll band, the *Girls* tour was probably our wildest outing in terms of excess.

After a week of technical run-throughs and rehearsals at arenas in San Diego and Arizona, the *Girls* world tour kicked off on June 19, 1987, in Tucson. Ex–Deep Purple frontman David Coverdale's Whitesnake was our opening act. The plan was to tour the U.S., then head to Japan in December, then on to Europe in January. We'd return home in early February for a couple of months off before a further American leg with Guns N' Roses.

Of course, that's not exactly how things went down.

We took the largest—and loudest—PA ever assembled out on the road with us. The stage theatrics included a giant inflatable Harley-Davidson motorbike and a spinning drum cage for Tommy, who first imagined the setup in a dream. Developed by an ex-navy submarine hydraulics specialist, it cost around eighty thousand dollars. It was welded onto a forklift, mounted on yokes from a garbage truck, and connected by microphone cables.

The success of the *Girls* album also meant yet another touring upgrade. We crisscrossed American airspace in an eighteen-seater Gulfstream One jet fitted out with beds, couches, and a plush black leather interior. We even had our own stewardess whose job it was to lay out drugs and drinks on each band member's meal tray before we boarded. Nikki got white wine and zombie dust (a mix of Halcion and cocaine); Tommy got a cocktail and a helping of zombie dust; Mick got his vodka—he always carried his own prescription pills; he was like a pharmacist. I was easy to please.

Just give me a drink and a sleeping pill. Like I said earlier: My destination of choice tends to be Planet Oblivion.

The jet's exterior sported a radical Mötley logo design with a scantily dressed cowgirl riding a bomb, a takeoff on those old World War II bomber planes. We soon began referring to this junket as the Airport Blow Job Tour. Every time we'd land at the airport there'd be a line of hot chicks waiting for us, and we'd oblige them by taking the best-looking ones into the airport's private VIP bathrooms. I can't imagine what would possess a young woman to drive in the night to a private landing field with the intention of sucking a stranger's dick. Thinking back on it, however, I can't say I ever took the time to ask.

And so it would go, one city after the next, a trail of debauchery, the rock 'n' roll lifestyle. It's such a haze to me now, gig after gig, place after place, a parade of different drugs and different female parts, each of them wonderfully different, like snowflakes. It would make a great, like, dream sequence in a movie—the carnal slide show of all the girls I've ever known. I'd pay to go to that flick.

As you might expect, things began to get a bit sloppy. In Rochester, New York, I ended up severing tendons, nerves, and an artery in my right hand and almost losing a finger when I threw a temper tantrum over a glass jar of GREY POUPON mustard. I was just being an asshole, but I did have a point. For a week or more I'd been telling everybody that I didn't like GREY POUPON. They had this food set up; I liked to eat something before the show, but I like yellow mustard. And every day there was only GREY POUPON, which I do not like. And call me an ass, you know, but who was the food supposed to be for? Me and the other guys, correct?

Finally, one night, I just lost it. I was all dressed. I was ready to go onstage. I was in my stage clothes. And I was like, "I fucking told you I hate fucking GREY POUPON!" I threw it against the wall, but I threw it really close, or I don't know what happened, but it cut my finger bad—to this day I can't even stretch my finger. There was a lot of blood. It basically severed the finger. *Fuck* yeah, I freaked out; I was in shock. They rushed me to the hospital and they had to operate, like, instantly. Obviously the show was canceled that night. The doctors managed to repair most of the damage to my hand, but I had to wear a full cast up to my elbow for a month. But they never had any GREY POUPON there again.

In Chicago, we were hanging out in a transvestite bar, drinking vodka and eating caviar and doing tons of coke, when the cops came bursting in. The officer in charge turned out to be a huge fan of ours, so he let us off. In Nikki's hometown of San Jose, they weren't so nice. We were playing the Great Western Forum; Nikki decided to ride to the venue on his Harley. On the way a cop pulled him over for speeding. When he couldn't produce his driver's license, he was arrested. Thankfully Doc McGhee got there in time to sort the situation out.

When we hit Japan things just got even crazier. There's something about the Japanese—they were so polite and worshipful that I think it made you want to act out even more than usual. The stories about that trip are well known—if not exactly accurate. It is true that the first official happening of our Japanese tour was Tommy getting busted by customs officials at the airport; they found some marijuana in his drum kit. Luckily, he was saved by our Japanese promoter, who managed to smooth things over without any charges being laid. When we got to the hotel, Tommy's foul mood became his great idea of fun—dropping a wine bottle out of a tenth-story window. Nikki, meanwhile, shortsightedly made the trip with no stash of heroin. By the time we landed, he was going through withdrawal.

There is another story about me getting drunk at a Roppongi restaurant and getting into a fight with a crew of Yakuza gangsters. I have no idea where that one came from. Nikki, on the other hand, had quite a night—his birthday. I guess he was drinking to fight down the withdrawals. He was like a bear woken from hibernation. First he comes to blows with Tommy. There is a historical dispute about this fight. Tommy says Nikki hit him in the mouth. Nikki says that Tommy was so drunk he fell over on his own and smashed his face into the floor. Whatever. Neither of those pussies can fight.

Before leaving the club, Nikki got into a second altercation with an American tourist, whose head he directed into a steel pole, cracking it open. Leaving the club wearing a Godzilla mask, Mick terrorized people in the street. Reportedly with his pants around his ankles, he was apprehended by police as he was urinating along the side of the road.

Later, after a show in Osaka, heading back to Tokyo by high-speed bullet train, Tommy and Nikki got roaring drunk on sake and Jack Daniel's. They poured liquor over the heads of several Japanese commuters—and also on Mick's girl, Emi. Emi Canyon was a backup singer in Nasty Habit, who were on tour with us. We had this rule where we weren't supposed to sleep with anyone who works for the band. Tommy and Nikki gave Mick a lot of shit, even though Tommy usually slept with anyone he wanted, as we've well established. They punished the couple on tour by pouring drinks on them and smearing food over their luggage. At one point Mick was so pissed he almost walked.

Now, on the train, Tommy and Nikki ordered curry and smeared it all over the walls. Then Nikki threw the Jack bottle and it hit a businessman; the guy went down like he'd been shot, bleeding copiously from a head wound. At this point our Japanese tour manager used a martial arts pressure-point move on Nikki and Tommy, pressing his finger onto a point on the backs of their necks, rendering them unconscious. When the train stopped in Tokyo, Japanese police took Nikki into custody. When Doc McGhee went over to do his thing—take responsibility and deflect blame—they took him into custody, too.

It took them like twenty-four hours to get out of jail.

In the meantime, I hooked up with this beautiful Japanese chick. I brought her back to the hotel, but when I got there I realized, *Holy shit!* Sharise was in my room!!!! I'd forgotten I'd told her to come visit.

I went to Doc's room. He'd just gotten into bed. I asked him if he would be a good manager and give me his room so I could fuck the Japanese girl.

Doc looked at me like I was crazy, that little fucker. Then he punched me in the face and closed the door.

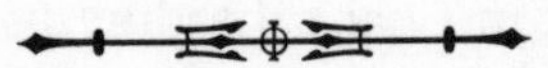

Sharise Ruddell Neil
Vince's Second Wife

It soon became obvious that he was hugely famous. We couldn't go anywhere without people stopping him and wanting his autograph and freaking out.

He wanted me to go to rehearsals with him—they were recording *Girls, Girls, Girls*. He made me go every single day to the studio with him, and I'd sit there for hours and hours. Parts of it were boring, because they sing the same line over and over and over, trying to get it right. But then again, this is a whole new world for me, I was getting to know Tommy and Nikki. Tommy's wife, Heather Locklear, was just a doll to me. Here's this big star and she's coming up like, "Hi, my name is Heather." She treated me like I was gold. She made me feel so welcome. And that became my life. Him saying, "Don't go to work tonight. How much you going to make? I'll pay you to stay with me." I was like, "Okay." Soon he was like, "You know what? I really don't want you to work there anymore." And I was like, "Okay." What would you say?

We got married on April 30, 1988. The wedding was beautiful. It was at the Hotel Bel Air, by the lake with the swans. We both spent the night there before the wedding and he got really drunk, which made me mad—he was superhungover at the wedding.

When I first started dating him he was still coming off of being a sober guy, so he was limiting himself, regulating himself and his drinking. I didn't really know as I was falling in love with him how bad it was. When I started to find out, it was devastating to me, because I had never seen him do the switcharoo he does. It's like a switch he has. We would have a few drinks and he would be fine, and then one time out of maybe ten times he would get too drunk and then I'd be like, *Whoa. Did* that *just happen?* He needs somebody to babysit him. He was fine drinking between maybe one and four drinks. Around five, six, seven he gets sloppy. When he goes all the way to twelve he's just belligerent; he doesn't remember anything; he takes swings at people. He becomes psychotic, really. And he never remembered a thing.

He loved to fight. And let me tell you something—if he couldn't fight with somebody else, on the way home he wanted to fight with me. That happened so many times. He just picks a fight.

I remember our first big fight. That's when I saw the ugly side of him. We had gone to an event, some kind of an awards event. We sat at a table with the Mötley guys and I happened to be sitting next to Tom Werman, the producer of the *Girls, Girls, Girls* album. Vince was on my other side. It was a dress up event. We took a limo and it was just a really nice night. And Tom Werman was just making conversation with me because I'm sitting next to him, and that's polite, right? I don't even remember what he was saying. I might not have been even listening very hard. But all of a sudden Vince leans over to me and he says something like, "Why don't you just go fuck him!" And I was like, "What?" I was shocked. He starts saying all these really mean things to me in my ear; it was just unbelievable stuff. The next morning he starts calling me. He leaves messages. He doesn't seem to remember anything; he doesn't remember saying those things. I don't think I answered the phone for three days. He kept leaving me messages: "Why won't you call me back," blah blah blah. That's like the first time I saw the ugly side of him. Which I was to see many, many, many, many, many more times. But when you're twenty and somebody says, "I don't know, I don't remember," and you love them, you kind of just say that must be a one-off. You know, "I'm just going to forgive him because he didn't mean to do it and he apologized," and blah blah blah. So by the time I was planning the wedding I had seen this a couple more times and I had a bad feeling. But the wedding was planned, do you know what I'm saying? The wedding was paid for.

Let me tell you about the first time he brought me to his house to meet his parents. They were very welcoming. His mom brings me into the front room; it's very nice. She goes, "Have you seen all these magazines with Vince in them? Let me show you." She starts pulling out scrapbooks and pictures, showing me pictures of him when he was little. Then she whips out the magazines; Vince and I are sitting on the couch and she's like, "Oh, and here's Vincent on the cover of *Metal Edge*," here's him on the cover of this, here's him on the cover of that. And then she, like, starts to cry. And she looks at Vince and she goes, "What would you do if I died?" I was like, *Whoa, whoa! Where did that come from?* And Vince just goes, "Mom, Mom, what's wrong with you?" And then he gets up and leaves. He just leaves me sitting with her.

Odie is very nice. He's tall; you could tell he was a really good-looking man when he was young. Very quiet man. Very passive and quiet. And he likes his drink. They both do. I've never seen Odie lose control or anything. But they're both drinkers. I don't know what Vince had to grow up with in terms of dealing with all that.

The second we'd have a fight, Vince would be on the phone to a friend calling him to come out to our house and sit with him. He's very co-dependent. He's just a very insecure person. I was constantly having to beef up his ego. You'd think when you're singing in front of twenty thousand people who are screaming how much they love you—you'd think that would fill the hole. The girls are out there showing their boobs. He could have his pick of any of them. But he was like, "People only want something from me; I have no friends; nobody likes me." I heard that five thousand times.

When he was on the road he wore my pants. He was that small. He could wear my stuff. He took my leopard-skin leggings and he would wear them onstage. He only ate once a day; he had a tuna sandwich. He never drank before the show back then. He'd only drink after. We had a trainer who would come to the house. He would train both. But before that Vince used to do this kind of karate or martial arts thing. I think that was when he lived at the beach with Beth.

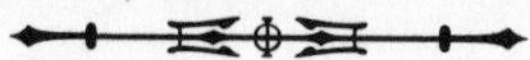

I was the first to hear of Nikki's death.

It was December 23, 1987, when I got the call. I was sound asleep, at home in bed with Sharise.

The call came from Nikki's driver, Boris, who'd been parked outside the Franklin Plaza Hotel, where the guys from Guns N' Roses stayed. "The dealer just ran past me screaming that he killed Nikki," is how Boris put it... I think. He had some kind of accent, so it was hard to make him out.

I was like, *What the fuck?* I'm sure I'd been drinking earlier. You know how it is when you wake up in that haze.

Apparently, after a night on the town with Slash and his girlfriend—and some time spent at the Cathouse, another popular strip club we all frequented—they came back to the hotel and did some potent gummy Persian heroin. The dealer shot up Nikki, who passed out in front of Slash's room and began turning blue. Seeing the turn of events, the dealer jumped out of the window and hightailed it over the balcony. He's running down the street, yelling, "I just killed Nikki Sixx!"

"They wheeled him out with a sheet over his face," Boris reported. He'd driven me around a couple of times. I guess mine was the only number he had. I was like, *What the fuck do you want me to do about it?*

I woke up Sharise and told her what was going on. I think we got hold of the tour manager, Rich Fisher. I was pretty good friends with him. He'd later turn me on to offshore speedboat racing, which was really a rush, just really fun. We had Rich call all the hospitals and find out what was going on.

In the meantime, I guess, a whole lot else was happening. News of Nikki's death spread fast, quickly reaching radio stations, causing a minor stir around town; impromptu memorials went up along the Strip. Slash called Tommy and explained how they'd tried everything to keep Nikki alive. Doug Thaler called Doc McGhee, who had just finished dinner with Bob Krasnow of Elektra Records. Then Fisher called Mick. Somehow, it was decided that the original Cousin It—the person who had always talked the least of everyone in the band—would call England and cancel the European leg of the tour, due to start in like two weeks. Mick called our old friends at *Kerrang!* magazine and made up some lame excuse for why were weren't coming.

After what seemed like an eternity, Fisher called me back. "Yeah," he says, "Nikki ODed, but he's not dead."

I'm like, *All right, cool.*

Then I went back to bed.

(To finish the story, as many of us know, it turned out the paramedic was a Mötley fan. He wasn't going to let Nikki die in his ambulance. After a second attempt at a double-dose jab of adrenaline, he managed to...kick-start Nikki's heart. A few hours later, Nikki discharged himself from the hospital and was picked up by two female fans who thought he was a ghost, having just heard on the radio the news of his demise.)

The next morning, Christmas Eve 1987, the members of Mötley Crüe, looking more motley than ever, assembled in Doc McGhee's living room for a hastily called meeting. We were informed that the *Girls* European tour had been eighty-sixed; compensation to the promoters over there would be coming out of our own pockets.

And then our esteemed management dropped their bombshell: They were prepared to resign if we didn't get our act together and get straight before going into the studio to start recording the next album, *Dr. Feelgood.*

If you ask me, compared to the other guys I wasn't really in bad shape. I wasn't totally sober anymore, but it didn't rule my life. I didn't sit and drink all day long. I have never been the kind of guy where you're like, "Okay, it's ten in the morning; I'm going to have my first drink." It was never like that, never in my life. I usually woke up, and then I went and worked out. I went to lunch; I did things. I didn't start drinking until the show...or really after the show for real. If you watch the "Wild Side" video, or other videos from those days...I looked fucking great. I was a young guy with my shirt off, fucking running around the stage. For me the drinking was always after the show. It was a way to keep the excitement going. It's not for before the show. Maybe just one drink. Or two. Like a glass of wine. But traditionally, for me at least, drinking was done after the show.

The truth is, I can't sing drunk. I mean, I've done it. Don't get me wrong. But not with Mötley. I've done it with my solo band—sometimes it has happened. Especially during the early solo band stuff. I was pretty messed up during that period. So maybe I've sung drunk on early solo band stuff. And maybe with early, *early* Mötley Crüe stuff, you know, 'cause you're drinking when you get to the gig and you might be a little more buzzed than you want to be when you're onstage. But after thirty years I can maybe remember two times that I might've been really drunk onstage.

Thinking back about what happened next...we may or may

not have gone to different residential rehabs. I can't remember. All the times in rehab blur together for me. It seems like I've been to five or ten different rehabs over the years. Maybe I've intentionally blocked it out, I don't know. But I do remember that at some point, before recording the album, instead of going to rehab, per se, we worked with this counselor named Bob Timmons. It was fucking lame. Nobody wanted to do it.

Timmons was an ex–Hell's Angel who'd done thirty years in prison. He'd killed some people. He was an imposing dude. He would come to rehearsal or we would go to somebody's house. He specialized in rock bands. He did Aerosmith; I think he did a thing with Metallica; he'd seen a lot. Also at that time, there were these special AA or NA meetings we went to. They were like private meetings held at people's houses—because if you're a celebrity and go into a regular meeting you're not going to be able to open up about yourself 'cause you're famous. We would go to one house one week and another house the next. Kind of like a movable meeting. My future roommate the actor Rob Lowe was there... all kinds of fucking people showed up at these meetings. I took my turn hosting them, too.

At the time, I had this huge house in Bell Canyon, near Chatsworth. It was an amazing house in a gated community. Forty minutes out the 101 from Hollywood, there were boulder-capped hills and verdant oak-lined forests—it was very rural out there, what they call horse property, five-acre lots. The actor Jamie Farr, from the old TV show *M*A*S*H*, lived across the street. Our house had a church steeple, its own moat, waterfalls, a stream running through the backyard. The front door was nine hundred years old; I had a train track with big electric trains that ran around the ceiling in one of the rooms. It was pretty cool, a great house—only a couple million bucks, I think.

The only problem was the house was haunted. I don't know who the ghost was—friends would stay in the guest bedroom and they would hear things hit the wall and slide down. They'd turn on the light; there'd be nothing there. Or the master bedroom—that was weird. My dog used to always bark at the TV nook. See, the master suite was almost like two rooms; there was a part where the bed was, and then there was like a pony wall, and then there was the nook, the place we had a TV and seating area. The dog would bark always at that section.

One night Sharise was in bed and she heard a baby crying in that corner. And she froze, you know, because I wasn't there or whatever. She didn't even want to look in that direction. But then she said she felt a hand turn her face toward the direction where the sound was coming from, where the baby was—actually physically turning her face. It's like, *Holy shit!* I still get goose bumps thinking about it.

We got outta there and found a new house. It was even better. It was in this community called Summit Ridge. It was in Chatsworth, at the very top of this ridge. It overlooked the whole Valley—kind of like the way Lovey's parents' place had back in the day. I guess in a way I would become a prisoner of this house, too. But what a prison: The place was even featured in the *Robb Report*. I had a car collection by then of like thirty-five cars. The house had a huge garage. I had cars stacked on top of each other, using those lifts they use in New York, Ferraris stacked on Ferraris, Lambos, what have you. I had a whole bunch of cars. It was lifestyles of the rich and famous.

In March 1989, we all picked up and moved to Vancouver to record *Dr. Feelgood* at Little Mountain Studios with Bob Rock. It was amazing. All of us were actually sober.

We brought our motorcycles. We were up there a long time—eight months or something. We went through the seasons; we saw winter and spring and summer. It cost like around six hundred thousand dollars to produce that album—I always think about the three days it took to record *Too Fast for Love.*

Rock's demanding work ethic pushed us to new limits, I think. I feel like he brought the best out of Mötley Crüe. I'm sure the sobriety helped, too. We still managed to have fun, though. We went out every night; we just didn't drink or do drugs. But we still had hookers come in and we still had fun. Aerosmith was recording next door. They were working on their big comeback album, *Pump.* It was pretty cool that we both came out with important albums from the same studio at the same time. Steven Tyler came and sang on a couple songs on our album; Bryan Adams came in and sang after Tommy met him in a Vancouver strip club. Cheap Trick came in also. And Jack Blades from the Night Rangers. While I'm being interviewed for this book, Blades is here in Vegas, producing the audio version of *Tattoos & Tequila.* He has been one of my closest friends for years. He is the fuckin' man.

The cover artwork for the album was originally going to have our band mascot, Allister Fiend, drawn as a mad doctor holding a big syringe. However, the final design—a dagger and a snake—is a piece of tattoo flash, designed by Sunset Strip tattoo artist Kevin Brady, who also designed a new Mötley Crüe logo. In August of 1989, the first single from the album was released: "Dr. Feelgood" became a huge hit, reaching #6 on the *Billboard* chart—our first gold disc for a single.

The album by the same title was released one month later. By October we had our first #1 album on the *Billboard* charts. By November it hit double platinum, 2 million copies sold in the U.S.

In early September of 1989, Mötley was invited to present the award for Best Heavy Metal Album at the MTV Music Video Awards at the Universal Amphitheatre in Universal City. It was a huge honor. We were stoked to get the exposure.

After we did our bit, we were sitting in the audience when Guns N' Roses came out to play with Tom Petty. Earlier in the year, while I was away on a white-water rafting trip with some guys, G N' R rhythm guitarist Izzy Stradlin had tried to pick up Sharise, who was partying with some friends at the Cathouse. When she told him she was married to me, it didn't faze him one bit. He was all over her; finally she pushed him away.

Izzy was really drunk, I guess. He starts this fight with Sharise—maybe not the best move. He pulled down her top in front of everyone. When she slapped his face, he fuckin' kicked her in the stomach. What kind of an animal does that?

One thing a lot of people don't know about me is that for years I studied Tang Soo Do, a Korean martial art. I have a red belt. Which isn't a black, I know, but I can still kick some ass if I want—I have the arrest record to prove it.

As G N' R was playing, I made my way back to the wings. When Izzy came offstage, I was like, "Hey! You fucked with my wife"—or something like that. I don't remember the exact words I said, but I said *something*. And he's like, "Fuck you!" And then I'm like, "Yeah, really!"

And then I fucking hit him with a solid right and he went down. He was out cold.

Suddenly there was security everywhere—these awards shows are lousy with moonlighting cops and other paid thugs. It was a fucking madhouse. Finally they take me into custody or whatever; there's a guard on either side, holding an arm. That's when big, tough Axl Rose comes up. He's so brave with the cops holding me back. He's like, "I'm going to fuckin' kill you. How could you hit my guitar player?"

What a fuckin' puss.

I'm like, "I'll fucking go right fucking now, bitch!"

And then security dragged me away.

As you might remember, this started a whole feud. I don't even know how Axl got into it. This had nothing to do with Axl. It was between me and Izzy. And as far as I was concerned, the Izzy shit was over. But Axl goes to the press and starts running his mouth, saying that I sucker punched Izzy and all this other shit. Fuckin' Axl—I had taken that ungrateful motherfucker under my wing when they were touring with us on the *Girls* tour. I helped him out with his throat when he was having problems; I showed him a few tricks to help his voice. And here he is, challenging me to fight him. He came up with several different challenges. He'd say Tower Records on Sunset. He'd say the boardwalk at Venice Beach. I actually went a few times, but fuckin' Axl never showed up. Meanwhile, Izzy called me and apologized for his behavior!

Finally I'd had enough. I went to my buddy Dr. Jerry Buss, who owns the Lakers, and we cooked up this scheme for a fight at the Great Western Forum—located in Inglewood, near where I grew up. At the time I think they had Wednesday night boxing at the Forum. Dr. Buss was one of my drinking buddies. Always a guy who admired a good-looking woman. He was like, "Come on, let's do this." I went on MTV and challenged Axl to a three-round fight. As far as I was concerned, it was *on*.

Bigmouth Axl never responded. My offer still stands. I'm sure Dr. Buss would help us get into the Staples Center if we wanted.

And so it went, basically, for the next three years. We kept on minting hits and minting money, filling arenas, filling the hallways of our hotels. It was like these girls were standing in line for the toilet, but they were standing in line for us. There didn't seem to be any limit to what we could achieve.

In December 1989, we celebrated our tenth anniversary with a huge sell-out show at the Meadowlands in New Jersey. In March 1990, *Dr. Feelgood* went triple platinum. By the end of the *Feelgood* tour, in August 1990, we were all feeling very good indeed: Despite the astronomical expenses associated with our upkeep—something like $325,000 a week, it's been said—we each walked with a payday of over $8 million. Not bad for a quartet of high school dropouts.

As we began work on *Decade of Decadence, Feelgood* hit quadruple platinum. Nikki's son Gunner was born. Nikki was writing more and doing his own thing. Mick was still in love with his Emi, whom he'd since married. She had her own band now called She Rock. We all fell off the wagon at different times in different places. I was drinking a lot again, and I was getting more and more into racing cars.

It was an interesting combination, I know, but I never did one at the same time as the other, despite what you might think. Maybe, as I entered my thirties, I was having an early midlife crisis, but I was at a point where I wanted to do some new, exciting things.

Obviously, being a rock star, having thousands of people cheer for you—it's a hard feeling to replicate when you're not onstage. It's a pretty powerful drug in its own right, sort of like shooting up heroin. The rush is hard to describe. So you go from the arena to the bar and you party as hard as you can and you fuck a lot of women, you try to keep the energy at a peak, you try to keep it arena size, if you follow me. You want that high to keep going.

What I found was that I got the same kind of buzz from racing. Drive 200 miles an hour with other cars just inches away... that'll ring your bell, I guarantee you. Plus, the drivers are all adrenaline junkies like me. *They* wanted to keep it revving at the after-party also. So not only did I like the driving; I understood the other drivers and they understood me also.

I started out with go-karts—I bought a kart and started racing at a track in Oxnard. Then I went to racing school in Sebring, Florida; after that I started racing Formula Fords. And then I kind of just started meeting people, and somebody asked me if I wanted to try racing Indy lights. These cars went like 200 miles an hour—it was nothing like driving a regular car. It's a lot of concentration, a lot of... everything. It's just very challenging. To be good you have to be in the car a lot. You have to practice. In my line of work I guess I had the time. I raced against a lot of pro drivers who are famous. Al Unser, Jr., helped me out when I was just starting. He gave me all these different tips on driving and stuff—we're still friends today.

Eventually I became the co-owner of an Indy car race team in Long Beach, with former Formula One driver Eddie Chiva. I raced on the circuit for like half a season, six or seven races. I raced in the Long Beach Grand Prix and in grand prix races in Phoenix, Portland (Oregon), and Milwaukee.

Our races were only like an hour and a half, but they were mentally exhausting. Yeah, of course I crashed. You can't *not* crash. If you don't crash you're not trying your hardest. I remember in Long Beach I actually slid my back tires around a turn and then hit the wall, which broke the rear wing. The rear wing keeps the back wheels on the ground. It's an aerodynamic thing. It helps traction at high speeds. It keeps you from lifting off the ground.

So I pulled in the pits. And my crew chief is like, "You're done. You can't drive without the wing, and we can't replace it here." And I said, "Well, fuck it, just take it off, I'll keep going." And they were like, "The car is going to be loose out there," meaning it wouldn't have good traction. But I decided to do it anyway. It's hard to argue with a rock star who wants his own way.

I pulled out of the pits, made a right-hand turn and another right, and then I was in second gear, gassing it down the straightaway. But the straightaway had a slight kink to it. And right when you were supposed to shift into third gear, you also had to turn slightly on the kink. I shifted into third, turned slightly...

And the entire back end of the car just spun out.

I wheeled around like a pinwheel. The car just spun, spun, spun. Then I slammed into the wall—it was on TV, the Long Beach Grand Prix. That was one of the wrecks. I think I crashed at Portland, too. And in some race in Australia.

What's going through your mind when you're hitting a wall? Well...nothing. You kind of know you're not going to get hurt. You're pretty strapped in there, to the extent that you feel like you're just going to bounce off. So it's, it's not like it's scary to crash. It's just part of racing.

December has always been a weird month for us, good and bad. December was the month of New Year's Eve-il, when we solidified our future as a band by bringing on Doc and Thaler. It was the month I killed a man in a car accident and permanently maimed two others. It was the month Nikki died and came back to life. And it was the month, in 1991, that Mötley signed a five-album deal with Bob Krasnow at Elektra Records, for a $25 million advance.

Then, on the afternoon of February 11, 1992, things took a bit of a drastic turn in the other direction.

I was living in Chatsworth with Sharise at the time, in the big house with all the cars, the one that was in the *Robb Report*. To get to the city it's a good half hour down the 101, and then you gotta go over Coldwater, over the Mulholland Mountains, from the Valley to get to Hollywood.

On that day, Los Angeles was under seige; bad storms and flash flooding was typical for this time of year, the rainy season in Southern Cal. This storm was especially bad, probably part of an El Niño;

on TV it was like a scene from a fucking disaster movie. You can look it up in the archives. Governor Pete Wilson declared a state of emergency and urged everyone to remain indoors. The entire Sepulveda Basin had been flooded; six people lost their lives. There were road closures. Plus, you have to remember, we lived in an exposed house on a ridge in a pretty rural area, so everything seemed even worse: It was literally raining so hard you couldn't see. As far as I was concerned, there was no need to risk my life to drive to rehearsal. There were plenty other days in front of us, you know? Why risk your life in a storm? I was like, *I'm not going out in this shit.*

The story goes that Nikki and Tommy and Mick waited four hours for me to come. Pissed, they had our tour manager, Mike Amato, send me a fax, asking where I was and ordering me to come to the studio immediately.

I was like, *What the fuck,* you know? *Who is* ordering *me to do shit? What the fuck do you mean,* immediately? *Nobody talks to* me *that way. I am a grown man.*

I called the studio hoping the fax was Nikki's weird idea of a joke, but of course it wasn't. Nikki started balling me out because my phone line had been constantly busy—maybe it was out. How was I supposed to know the line was out? And if it was out, how did I get the fax?

The funny thing about all this stuff—the thing that *nobody says*—is that the guys had been rehearsing with John Corabi this whole time. I didn't know about it then, but I know about it now. So if you ask me, you can tell this story one hundred ways, but there's only one truth. They just kind of masterminded some shit with this whole thing 'cause they wanted to get rid of me and replace me with Corabi.

I drove in to the studio. I don't remember if it was in Hollywood or in the Valley. I don't remember which one of my thirty cars I drove—probably one of the four-wheelers or the Hummer. When

I got there Nikki and them start talking all this trash about how I was out the night before drunk and how they are thinking of... *getting a new lead singer*!!!!

When I heard that I think I went deaf and blind.

I was like, *Fuck this shit, I'm outta here.*

It sounded to me like I'd just been fired.

On Valentine's Day, Mötley put out a press statement: "Race car driving has become a priority in Neil's life, and he's dedicated much of his time and energy to it. The Crüe's relationship to Vince began to deteriorate because his band-mates felt he didn't share their determination and passion for music. Vince was the only Crüe member who didn't regularly participate in the song writing process."

First of all, let me tell you, when they issued this, the racing season was *over.* I wasn't even driving at the time. Then they blame my tardiness all the time? Are you fuckin' kidding me? There was a fuckin' storm that day—did they mention that in the press release? Was I racing cars that day? They just wanted an excuse to get rid of me. And that was it, cut-and-dry. It was a them-or-me situation—and it's always been that way, since the accident days. It's always them against me. They're just not nice people. They don't know what friends really are. They think friends are, "What can you do for me?" It's like Tommy and Nikki were the center of things and Mick was the yes-man. Mick always agreed with whatever Nikki and Tommy said.

So when I got to rehearsal and it was basically just one of those situations. It was like: "Fuck you." *No. Fuck you.* That was it. And I drove right home. A lot of people ask the question, "Were you fired or did you quit?" Because those guys say I quit.

If you ask me, the fired came first. I mean, it was a little outrageous. I'm supposed to be 25 percent of this thing and you're firing me? And the band manager, Doug Thaler, was sitting right there!

And I'm like, *We're the biggest band in the world and you're going to watch it dissolve right in front of your eyes?* Great management, you know?

If I was the manager, I think I would have taken some control at that point. As a manager I would have told everybody to go home, take a week off, take two weeks off, calm down. I would have counseled everybody to chill out for a bit. I thought it was weird that he didn't do that, you know?

When I got home, Thaler called.

I take the phone, thinking he's going to say what I just said—take a couple weeks off, everybody cool down.

But that's not what he says. He says, "I think we're going to let you out of your contract."

That sounds pretty much like, "You're fired."

Don't you agree?

Chapter 8

WHO'LL STOP THE RAIN

If I told you the breakup of Mötley Crüe didn't affect me, I'd be lying.

At first I was pissed, especially about the way they announced it on Valentine's Day and said I was "the only Crüe member who didn't regularly participate in the song writing process." That's pretty funny, because when you look at all the songs, all the hits, you see the name Neil there. I wrote the melody for "Home Sweet Home." I wrote the melody for "Wild Side." I wrote the melody for "Same Ol' Situation." You look at all my songwriting credits and there can be only one conclusion: Fuck yeah, he contributed.

Then the anger cleared a little and I got excited. I realized maybe this was a blessing in disguise. I was finally rid of those bastards. Plus, I wasn't that great in math, but I understood the concept of division. When you don't have partners and you don't have to split the proceeds, you can make a whole lot more money!

Especially on tour. Lower expenses, higher share of the gate. The ticket prices are the same if you're one person or ten.

I called up the head of Elektra at the time, Bob Krasnow, and said, "I'm not in Mötley Crüe anymore, where do I stand? What are my options?"

And he said... all together now, "First you gotta find a manager, *then* we'll talk about it."

Krasnow did let me know that the company retained an option on me for solo records. Bottom line: I had value. With or without Mötley, there would be money coming in, I could earn, I could have a career.

Thus fortified, I did what I always did... I decided to celebrate.

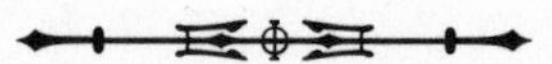

Sharise Rudell Neil
Vince's Second Wife

Skylar was no accident. We tried for Skylar. Vince had really wanted a baby. When I started dating him, Beth had left him a month before. She had taken Little Beth, obviously, and wouldn't let her see Vince. I got to see the fallout from all that—Vince crying, Vince begging to see his baby. And Beth saying no. She was calling him, leaving lots of mean and nasty messages on his machine, and he would call her back and they would fight for hours on the phone. And I remember it was Little Beth's birthday—I think it was her second birthday or maybe her third birthday. They were going to go to Disneyland together. So Vince went out to Toys"R"Us and bought her all these presents. One of them was this car that she could actually sit in and drive. It was like the BIGFOOT monster truck, you know, and you could press the pedal and it actually went—I think it was rechargeable. He bought all these toys and I wrapped them all for him, for her. And then that morning, the morning of her birthday, Beth tells him, "Don't bring any toys; she can't have them. I don't want you bringing all that stuff." So he was crushed. He wanted to be the daddy with the presents. I saw over the next two years him asking to see Little Beth. And I saw him be crushed every time that Beth said no. So when I became the age where I felt I was ready to have a baby, I wanted to have a baby; I couldn't *wait* to give that to him again. And he was excited, too. I mean, we were so excited we were having a little girl, especially.

I think that he never considered himself a married man. I think that he always conducted himself as if he was single when he was not with me. When he was on the road, he acted as if he was single. This is what I hear that athletes do—when they all get on the plane to go to the game, all the guys kinda say, "Hey, did you bring your road dick?" It's their opportunity to be bad together. And nobody's gonna tell. I think it's the same mentality for rock stars. They all are bad and they all keep the secrets. If I found out he did something one time, there were probably twenty or fifty or a hundred times that I *didn't* know about. But the one I did find out about happened. He was with that porno girl when I was pregnant. Before that, I thought we were doing great. Cheating on your wife when she's pregnant is really the shittiest thing you can do to a woman. I guess it's common. But I couldn't really deal with it. I guess that's when everything started to fall apart. That's when the shit hit the fan.

After that it was like everything came crashing down in a way. When you cheat on somebody, it's poison. It's poison forever to the relationship. Nothing is ever the same. I kicked him out of the house—that's where he lived, at the Bel Age, for the next six months. I said, "I'll never get back with you. It's not going to happen." He wanted to go to counseling; over the next six months we went to counseling. We eventually got back together, but the only reason I wanted to get back together was so that he would know his daughter. I was completely done with him, really.

The weird thing was, Vince called me twenty times a day. This is why I could not believe that he would ever even cheat on me, because the guy stayed in constant contact with me. He was always like, "Come down to the studio." He always wanted me right next to him. When he was on the road he would call me when he woke up. He'd call me before he ordered breakfast, when he got breakfast, or after he got breakfast. Before he went to the gig, when he got to the gig, before the show, after the show, and then when he went to sleep. Like that's how many times a day he called me? So where was he fitting in time with girls? Like I just didn't even think that that was possible, right? Why would he be calling me if there was a girl right there? That just doesn't make sense in my world.

Then you know where he went the night that I had Skylar? He went to the porno chick's house, but he told me he was going home 'cause he couldn't sleep in the hospital bed. But later I found out that's not what he did. I mean that's just so . . . sick.

It was seven years of my life. I will say this: When I watch our home videos we were really good friends. We really got along great. We cracked up together. Every day of my life he told me, "You're beautiful; I love you." There were some great parts to it, which is why I stayed for as long as I did. You don't stay for seven years if it's just ugly, ugly, ugly. But these ugly experiences would come like every couple months. It got to a point where I was trying to control him because I didn't want him to do something that would ruin the marriage. Because if he did that, I would have to leave. I would say, "Don't go to strip clubs." Because I knew that once he had nine drinks at a strip club he would have no control over what he did next. Girls just threw themselves at him. Then he would end up in bed with one. And he'd be like, "Ooops, I'm sorry. I didn't *mean* to. It just happened."

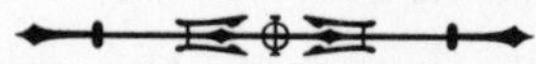

It was essentially over with Sharise. Right before Mötley fired me—three days before, to be exact—we'd been celebrating my birthday at the Roxy with Robert Patrick, who played the mercury-based villain in *Terminator 2*, and a bunch of other people. At one point, me and Patrick were chatting up this porn star named

Lenay. Sharise must have been pretty drunk. When she spotted us, she came storming across the room and threw a drink in my face, glass and all. She's a big girl, remember. That glass had some force behind it. I was stunned. The next thing I knew the whole place was in an uproar; we both got thrown out of the club. Nice, right?

Around that time, I'd been hanging out with a girl named Shannon Wilsey. To the rest of the world, she was known as Savannah. She was this amazingly beautiful platinum blond Vivid Video star—that's the company that features only the really hot-looking women. Savannah was one of their first big stars. The thing about her was she didn't look like a porn star. Not at all. I have always been a sucker for a beautiful face, beautiful eyes, beautiful lips. She was the California dream girl personified. And she was hot. It was a sex thing between us, but she was cool, too. I mean I *liked* her, you know?

Savannah was sweet and she was funny, but she did *way* too many drugs. She was a heroin addict. Plus she was really into the coke. She had this friend, another porn star, Gina Fine, a brunette. They were a couple. The three of us would hang out and drink and do drugs and have sex at Savannah's apartment on Laurel Canyon Avenue. We just had a lot of great adult fun.

When Savvy and I went to Hawaii after the Mötley breakup, the party was on, no holds barred. I was in full-rage fuck-the-world mode. We checked into the Maui Hilton; we partied four days straight on pills, alcohol, heroin, and cocaine. I remember on the fourth day, I think it was at nighttime. I might've been in the bar or something, I can't recall where I was. But I remember they came to me and told me that somebody had called 911 for Savannah—she'd had a seizure or something in the room.

By the time I got to the hospital, she was already released. We went back to the hotel and they had packed all of our bags and put them at the front desk. They were like, "Good-bye, you're out of here." They actually kicked us out! So we checked into the Four Seasons Maui. Fuck 'em. The Four Seasons is one of my favorite hotels in the world—much better than the Hilton.

I never knew a girl who could party like Savannah. She had a seemingly bottomless capacity. She didn't especially love sex on camera—she always looked bored and distracted in her films—but what a specimen she was, this gorgeous Barbie doll come to life. You just wanted to devour her. After we got back from Hawaii, she picked up Gina and met me up at Oxnard, where I was racing. While we were there, Sharise showed up with Skylar in her arms—our daughter was just about one year old at the time; her birthday was March 26, 1991. Luckily, when Sharise got to the room—she got access because she was my wife—me and the girls were not there. We were somewhere else. I can only imagine the look on her face when she found all these girls' purses and clothes and all that stuff. I'm real glad I wasn't there.

I'd see Savannah on and off for the next two years. In July of 1994, she asked me to be her date to the Adult Video News porn awards in Las Vegas. By then I was divorced; I told her I'd go. At the last minute I canceled. A few days later, after totaling her Corvette and banging up her face, Savannah shot herself in the head with a Beretta 9mm automatic pistol. She died in the hospital on July 11, 1994. I felt terrible.

I have always wondered secretly if I somehow contributed to her death. Another piece of guilt I guess I carry around. Everybody said she was really fucked up; she had a lot of problems. I think she was molested as a young girl. When someone becomes a porn star, you have to wonder. A lot of these girls really have deep issues. There is a sweetness inside of them, though; I think it's part of what attracts me to these types.

Though I went to rehab one more time to appease Sharise, we finally separated.

In the spring of 1992, I got out of my house and moved in with Rob Lowe, who was sober after his own well-documented fall from grace. Looking back now, Rob's was probably the first public sex tape scandal—an encounter with two women, one of whom was underage, at the 1988 Democratic National Convention in Atlanta. (How's this for coincidence: You can read about Lowe's sex-capades *and* about Savannah's life and death in Mike Sager's collection, *Scary Monsters and Super Freaks.*) In the aftermath of a lawsuit, the tabloids had latched onto Rob's story. The former Brat Pack matinee idol took a hard fall. It's one thing to be a rock star, another to be a squeaky-clean actor type like Rob. It was devastating to his career and personal life. As a result, his wife, Sheryl, left him. So here we were, the odd couple. Two studs at large on the town.

At the time, I think I was still flirting with sobriety; I was sober on and off. Rob was definitely on the wagon. He wanted to get his life back on track. I'm pretty sure I originally met Rob at an AA meeting; that's how we became friends. It was really good of him to extend his hospitality. I could have gone to a hotel, but I didn't want to be alone just yet.

Rob's house was in the Hollywood Hills. We'd wake up early and go work out every day together. We'd go to meetings together. We also went out a lot. I would take him to the Rainbow. He was a total fish out of water there, this really handsome preppy clean-cut guy. And then he would take me to, I don't know, somewhere like Nobu, that famous Hollywood sushi restaurant where all the mainstream stars like to go. I mean, you don't ordinarily catch me eating sushi all that much. But it has always been fun for me to see the other sides of life. I have always enjoyed trying new things—up to a point. I'm not the most adventurous eater. With me and Rob, it was kind of a cultural exchange for both of us. I'll tell you this:

That guy was a chick magnet. We always had girls over at the house; it was a lot of fun. It lasted for a while—until he got back together with Sheryl.

By then I found a manager, a guy named Bruce Bird. And I got a contract...for $4 million, thank you very much. I ended up signing with Warner Bros. because it was all part of the same company, Warner/Elektra/Atlantic. Warner Bros. and Elektra kind of shared me. I got a $2 million advance. The rest would come upon production of the albums.

I was like, *Fuck Mötley Crüe!* I didn't need them anymore. I don't know what happened to those guys. Once upon a time it was great. They just changed. But I was good with it. I was fine with it. Like fuck them, you know? This is the new chapter in my life. For good measure, my lawyer sued Mötley for 25 percent of their future profits and $5 million in damages for firing me. A man's gotta do what a man's gotta do.

Within a month I had a hit single, "You're Invited (but Your Friend Can't Come)." I wrote that song in twenty minutes with Jack Blades and Tommy Shaw from Damn Yankees, for the soundtrack of the Disney movie *Encino Man,* starring Brendan Fraser and Pauly Shore. (Incidentally, Pauly Shore took up with Savannah after we stopped seeing each other on a regular basis—Hollywood *is* a very small town.) That year, me and my solo band performed "You're Invited" live on the MTV Movie Awards. Don't tell me I can't write songs, motherfucker. Vince Neil was back.

I moved into the Bel Age hotel in West Hollywood. The people at Bel Age were great. They let me keep all my cars there—my Ferraris, my Rolls-Royce—my custom chopper, a bunch of vehicles. I even had a phone line put in so I didn't have to go through the operator. Plus, they had that great restaurant, the Diaghilev. They'd let me come in after hours and order anything I wanted. The Bel Age is where I first actually met Anna Nicole Smith. She was staying there when she'd just become Playmate of the Year. They gave me a deal to live there, but it still cost a shitload of money. I paid by the month rather than the day.

I guess you could say this was the beginning of my Hollywood phase. I hadn't really spent much time there since the early days of Mötley. Of course, now that I had a lot of money, it was like a different part of town had opened up to me.

My favorite new spot was this place called Bar One. I was always hanging out there. It had a five-star restaurant on one side of the room and a bar and dance floor on the other. All the celebs used to come in; there were always paparazzi waiting outside. One night one of the owners asked me if I wanted to buy in; that was pretty much it. It seemed like a good idea. It worked for me for a while; without the band, maybe I was a little untethered. It gave me a sort of home base.

Appropriately enough, Bar One was at the fork of Sunset Boulevard—just west of the Strip, closer to Beverly Hills. There's a big bank there on the corner, across from where the trendy restaurant BOA is now. I met so many famous people there. It turned out that having a club *was* sort of like being in the band. You owned the joint, one way or another. It was a great way to meet chicks, many of whom I went on to date. You're the host. You can approach anyone.

Remember Ann Turkel, remember that name? According to her Web site, she had one of the most interesting and diverse careers in the entertainment industry. A six-foot former *Vogue* cover girl who has been around TV and film for years, she is the original cougar—she actually went with me to Europe. I had dinner at Bar One with Sly Stallone. I made out with Tori Spelling and Shannen Doherty in the private back room, though not at the same time. After Shannen married Ashley Hamilton, George Hamilton's handsome son, I let the kid's band play at the club.

There was Vanessa Marcil, from *General Hospital*, and supermodel Christy Turlington. I dated Pam Anderson *before she married Tommy.* This was way before she was even on *Baywatch*, when she was the Tool Time Girl on *Home Improvement.* On our first date we went to see Tim Allen do stand-up. She'd come to the club or she'd hang out at the hotel. At one point I was shooting a video for one of the songs on my album, "Can't Have Your Cake." I asked Pamela to be in it, along with my daughter Skylar, who was now about three. There were some other girls in the shoot; I was also dating them—though none of them knew. (At least that's what I thought at the time!)

As you probably know, Pamela is close friends with the whole Playboy organization. She's been in the magazine a million times; they kind of take credit for her. She's great friends with founder Hugh Hefner. After she introduced me to that world, I went on a little run of dating Playmates. Let's face it. Playmates are a lot more beautiful than most porn stars. Plus, they don't fuck for a living. They seem sort of more wholesome, if you know what I mean, even though they're posing nude. It's tasteful nudity, like everyone says.

Carrie Westcott was Playmate of the Month, Miss September, 1993. A beautiful wholesome blonde with a big smile and red lips. She was a really funny girl. She had personality. In her centerfold she was wearing one of those yachting hats with the gold filigree on the bill. What happened was, I was reading her spread, her centerfold thing. And you know how they have the write-up with their turn-ons and stuff? It said that her dream was...to date a rock star.

This girl was smoking hot and beautiful. I called the Playboy Mansion. I said, "Can I speak to Carrie? I'm the rock star she's been looking for." And that was it. We started hanging out together.

One night Carrie and I went to the mansion for the Midsummer Night's Dream party, where everyone wears lingerie and stuff.

After that we went to Bar One, still wearing our pajamas. Carrie got pretty drunk; she started dancing on the pool table. I'd been driving my Ferrari Testarossa that night. She was like, "One of my fantasies has always been to drive a Ferrari." I was pretty drunk, too, I guess. I'm like, "Let's do it!"

She gunned it down the Strip, made a right on one of those streets that are perpendicular, then made a right on Fountain. As she made this last turn, there was water on the street, a big wet spot—here we go again, right?

She downshifted....

The car spun out.

My two-hundred-thousand-dollar Ferrari slammed rear-end first into a parked car. And then, because Carrie was out of it and still had her foot on the gas, my car proceeded to bounce off the first car—and hit another car, this time with the *front* end. At this point, my Testarossa was totally crunched.

Finally it was over. We clambered out of the car, sat on the curb. Neither of us was hurt. Here's this beautiful girl, sitting on the curb in her lingerie, crying. Her makeup was all over her face. "I'm sorry. I'm *soooo* sorry," she kept repeating.

I'm wearing my boxers and a robe. In my mind I'm cursing a blue streak. *You stupid fucking bitch! What the fuck is wrong with you, you fucking asshole!* Externally, I remained calm. I tried not to show it. I put one arm around her to keep her warm.

Then the cops came. They handcuffed her and took her to jail. Do you think they really needed the handcuffs? They got a Playmate in their car in a nightie and they need to put her in handcuffs?

I'm like, *Fuck it. That was an expensive evening.* One of the cops called a tow truck and offered to take me back to the hotel.

About an hour later, I started thinking about Carrie, you know, and how hot she looked in her nightie with the cuffs and stuff. Damn, you know, she was pretty amazingly gorgeous.

I got another of my Ferraris out of valet parking. I went and bailed her out of jail. Then I brought her back to the hotel. I at least deserved a little sex out of this whole deal, don't you think? We kept dating for a little while after that. Situations like that tend to bring people closer.

Not long after, Carrie and I were in my suite at the Bel Age listening to some tracks with the son of a major music industry executive. Along with Carrie we were hanging with another *Playboy* girl, who went on to do some minor acting.

What happened was, the guy was listening to the music. It seemed like he was drunk or high or something—he'd be listening, and then all of a sudden he'd start to kind of nod out, and then he'd wake up and listen some more, then he'd nod out again.

At one point, he went into the bathroom and stayed there for a long time. When he came out he started to twitch; his head was twitching and his eyes rolled back in his head, and then he fell over and started foaming at the mouth.

I'm like, *Holy fuck!*

I told the girls, *"Call 911 now!"*

I got him kind of propped up, so he didn't choke and stuff, and then I got him on his side, trying to clear his throat. When we heard the sirens I told the girls to get the fuck outta there because they didn't need to be involved in this.

They rushed him to the hospital; he'd ODed on something, I can't remember what it was—he was in a coma for a few days and then he came out of it; he was okay.

A few days later I got a call from his mom and I was like, *Shit! Why is she calling me?* I thought I was going to get yelled at—"You piece of shit! What did you do to my son?"

But instead she thanked me. She goes, "Thank you so much for being there for my son."

It brings tears to my eyes now thinking about it. It was just like *wow*.

Believe it or not, during this time, I wasn't just partying. During the second half of 1992, I was working on my first solo album. After years of being the *guy nobody heard*, this was like a dream. For once I was basically in control. Everybody was sort of kowtowing to me, asking me what I thought. *That* was a first, for sure. The album was called *Exposed*. Because I was exposing myself, coming out into the light I guess you could say, coming out from under the shadow of Mötley.

We did it at the Record Plant with Billy Idol guitarist Steve Stevens, Vikki Foxx of Enuff Z'Nuff on drums, Dave Marshall on rhythm guitar, and Robbie Crane on bass. Foxx didn't last long; she was replaced by my old buddy Randy Castillo. The album included a cover of "Set Me Free" from Sweet's *Desolation Boulevard* album; "Forever" is a ballad about Sharise, who had just formally filed for divorce. The first single, "Sister of Pain," features a space-age-clad porn star named Janine Lindemulder in the video.

While I was working on the album, my new manager, Bruce Bird, was stricken with a brain aneurysm. It was weird. That afternoon we were working with him in the studio. By that evening he was gone. I hustled over to the hospital, but I was too late to say good-bye. It was like, *Whoa*, you know? That kind of thing really made you think. In the short time we were together, we had become close; I thought of him as a father figure. For a while after that I worked with Bruce's brother, Gary. Let's just say they were not cut from the same cloth. When you think of slimy people, you think of Gary. If you look it up in the dictionary, there's his picture. He was unbelievable.

I ended up with a mutual friend, Burt Stein. The idea was that Stein would step in to help out until I found a new manager—he ended up staying with me for the next sixteen years. It's only recently that we parted company; I still consider him a friend. He declined to be interviewed for this book.

As soon as the album was finished, I grabbed up Janine and went to Maui to celebrate. For fun, we brought along a friend of mine, a *Penthouse* Pet named Brandy.

Like many vacationers, one of the girls brought a video camera. One thing led to another; we shot a bunch of footage. We had a lot of fun together. A lot of fun. It was not a big drug binge like with Savannah. It wasn't an overindulgence thing at all. It was more like a little coke and some drinking and the girls would smoke some pot. It was more of a fun sex thing. Not dark at all, just innocent fun between three healthy and consenting adults. We'd flown there with my bodyguard; he would stand guard at a stretch of beach while we filmed. We had so much fun that we decided we all wanted to get married. So I went and bought three identical diamond rings and we gave them to each other. We were not a couple but a triple. For a little while I think we were serious. We were like, *This could work.* I was genuinely excited about it. And then . . . I don't know. Something happened. Toward the end of the trip things got a little weird.

After that we went our separate ways—until a little later we ran into each other in Palm Springs.

I'd gone out there for this annual party these guys throw. They call it the DASK party because those are the initials of the hosts. It's what you'd expect—wealthy people, hot women, rock stars, plenty of drugs, all of it in Palm Springs. So I'm somewhere around town the day before the party, I don't remember where, and I run into Janine and Brandy. They're together, vacationing in Palm Springs. Which is weird because before our little trip to Maui they didn't even know each other.

I was a few minutes into the conversation with them when it hit me: *These bitches are a couple! They're in love!* Suddenly their weirdness at the end of the trip made perfect sense...they'd fallen in love and they didn't want to tell me. (Or maybe they just wanted to be alone????)

The girls and I decided that we'd meet at the DASK party the next night. I was like, *See you at the party.* Then we went our separate ways.

During that same time, I also was seeing this girl named Shauna. She was a *Penthouse* Pet of the Month, a killer brunette(!). Me and Shauna always had fun together. That night, in Palm Springs, we ran into each other. We ended up going home together.

The next night we all met at the DASK party. It was a great party. Me, Shauna, Brandy, and Janine left together. We went back to my suite and had a foursome.

You might ask, just technically speaking, how does one man service three girls in a foursome? Could one man possibly even be up to that task?

I'll tell you this: It's fun trying. There's a lot of switching off. You're with one of the girls while the other two girls go at it; then you change up. There are periods of resting and hanging out in between, I suppose, which makes it as much fun as the actual fucking. There's lots of laughter and talking. I mean, look: I had genuine feelings for Janine. I still look at her picture and go, *Wow,* you know? The thing I find about porn stars is that they're just more open. There are no hang-ups. You can kind of say anything; you're not going to offend anybody. They're still like other girls, though. They still want to couple up and square up and get married. They're still kind of clingy and jealous. Maybe even more so because all of them are damaged in some way or another. It's just the nature of the beast.

Things were going along well when Shauna casually mentioned to the group, during an interlude, that she had just fucked me the night before.

Hearing that, Brandy and Janine freaked out.

It was like I cheated on them, even though we'd all just had sex. I didn't get it at all. Nobody was married here (well, I guess we'd play-married each other in Hawaii, but the girls had obviously dumped me for each other). I thought we were all just fuck buddies.

Brandy and Janine dressed in a huff and left, leaving me alone with Shauna.

I did my best to make do.

(You could imagine my surprise, a couple years later, when a Vince Neil sex tape surfaced for sale on the Internet. It turned out Brandy sold the tape for a lot of money to a distributor. I was pissed, kind of. But on the other hand, I didn't really care. There was nothing you could do to my reputation. What? I fuck women? Big surprise, right? That's what you expect from a rock star. The only thing that pissed me off is I didn't collect any of the profits.)

Exposed entered the *Billboard* charts at #13. After a warm-up gig at the Roxy, under the name Five Guys from Van Nuys, we went out on the road. At first there was some talk of a stadium tour, but that fizzled out. I ended up settling for second billing on the latest Van Halen tour—the first for their new lead singer, Sammy Hagar.

Opening for Van Halen was very humbling for me. I hadn't opened for anybody in a long time. It was tough because when you go see Van Halen it's like date night. That's who goes to see Van Halen—you're with your girlfriend. It's not like rockers coming out to hear you; it's more like yuppies. Plus, when I got onstage there was fucking *nobody* there. The hall was like less than half-full. Because nobody comes to hear the backup band, right? It was like playing with Y&T again at the Starwood. As I'm doing the last two songs, people start filing in. That's what they mean by starting over, man. I wasn't really starting over, but I was. But I didn't care. It was cool. I was just having a good time not hassling with those other guys, just making the music. It was like, *Wow, you know, this is a dream.*

For the first time in my life I started getting more involved in my own work. Now that I was a solo act, I had to do all the interviews, make all the creative decisions, write songs, approve concepts and artwork, deal with my manager and accountant and all that stuff. In other words, for the first time in my life, the buck stopped here. It was about time; I was well into my fourth decade.

I also started making more of an effort to be a father. I saw Neil on and off; my parents always made sure he was around. When I wasn't touring, I was seeing Skylar for my visitation rights. At some point, I decided it would be better for her if I had a house. Visiting me at the hotel was never much fun for a three-year-old. There was nowhere to run or play, and you felt like you had to keep her quiet, which is no fun for a little kid. After two previous ruined attempts at fatherhood, I was getting really close with Skylar.

I found a great place in Malibu, right on the beach. It even had a name: Sea Manor. This was probably the sickest house I'd had so far. It had a spiral staircase, a stained-glass dome, marble floors; the beach was just down the steps. I set up a room for Skylar with a little desk and a computer. We'd spend a lot of our time together on the beach. There is something so healing about the waves and the water. I have always been a big surfer; both of us just loved being there. There was a certain simple joy in fatherhood that I'd never understood. This time, I felt like I could appreciate things more; having a child was like a haven from everything bad. It was like a drug that was legal—you could escape the big bad world and go into the fanciful world of your beautiful daughter. Learning this helped me become a more balanced person.

When Skylar wasn't around, I liked to rent out my house to porn companies to shoot films there, and also to *Penthouse* magazine to shoot photo spreads. Because it was such a beautiful setting, on the beach and stuff, I kept it rented out all the time. There were always people in and out. I'd come downstairs from the master bedroom and there would be people fucking on my spiral staircase. It was fun. In some of the movies I'd be in little cameos. Usually it was Ron Jeremy's movies. We've been friends forever.

One time I went upstairs to go take a nap. All of a sudden I hear this *boom!* The whole house shook. I was like, *What the fuck was that?* I jumped up; I went downstairs, opened the front door. Now remember, my front door is basically on the Pacific Coast Highway, also known as Route 1. It's four lanes, with a small shoulder on either side—the cars whip by. When I opened the door I find this car. It's crashed into the pillars in the front. It had lost control and spun out. Another couple of feet and it would have been *inside* my house... on the fuckin' beach. I mean the car was literally—another couple of feet it would've probably killed somebody. I remember this girl, they were taking pictures of her for *Penthouse.* And she's standing at the front door, near this crashed car. She's naked, wrapped in a red towel. And she's like freaking out. *Oh my god!*

Around this period, at one of the *Penthouse* shoots, I got talking to this makeup artist. Makeup artists are cool chicks; a lot of them become celebrity wives. This girl was showing me her book—photos of makeup jobs she'd done in the past. One of them was the cover model for the April 1994 issue of *Playboy.* This girl was *amazingly beautiful.* I demanded a hookup.

Her name was Heidi Mark. We went out on a date...and ended up staying in bed for the next three days straight.

She was sweet. She was sexy. We were on the same page. She was unbelievably gorgeous. A cut above gorgeous. And believe me, I know gorgeous, I am a connoisseur.

Heidi was blond with a nice rack, but her body was little teeny-tiny. Brought up rough on the wrong side of the tracks in Florida, molested on and off by an assortment of stepfathers and other mother daters, she'd left home at fifteen to live with a *Miami Vice*–style drug dealer. When she was barely twenty, she found herself dating Prince. Later, she'd date O. J. Simpson, though that was long before the death of his wife Nicole.

Soon after we met, Heidi started doing the soap opera *The Young and the Restless*. Later, when her *Playboy* centerfold came out, in July 1995, she was fired by the stuffy network suits. After that, she had a busy career doing guest-starring roles on many popular shows and in several movies. She was always doing appearances and stuff. Though I didn't always like it when she was traveling, it was cool for once to have a chick who made money. Usually I was the one making the money. And right now, I was making less than I used to with Mötley, plus I had all kinds of lawyer bills and child support and alimony and whatnot. You wonder where the money goes. It's not hard to figure out. Most of it never even saw my pocket.

Next stop was the sixth annual Frank Sinatra Celebrity Invitational golf tournament at the Marriott's Desert Springs Resort in Palm Desert. I'm not a bad golfer; I've played a lot of charity tournaments over the years. (I've been hosting one in Skylar's memory for more than a decade.) Owing to Frank's involvement, this was probably the highest-ranking event on the Californian golfing calendar; it was a charity thing to raise money for two different hospitals. I'd been taking part since the second annual, I think it was.

Back when he was alive, the tourney was pretty special. Frank was like the ultimate rock star. Frank was so cool. He called me "kid." He was like, "Hey, kid."

Oh man. He was just *soooo* cool.

Frank only invited certain people to his house; I was shocked that I got an invitation. Here I am, this guy who's from Mötley Crüe. You're at his house. The party's in a big tent out back. To go to the bathroom you would go into the house and use the one in his office.

And you're in there taking a leak and there's like keys to the city from all these cities all over the walls, and all these awards that he's won over the years. And you're trying to piss. You got your dick in your hand... literally. It was unbelievable, all the memorabilia he had. I could've been in his office all day and all night just looking at stuff.

All the old stars were there. Robert Wagner. Sammy Davis, Jr. And... What's that guy's name? The *Unsolved Mysteries* guy, Robert Stack. Telly Savalas was there. I guess a lot of those people are dead now. I remember I was in Sinatra's backyard and I was slow-dancing with the singer Frankie Avalon. No. I'm sorry. I was slow-dancing with Mike Connors, the actor from that old show *Mannix*. While I was dancing with Mike, me and Frankie Avalon were singing "Strangers in the Night" to Frank Sinatra, who was standing there with a drink in his hand, just smiling and shaking his head at the big fools we were being.

Right after that I went to the Bahamas to hang out on this ninety-foot yacht with Michael Peters. He's known as the King of Strip Clubs; he owns all the Pure Platinum and Solid Gold strip clubs around the country. He'd been a good buddy ever since he vowed to play *Girls, Girls, Girls* every hour in all of his strip clubs across the country. I'd gotten the idea to shoot a tropical video for one of the songs on my album. So I said to Peters, "Let's go down to the Bahamas." We actually took a camera and a crew with us and stuff.

We jumped on a couple of Learjets. I think we took twelve girls, fourteen girls—we had the chicks put coke in their pussies so we could clear customs or whatever. We went to this secluded bay called Hurricane Hole, where a ninety-foot yacht called *Solid Gold* lay at anchor awaiting our arrival. It was a fucking madhouse—literally. It was just... Let's just say we didn't get a whole lot of filming done. Everywhere you looked there were girls doing blow and fucking. And that was pretty much it. I think we were there a couple weeks or something.

And then . . . what?

Heidi showed up? In the Bahamas?

Oh my god! That's *right*.

I completely forgot.

Heidi showed up on the beach with her suitcase while I was Jet-Skiing in the bay. I had this topless girl sitting behind me on the Jet Ski, her arms wrapped around my waist, one hand down the front of my bathing suit.

Heidi and I had only just started dating; I really liked her. I'd invited her to come to the Bahamas—only I'd forgotten all about it.

Shit! I can picture her waving to me from the beach, trying to flag me down, you know? And I'm with this chick on the back of the Jet Ski—I had actually invited this *other* chick down from Florida to come hang out with me, because Peters also had this house right there on the beach. I can't remember her name. She was this hot brunette. But when I saw Heidi I just knocked her off the back of the Jet Ski. I mean, it's not like there weren't other boats and people out there. It wasn't the middle of the ocean. It was just this little bay. It was purely an instinctive move. There was no thought about it. I was in survival mode at that point, I guess.

And then I Jet-Skied onto the beach to where Heidi was waiting. I was like, "Hi, honey. What's up? How was your flight?"

Heidi put the bimbo eruption behind her . . . this time. We took up residence in the beach house—after the other girl's shit was discreetly removed.

That week, and for the next six or seven years, our time together would be a mixture of heaven and hell. There were wonderful, tender moments and wild, over-the-moon moments; we'd go days sometimes without getting out of bed. And there were drunken arguments and lots of women and lies and her nagging the shit out of me. You wouldn't think a woman that beautiful and successful would be so insecure, but that's the way it is with a lot of beautiful women. I think the most beautiful ones end up getting abused in some way when they're young and it damages them forever.

Our Bahamas sojourn ended with me running the Jet Ski into a coral reef. I banged myself up pretty good—I think I cracked a couple of ribs. Heidi said it was probably bad karma. The truth: I was pretty drunk.

Heidi would become wife number three, the woman who stuck by me during my lowest times—until she left me for a fuckin' plastic surgeon, the bitch. Some people say Heidi was my one true love. I know I told her that a time or two. People say a lot of stuff in the course of a relationship. I know one thing: You don't stop loving people. They just sort of outlive their time. You grow apart. You move on.

Heidi Mark
Vince's Third Wife

It all started when he called the Playboy Mansion looking for me. He'd seen my picture; he knew my makeup artist—she'd been working on a shoot at his house when he was renting it out. He saw a picture of me and he told my friend, "That's the girl I've been looking for." But I have to tell you: I was not initially into it. I was not a Mötley Crüe kind of girl. I grew up in Florida. Orlando, Palm Beach. I listened to dance music, Stevie B, Stacey Q, those kinds of things. I remember I asked around at the mansion and somebody had a Mötley Crüe album cover—I think it was *Shout at the Devil*. There was a picture of all four guys, three dark-haired and a blond. Vince had said he was the blond. So okay. They all looked pretty much the same to me. But my friend said he was cool, so I said I'd go out with him—though I lied and said I had to be home early because I had a photo shoot the next day and I had to get my rest.

Vince picked me up in a white Testarossa. He pulled through the gates of the mansion; they let him in. I was staying in the guest cottages. At the time Hef was married and there was a sign that hung in the kitchen: "If mama ain't happy, nobody is happy." I never ate in the house; I never hung out in the house. I never sat down with Mr. Hefner. If he passed by I was like a little mouse: "Hi, Mr. Hefner." I stayed in my room. I wanted no trouble. Kimberly and I were friends. And people who didn't respect their marriage tended to have trouble.

I remember Vince picking me up and he pulled around to the very back and that's where the back gate is. There's nothing pretty or nice about that area; that's like where security is, where the dog pens are.

Vince seemed very nice. He got out to help me in the door because the Testarossa has weird door handles. But I was from Palm Beach. I knew how to open a Ferrari. Vince seemed soft-spoken. Charismatic. Not weird at all, very normal. When I was with Prince, he was just strange. I met Prince in his club in an upstairs room. And he's literally sitting in a throne with like a big picture window overlooking the club and a seven-foot-tall Hare Krishna bodyguard next to him—he's the one who pulled me off the dance floor. But Vince had on a suit, which I was very surprised at. I thought he was going to show up in some sort of rock star gear, whatever *that* was.

We get in the car and the first thing he says is, "I don't think I want to drive this car tonight. I think I'll go home and switch cars." I didn't know it then, but it's not like it was around the corner. We're in Holmby Hills. He lived in Malibu. So, we drive all the way to Malibu and switch into his convertible Rolls-Royce. And I'm like, *Okay, we switched the cars....*

He smelled so good. He was so polite and so kind. We ended up at this party. There was a girl dancing on our table and I'm like, "Give me a hundred." I put it in her G-string, and he was like, *Wow, this girl is* cool. I was always a man's woman I guess, for better or worse. I drank beer. I liked to party. Like one night we actually both drank a bottle of gin. Vince and I both had our own bottles. We were in Hawaii. And we finished at the same time. I smoked cigars sometimes with him at the Havana Room. My mother was married seven times. I ran away at fifteen to live with my boyfriend/drug dealer. Then I'm like twenty-three and I'm on the cover of *Playboy*, you know? I've lived a lot of life. I think that's why I understood Vince.

Vince was very gregarious. That first night, we were making out. And I'm like, "What the fuck's in your tooth?" And he's like, "A diamond." And I was like, *Who puts a diamond in their tooth?* That was our very first date. After that, I didn't leave his house for a week.

After that, I was going back to Orlando; I was shooting a TV series with Hulk Hogan called *Thunder in Paradise*. I was leaving and I go, "You have to swear on this Bible that you will never cheat on me." And he swore on the Bible. And I was like, "Okay, we're done. Okay, perfect. I love you. See you soon."

I was the first woman Vince had dated who had her own established career. I'd been a working actress for a long time. Vince didn't have to support me at all. He was very proud of that. He was like, "You're the first girl I've ever dated who paid for shit." And I did. I paid for my own shit. Vince had the divorce and the doctor bills. He wasn't in Mötley anymore. I paid for my own car. I bought my Mercedes E55 *before* it was in production—it was a year before it was in production; I paid a little extra; I didn't care, I had the money. I remember him just being like so proud of me, because he loved cars, too.

Then I got this amazing job with Aaron Spelling. Mr. Spelling adored me; he was the sweetest man. He was like, "Heidi, we need to make you a star." So I got on his new show, *Love Boat: The Next Generation*. They wanted to sex up the show, so Mr. Spelling brought me in and basically told the network, "This girl is my only choice; there's nobody else I want but Heidi Mark." When I went to the network, Mr. Spelling was on the phone waiting when I got out of the meeting. He told me I got the job. It was just so amazing.

When I got home, Vince had painted a picture using my paints—I was all into painting and still am. He had gone through the *Robb Report* and cut out a cruise ship. He'd glued it onto paper; he'd even written: "Congratulations. I love you." And he put it in a frame. All in a mat—the whole bit. All of that in the time since I had called him and told him I got the job. He drew the ocean, the sky, some clouds, a couple birds. Like the works. Those are the things that he did. You know?

It's sad, but when you look back at our like wedding pictures we looked really in love. We did the whole rock 'n' roll wedding. Vince started crying—I don't have a copy of the videotape anymore, but I remember being in front of the minister and going, "Are you crying? Oh my god, you're really crying?" Like at first I thought he was kind of being funny. Then I realized he was really crying. And I was like— I forgot all about the video camera, which is a telltale sign of being in the moment. I really forgot what we were doing. For those few seconds, it was like everyone was gone, all the guests and the minister and everyone, and it's just me and Vince and I'm like, "Babe, you're really crying, oh my god, honey." Because I didn't mean to make fun of him—he was really crying. There's this one picture of us at our wedding and you just see the whole room going crazy. Not crazy like bad, crazy like fun. The picture is taken from behind us, so all you see is the backs of our heads. He has his arm around me and I have my head on his shoulder and we're doing nothing, absolutely nothing, just looking on while the entire rest of the room seems like people in a nightclub in New York City. All the guests are at their tables drinking and talking, just having so much fun; you can tell. It was a great great great night. We got married to Van Morrison's "Crazy Love." I remember walking down the aisle and the words to the song talk about a man who is so imperfect and how much the woman loves him anyway. And I just remember seeing Vince and he was already bawling so hard. And I just remember thinking, *He's so imperfect but he's perfect for me.*

Unfortunately, it turned out the only way our marriage would've worked was if I quit working. He couldn't understand that I had to have space to do my thing. He was proud of me. He bragged about me constantly: He loved the fact that I was a Playmate; he loved the fact that I was on the cover; he loved the fact that I worked for Aaron Spelling; he loved the fact that I did movies. He loved all that. He loved it. But he wanted me home. He didn't want to be there by himself. To him, that's what your woman is for. A woman. Any woman? It was hard.

One time—I think I was doing *Beverly Hills 90210* at the time. I came home late from the set and let's just say there was a lot of damage. You look around the house; you look in the garbage. It doesn't take a rocket scientist to figure out that your husband has been fucking someone in your house while you've been gone. I check his phone and he'd been with a girl that day. He'd gone shopping that day and bought me a Louis Vuitton purse, so his intentions were good. But somehow he hooked up with a girl and he brought her home. You know, I listened to his messages. We had this deal that if he was going to have a cell phone, it was under *my* name and I had the code to the message box. Now he could've been sneaky enough to hide things from me, but he didn't.

So I get the messages and one is from this girl who is actually the girlfriend of Randy Castillo, the drummer who passed away. He even played with Mötley for a while. He was a friend of Vince's. Anyway, it was his chick. I knew the girl. I forget her name. Honestly, I would tell you. But she leaves this message, like, "I left my keys in your car. You have to get them out of your car before Heidi sees them." I was like, "Oh really?"

And she goes on in her message about like how important her keys are. She's listing every key she has. There are a lot of them. "My front door, my mailbox," my this, my that. And then she's like, "Make sure you hide those keys and I'll get 'em from you as soon as I can."

I went out to the Rolls, opened the door, saw the keys, grabbed them up.

Then I walked down the street about four or five houses and dropped them in a trash can.

The next morning, I'm like, "Good morning." And then I'm like, "By the way, if your little girlfriend wants to know where her keys are, they're in a *landfill* somewhere."

And he's like, "What you talking about?"

And I go, "I got your messages last night off your phone."

And he goes, "I don't know what you're talking about."

Vince is a huge liar. He is a huge denier. Deny Deny Deny. That is Vince.

After being with Vince close to a decade, I started to notice the different "tics" you might say he had when he was lying or embellishing. He will start blinking a lot; he'll rock back and forth, one foot to the other. He does this thing where he rubs his chin. And then he does this other thing where he kind of talk/laughs. It's like laughing and talking at the same time. When he greets somebody, he'll be like, "Hey, man, hey, buddy," using his laugh/talk voice. And if he's lying to you he uses the same voice, like, "What do you mean?" laugh/talk. If he's going to lie to you, it's like his brain has already started spinning before you confront him. It's like he knows what he wants you to know. If you look at him closely, the outer edges of his eyebrows are missing. He pulls them out obsessively when he's lying/thinking of what lie to say. It's like a sort of a reverse Pinocchio syndrome, only it's with his eyebrows instead of his nose. His eyebrows quit growing back a long time ago, so I guess he's been doing it a long time. He would have to draw them on before going onstage. Along with all of the other makeup—the eyeliner and stuff. I always thought he looked so hot with his eyeliner just a little smudged. He has nice green eyes. If there is a lot of drinking involved, look for...I believe it's his left eye. It will start closing or getting sort of lazy, like there's smoke in there. That's when you know you are entering potentially dangerous territory. He will either be your "brother" or your "buddy"...or turn into a spiteful, mean, and sometimes violent Vince.

Vince would try to tell you that it was night and not day. Like, one time, he was on TV. I saw the interview; it was live. And Vince was on TV talking about all the porn stars he'd banged. Now, Vince and I had an agreement—he was not supposed to talk about banging porn stars and all the women he fucked. Because at one point I said to him, "Look, I have a career. I kinda want to keep it untainted." This was after Tommy and Pamela had had their blowout and Tommy beat her up or whatever and I didn't want to be another actress, another *Playmate*, who got her ass kicked by a member of Mötley Crüe. So I tried to keep Vince out of like dumb interviews, unless it was positive. But then he goes and does an interview about his buddy Sam Kinison, the comedian who died.

Vince was a good friend of his. They were doing like the *E! True Hollywood Story* and Vince really cared about him. Vince thought it would be a good idea, great, go. So of course, E! being E!, they start asking him about when he fucked Savannah. I don't remember what exactly he said; he just said a couple lines that I thought were really rude about the girl. I mean, she was dead by this time, so I was actually angry that I was watching this footage on TV where he's saying rude things about a dead girl that I didn't even know. But it reflected on me, you know? How can it not? Plus, we had an *agreement* we're not talking about chicks that he fucked in the past, especially porn stars. I remember I told him, "All you have to say is, 'I'm not answering that question.' Look, I am in the business, too. I know what you can say to a reporter or a journalist. You can say, 'No, I'm not answering that.'"

He says, "I didn't say that about Savannah. That wasn't me." And it was like that was the kind of shit he pulled on other people, but he couldn't play it with me. I go, "Vince, I have it TiVoed; you're wearing a shirt I bought you."

"It wasn't me, Heidi. I swear."

And this is on the phone, so I go, "I'm staring at you right now, you're on TiVo. I'm watching you on your own television set. You have on an orange and yellow Hawaiian shirt I bought you. I'm looking at you."

And he's like, "I swear, that's not me."

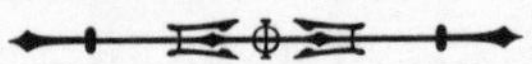

In April of 1995, I was once again entered into the Long Beach Grand Prix, an amateur celebrity race. There were a lot of big people entered in the race, including the actors Cameron Diaz, Anthony Edwards from the TV show *ER*, and Matt LeBlanc from *Friends*. Everybody raced in identically prepared Toyota Celica GT Liftbacks; it was a ten-lap race.

I finished in second place; I was totally stoked. There was a big party that night at the hotel where most of the drivers were staying. As you can imagine, I partook of the festivities full-heartedly.

All in all, this was really a good time for me. I was living in this big house on the beach in Malibu with Heidi, the kind of woman who likes to please her man in every way. I was seeing a lot of Skylar—Heidi was great with her; it really helped to have the mother figure around to do the things that needed to be done for a little girl. I could tease hair and spray it with Aqua Net and I could dye hair with packaged color, but that was about the extent of my Barbie doll skills. Now that I'd been in Malibu for a while, I'd gotten to know my neighbors. As I said earlier, I loved hanging out at this place called Moonshadows—it was walking distance from my house, like a quarter mile. You'd see actors like Fran Drescher, Gary Busey, and Kelsey Grammer all the time; it was our own little version of *Cheers*. It sometimes felt like I knew everybody in Malibu and everybody knew me. At least all the barflies. Every time I came in, everybody would call out, "Vince!" I was like Norm. Everybody knew me.

Around this time, Warner put me together with the Dust Brothers, thinking we could make good music together. They'd just produced a Beastie Boys joint; they'd also worked with Beck and Hanson. They smoked a lot of pot. They reminded me of Cheech and Chong. We didn't connect well. It was like apples and oranges in a way.

Somehow we ended up with a pretty good album—that nobody understood and nobody *bought*. If you ask me, it was way ahead of its time. Mixing rock guitar with rap beats—people were horrified. It makes me laugh now. Eight years down the road you'd get Kid Rock and Limp Bizkit. Even Lil Wayne just released a rock/rap album. Mine was titled *Carved in Stone*. Warner didn't know what to do with it. After some delay, it would be released. Fewer than one hundred thousand copies were sold.

After the album tanked, Warner released me from my contract. . . .

But none of that was on my mind as I partied in Long Beach after my second-place finish at the celebrity Grand Prix. About an hour into the party, I was summoned to a phone call in the lobby. I thought at first it was Heidi. Remember, this was a time before cell phones. I thought she was calling to find out how I'd done in the race.

But it turned out to be Sharise.

"Skylar's in the hospital," she sobbed.

Sharise thought Skylar had the flu. She told her mom she had a tummyache and a headache and that she felt like she was going to be sick to her stomach. Sharise took her to the doctor. Everybody figured it was her appendix.

I got to the West Hills Hospital pretty fast, thinking things were serious but routine. Anytime a child goes to the hospital it is scary. I told myself everything would be okay. She'd have her appendix out. She'd be healthy again in a few weeks.

But her appendix turned out to be healthy and intact. The problem was a cancerous tumor, the size of a softball, wrapped around her abdomen. Some of the tumor had ruptured, spreading cancer all through her body. It was about as bad as it could be.

When they finally let us into the intensive-care unit I couldn't believe my eyes. My four-year-old was lying there surrounded by machines, all these tubes sticking out of her arms. I felt absolutely powerless. I didn't know what to do. We'd given her a birthday party the weekend before. It was unbelievable. By the next morning,

Skylar was looking a lot better. She wanted to know why she wasn't at home in her room and what all this stuff sticking out of her arms was for. We explained to her as best we could. There was no way a four-year-old was going to understand something like cancer, so we said she had something growing inside her stomach, like a flower, that wasn't supposed to be there.

They transferred her to Children's Hospital in Los Angeles. By then, Heidi had returned from Florida and she met up with us at the hospital. It was awkward and a little uncomfortable, but everybody acted like adults. The CAT showed that Skylar had tumors on both kidneys. An operation would be needed to remove them immediately. When the doctors got in there, they discovered that the tumors were so large that removing them would have killed her immediately. There was nothing the doctors could do except sew her back up. They recommended radiation treatment to reduce the size of the malignancy. Maybe then, they said, the tumors could be removed successfully.

Skylar's hair fell out. She complained she looked like a boy. But I would tell her, "No, honey, you're still beautiful." And she was.

The hospital became the center of my universe. My entire being had been reduced to three emotions: anxiety, depression, and anger. Every day, Sharise, myself, our parents, Heidi, some combination of people, would sit with Skylar.

Finally, Skylar took a turn for the worse when the tumor on her right kidney began pressing against her lungs. By this time she was on a morphine drip; at least we knew she wasn't suffering any physical pain. It was becoming harder and harder to remain upbeat for her, but when I was at the hospital I was determined to keep my baby smiling. I brought her favorite clothes and toys and surrounded her with them, and we'd watch her favorite Disney videos, sing along with the songs. Using connections, I got Warner Bros. to bring in Bugs Bunny and Sylvester. On Easter I went to the hospital dressed as the Easter Bunny—fuzzy costume, the whole nine. Skylar didn't even recognize me until I started talking.

Of course, she kept asking when she could go home. I got so used to that question. It killed me every time. "Soon, honey," was my automatic response. But one morning she looked up at me with the most grown-up look in her eyes. And she said, "Daddy, I'm never going home, am I?"

After that, you can damn well believe that I made *sure* we took her home. She'd been in hospitals for nearly a month at this point. The deal was we'd take her home, but we would come back for more chemotherapy. I could see the joy on her face—unfortunately, she didn't last long. Every day the pain just got worse; she couldn't sleep because her stomach hurt so much. We couldn't stand to see her suffering; we brought her back to the hospital.

The doctors said they needed to perform another operation: The scar tissue from previous surgeries had formed on her intestines, twisting them and obstructing her bowels, the main source of her pain.

After that, Skylar looked even worse—if that was possible. It was as if she herself had given up. Lord knows she was a fighter, but I guess her little body just couldn't keep on taking it. The life had drained from her face; she was just skin and bones. Three days later they took her, this time to remove her kidney, they said. Once inside, they discovered that the cancer had spread—it was in her liver, intestines, and dorsal muscles.

I was at home a few days later when the oncologist called to tell me they'd placed Skylar on a ventilator. He suggested one last operation. They warned us the procedure was extremely dangerous. However, they said if Skylar made it through, it was very likely she would survive.

Those eight hours in the waiting room were the worst of

hundreds. Sharise and her family, my family, Neil, Heidi... all of us sat huddled together anxiously waiting for word from the doctors.

They managed to remove the tumor. It weighed an incredible six and a half pounds (about the same as Skylar's birth weight). They'd also been forced to remove her right kidney, half her liver, some of her diaphragm, and a muscle in her back. How many organs could she lose and still be alive? Somehow she managed to survive.

I know it sounds gross, but I wanted desperately to see the thing that had slowly been sucking the life out of my daughter. After some discussion, the doctors took me down to the pathology lab, where the monstrous tumor was spread out in a metal pan. I had never seen anything so ugly and vile in my life; I felt like I wanted to vomit.

As you can imagine, at this time I wasn't taking things very well. I was going straight from the hospital, where I'd put on a good face, to Moonshadows, where I'd drink myself to oblivion. At least I had a place to go where people knew me and cared about me. I got so drunk one night the cops drove me home. The hurt and pain was more than I could take. I felt like God was punishing me. I know I've done a lot of bad stuff in my life, but why take my little girl? What had she done to anyone?

After this surgery, for a little while we thought things were looking up. Every day Skylar seemed to recover a little bit more. She was breathing on her own; the color had returned to her skin. She could again speak and smile. Every gesture, no matter how slight, felt like a gift. I spent the next few days cleaning up the house in readiness for her return.

I was walking into the hospital carrying a giant stuffed panda when I was greeted by the team of surgeons. An infection had formed on Skylar's left kidney, they said. They needed to operate again. They had already operated on my baby five times, and I was terrified that she wouldn't be able to take any more.

After this sixth major surgery was performed, she went into a fast decline. She was suffering from sepsis at this point. The infections were too great. Her remaining kidney, her lungs, and her liver began to fail and she slipped into a coma.

I stayed at her bedside all that day before heading out to Moonshadows with Heidi. Sharise and her family kept vigil; I said I'd be back—I meant the next day, same as usual.

Heidi and I had barely sat down at the table when the bartender said I had a call. It was Sharise telling me to get back to the hospital. Skylar's vital signs were slipping fast.

There was a lot of traffic on the way back from Malibu. Skylar was gone by the time I arrived. The date was August 15, 1995. I will never forget her.

It kills me that I never had the chance to say good-bye to her, to tell her one more time how much I loved her. Wherever you are, sweetie, I hope you know that. I'm pretty sure you do.

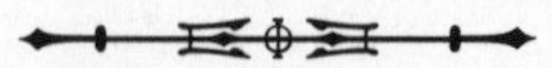

Sharise Ruddell Neil
Vince's Second Wife

I had already left Vince; Skylar and I were living in a house I'd rented in Studio City. She had a stomachache at like two in the morning. I lay in bed with her, because I'd never seen such a bad stomachache. I didn't want to bring her to the emergency room because I thought it was cramping and the flu. The flu had been going around at her preschool. They get sick all the time when they first go to school. And I had already brought her to the doctor two weeks before for the flu, so

I thought, *Oh no, here we go again; she's got another strain of it.* So in the morning I brought her in to the doctor.

The doctor said he couldn't hear the sounds he was supposed to be hearing. Later we find out it's because there's a tumor, but we didn't know that yet. The doctor was like, "I want you to go across the street to the hospital, to the emergency room." And I was like, "Why why why?" He was just, you know, "I want something to be checked out." So we go to check her out and, oh, I'm going to cry. . . .

The doctor said she needed her appendix removed. I was freaking out because I was like, "Why?" I was thinking about how hard that was going to be for my little girl to have to be cut open. And so I went home to get some of our things, and and when I came back my brother was waiting for me. And he said, "It's not her appendix. She has cancer." It was just so shocking, because she was always the strongest and tallest kid in her class. Other than this flu the other week, she was a kid who never got sick. It was like, "What? Are you talking about the right little girl?"

She was admitted to the hospital, they put her in surgery right away. I called Vince. He was at like a race, the Long Beach Grand Prix; I couldn't get ahold of him for the longest time. Finally I did. He came to the hospital.

They opened her up and oh my god, it was just like nightmare after nightmare after nightmare. They couldn't get it all; it was actually a tumor that had ruptured; it was stage four already. It was all throughout her body. It was leaking everywhere. It was just like unbelievable.

We never wanted her to be alone in the hospital during visiting hours. So I would take the mornings, he would take the afternoons, and then vice versa every single day. So he would sit there for—you were allowed to be with your child ten hours a day. Vince would take five hours and I would take five hours. And we would sit there with her mutually for a little while, during the overlap. It would be like the changing of the guard. It's a really hard thing to, to just watch your child deteriorate. We managed as much grace as was humanly possible.

After that it was pretty much over between us. We went our separate ways. One of the weirdest parts of our relationship I felt was that he never even mentioned to me in seven years the stuff about the accident with Razzle. He never spoke about it, and I didn't really bring it up because I didn't want to bring up bad memories or whatever. Vince doesn't like to deal with emotions like that. He doesn't like to vent verbally. He keeps everything at like a level five. You know? He doesn't, he doesn't ever feel things deeply, maybe. He doesn't let himself. I mean, he would show emotions. He would cry; he would cry when he was in trouble and he wanted you to know he wanted to work stuff out. He showed love and affection, but he didn't show sadness. He was comfortable with anger. You know: "Fuck that guy, fuck these people, fuck you." But never sadness. Not a very deep guy.

When I first got with Vince I thought it was going to be so great because I was in love and he was a great guy and I had this little fairy tale, and it just didn't quite turn out that way. Life is an adventure. You never know where you're going to be even ten years from now; you can't even imagine.

Even though there was a lot of, of heartache and trauma being with Vince, I had such an amazing ride. It was hard losing somebody who I was really, really in love with. I was really in love with him. I didn't want to let go. He dictated the terms himself by cheating all the time. He always thought I was just with him for his money. The managers used to say stuff. And he would say it in a fight: "You're just with me for my money; that's what everybody thinks." Of course it was never that. He couldn't see he was wrecking something with someone who actually loved him. He's done this probably over and over and over. I know Heidi really loved him. By the time she got him, he had no money and he was fat. And he was a total raging alcoholic all the time, and she paid for him and put up with him... and look, he threw away that relationship, too. It's just like what a waste this guy's life has been.

At least I had some fun times. I had all the limos and the jets and the helicoptering into the gigs and... that was awesome. And while I was with Vince I was designing some of his gear and stuff to wear for photo shoots. I'd always kinda done that. Today I am a successful designer and businesswoman. I have three companies. Pink Polka Dot is the largest. I sell to over five hundred stores in the U.S. and abroad.

It bothered me that in *The Dirt* Vince wrote about how our whole relationship we fought all the time. But really I would like it to be said that the reason that we fought was because his stories didn't match up. I'd ask questions and his stories wouldn't match up. It was eating me up inside. He was being unfaithful and that's what we would fight about. If you're being unfaithful, don't you think you're going to fight with your wife?

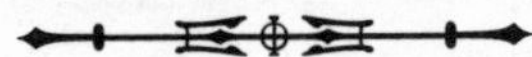

Chapter 9

BITCH IS BACK

After Skylar died, we put her in the ground in a little pink coffin. My drinking got steadily worse. I added pills, any kind I could get my hands on.

I knew I was on a path to self-destruction, but when the love of your life has just died, rational thinking doesn't enter the equation. I blamed myself for Skylar's death. I was her father. I was supposed to protect her. That's the toughest part about being a parent. You're there to protect your kids, but you really have no control. Life dishes out what it gives you; you do the best to deal. Skylar had the best care in the world, but we just couldn't save her. Her medical bills, even with insurance, came to something like $2.5 million. Between that and the cost of my divorce, I was almost tapped.

I couldn't stay at Sea Manor; the memories were too painful. I fought with my neighbor; there was legal action back and forth; we'd had a fight after he told me that Skylar was better off dead so that she wouldn't end up like me.

I checked in and out of rehabs. At one point I spent an entire month in Palm Springs by myself—playing golf every day and drinking every night until I passed out. I must have been wasted; it was the longest in my life I'd ever been alone on a consistent basis.... Of course there was never any shortage of barflies, fans, and professionals to warm my bed. I was still deeply in love with Heidi at this time; of course that had nothing to do with the other girls. I was confused and fucked up. Women, alcohol, and golf were my tickets out of Realityville. One sunny morning, out on the golf course, I shot a 76, my best score ever. I was momentarily elated.

And then the guilt hit me. *What the fuck is wrong with you, man?*

My daughter was dead, and here I was hiding away from the world playing golf, drinking, and fucking to oblivion. I was never really one to be objective about myself, but right then and there it occurred to me that maybe I really *did* need a better way to work through my emotions. I might have had a relatively normal childhood in a loving middle-class family, but shit, I had sure been through a lot since. The death of Razzle, the death of Skylar, the broken marriages and children left behind... there was a lot of grief inside of me, though it didn't really occur to me then. I was focused on Skylar—it would be years before I would realize the toll of a lifetime of strife. I went back to the hotel and called Heidi and my old drug counselor Bob Timmons. They flew me to yet another rehab.

This time, rather than asking me bullshit questions about why I liked to get high and if my mother loved me, the counselors told me the treatment they were offering wasn't so much for alcohol or pills—it was to deal with grief. They suggested I should write a letter to Skylar and then set it on fire. I sat there watching the smoke drift up into the air; I think that was the beginning of my being able to accept Skylar's death, learning to accept a past I couldn't change. They suggested that I begin to think about her life in a different light, and to thank God for the four years I had with her.

When I called Heidi and my parents, they could sense from my voice that I was back in the land of the living. I had made it through to the other side. The first thing I did when I got out of rehab was visit Skylar's grave for the first time. I'd missed her funeral. There was no way I could go at that point. I was in no condition, even I knew that. Now, instead of bursting into tears, I was able to smile as I talked with her and remembered all the things we used to laugh and joke about.

While I was in rehab Sharise and I finalized our divorce. We hadn't gotten along for years, but Skylar's illness created a strong bond between me and Sharise during the last months of Skylar's life—I was so glad we could at least give her that much. Once our baby was gone, there was nothing to tie us together anymore. There was nothing more to say, you know?

On the other hand, Skylar's illness and death brought me and Heidi closer together. It's kind of funny that it takes a death of someone close to you, or some other tragedy, to make you appreciate what you have in life.

Another—and more permanent—good thing to bloom from Skylar's death was that I pledged to commit a greater percentage of myself to charity work, to help other children and parents who were going through what I'd been through. It started while Skylar was in the hospital. We had Disney bring in first-run movies such as *The Lion King* and Warner sent the characters in person, as I already said. As the hospital only had one TV for the whole ward, I bought TVs and video players for every room. It doesn't seem like much, but little things can make a whole lot of difference when you're a kid in the hospital. In 1997 I would begin hosting the Skylar Neil Memorial Golf Tournament—we've done it every year since; it's become a huge deal, raising millions for charity. Together with "Skylar's Song" on *Carved in Stone,* those things are my daughter's legacy, my monuments to her memory.

Skylar's illness had also served as a distraction from work. I still had the lawsuit going against Mötley Crüe. During the whole business with Skylar's illness, over the agonizing months that my little girl lay dying, *I never once heard from any of my former bandmates.* Not one of them bothered to call, write, send a fuckin' flower, or do jack shit. Sure, we were at war, legally speaking, but as far as I was concerned, all our petty squabbles and hissy fits paled in comparison with what I was going through. Nikki had kids. Tommy had kids. When you have kids you know what it means for someone else's kids to get sick. You can't convince me they didn't know what was happening—for years, those guys had been like family to me. Maybe it was because they didn't know what to say, but they should have manned up and said *something*. I know that feeds into my whole resentment of the band as well.

As history shows, the John Corabi–led version of Mötley Crüe went over like a lead balloon. Although the album *Mötley Crüe* hit gold status, sales were pitiful compared to the albums in our past—Crüe had a built-in audience because we'd earned it over the years, but you give your fans too much dog shit and they're gonna all be gone, as far as I'm concerned. I hated the idea that Crüe was letting down the fans, but of course I was also secretly cheering. "Secretly" being the operative word, because if you asked me about the band directly I'm sure I would have feigned ignorance about any and all happenings at that time. The band blamed Elektra for not promoting the album. Then they turned on producer Bob Rock and blamed him for the album's failure. It couldn't have been the songs, because Nikki had written them, so it *had* to be the production, right? Next they decided that manager Doug Thaler was the problem. They fired him and brought in Allen Kovac. Kovac's record was impressive enough—he'd resuscitated Duran Duran and breathed life into Meat Loaf's dead career. But like I said, I was not really interested.

The story goes that Nikki had signed on with Kovac only given the proviso that Kovac was committed to keeping John Corabi as the singer. But Kovac was and is a smart and slippery motherfucker. In his opinion, only one thing would restore Mötley Crüe back to their former glory... a reunion with Vince Neil.

It was the spring of 1996. I was thirty-five years old. My career was going nowhere fast. There was new management at Warner Bros.; when new folks come in, all the old shit goes. If it's not selling, they don't want it—no matter what it is. And I'd gotten caught up in that. One minute I had all these friends at Warner Bros.; the next minute I had no friends at Warner Bros. And nobody gave two shits.

Around this time, my manager, Burt Stein, got a call from Kovac saying he wanted to meet and talk about me maybe coming back to Mötley. I think I happened to be in New York City at the time. Maybe I was doing press for a solo tour, I can't remember. I don't think I made a special trip out to New York to see Kovac. I will say this: You know that whole story about me being in the lobby of a hotel with Burt and running into Kovac and how sneaky and clever he was and how they duped me into taking this meeting? That's right, the famous story about how brilliant all the managers were for plotting to get us back together? And how they tricked me into a meeting? You know, *that* story?

That story is total bullshit.

I knew about the meeting the whole time. I knew that the only reason Kovac took on Mötley was if I was going to be in the band, okay?

So we went to Kovac's hotel to meet him. He'd asked Burt to bring me and I'd agreed.

We ordered room service and made small talk until the food arrived. Then Kovac wasted no time: "Would you consider getting back with Mötley?"

Now lemme tell you. I didn't trust this guy. And I had no interest in being anywhere near any member of Mötley Crüe. Ever again! I remember at that time I hated every guy in the band and every person who worked for them. Even though I'd been released by Warner, I didn't care. I could tour. I could always get another solo record deal, I was sure. There was no amount of money that would make me get back together with Mötley. That's where my head was at. I let it be known.

Kovac remained calm while I went through my rant. Once I finished, he looked at me calmly. "Vince," he said, "you can get as angry as you want with me, but you have to ask yourself, are you a star as a solo artist?"

I answered him with a glare. He knew he had me. Okay, so I hadn't exactly been filling arenas with the Vince Neil Band. One tour had to be closed down halfway through 'cause we were spending more than we were making. More recently I'd brawled with my bass player, Robbie Crane. After quitting the band he would tell the press, "The only thing I look down on him for is that he can't handle his alcohol. I'm a drinker, too... but I don't get violent and I don't take my problems out on other people. He does and that's not fair."

Kovac continued. "In the environment of four guys in a band called Mötley Crüe, you are a real star. The audience that comes to see you gets its money's worth. Is the audience that comes to see the Vince Neil Band really getting what it pays for?"

The same, he went on to say, was true of Mötley Crüe *without* me in the lineup. The paying public had voted resoundingly, as was evidenced by sales and critical reviews.

Looking at the big picture, he concluded, there was only one rational thing to do. I had never given any thought to rejoining the band. All I wanted was my quarter share of the brand name and the money they owed me. I just wanted to get on with my life. But Kovac had talked some sense. A seed had been planted.

Allen Kovac
Vince's Manager,
CEO and Chairman of 10th Street Entertainment

Yes, the story about the chance meeting is BS. I had Burt Stein's commitment to deliver Vince Neil. That's why I threw the other guy (John Corabi) out. I felt Vince Neil was Mötley Crüe. I felt the other guy was like some placeholder that didn't hold the place well. So for anybody to say I just stumbled into a hotel or they just stumbled into a hotel is kind of off the mark. The only reason I knew Vince was at the hotel, or that I could guarantee his participation in the band, would've had to come from one of his representatives. It was never a chance meeting. It was premeditated with me and Burt Stein.

As I saw it, things at that point were a little two-sided. Because here you have Vince's manager, Stein, telling Vince, "You don't need to be in Mötley Crüe; you can make it on your own." Meanwhile the same person is telling me, "Look, just drop by, give him your presentation, give him your take, and we can make this happen." 'Cause I called Stein up and I told him how silly it was that he was making no money with Vince Neil. I told him the only way Vince was going to make any real income was to join Mötley Crüe. I told him, "I'm going to get the guys to New York to meet with Doug Morris and Sylvia Rhone at Warner. How can I meet with Vince and you and get this done?" And he laid it out for me.

I was honest with the band. I said, "Look, I'm willing to do what you guys want. I work for you. But this is *my* opinion." At first they wanted to make a go of it with Corabi; as I saw more and more issues arising I'd of course point them out to the band. And finally they started to understand the same thing I understood. The reason I had that meeting with Vince was because they had turned around.

They finally saw what I saw, which was: Yes, Corabi's a really good guitar player; yes, he can sing; but he's not the frontman that Vince Neil is; he's not a frontman like David Lee Roth. And if they needed someone like David Lee Roth, then why not go get the *real* guy, the original guy, the guy we knew who worked, at least musically.

As I remember the meeting, I laid out to Vince why I thought it was silly for him to go on solo when he and the band together could make him 500 percent more than he was making on his own. At the time I think I was managing the Cranberries, Duran Duran, Mellencamp, and Luther and Meat Loaf, so I was managing a lot of artists, and Mötley Crüe wasn't a big part of my client base. They were a part of it, but not a big part. And Vince was playing small venues and fairgrounds or whatnot. I'm sure Vince understood this. Especially in light of who was representing him.

I tried to get across to Vince that whatever his perception of why he wasn't in the band didn't matter. That was baggage he had to pack away. He had to decide whether or not he wanted to be involved in an asset that he'd built. It was a straight business conversation; I told him, "I have nothing to do with the past; this is a clean slate." The way I positioned it was, "You'd be crazy not to have a guy like me sit down and work with you and your manager." So Burt and I negotiated a deal. I had to pay him a point or so of course. But, you know, it was basically a business discussion. A discussion about moving forward and forgetting about the past. It was irrelevant to me *why* they broke up. I got Vince past *that* and got him to realize that I wasn't a part of whatever had happened in the past. I explained that I could be a part of bringing him back into the band. Eventually he started believing that was a good idea.

Look, I'm not Vince's friend, you know? I told Vince during that first meeting, I told him, "I think I've been to Mick Mars's house in fifteen years twice. I've been to Tommy's house twice, and I've been to Nikki's house twice. None of them have ever been at my house. So I'm not their friend. That's the way it should be." I'm not their friend. I'm the person who is helping to guide their career. I'm not really involved with the day-to-day activities—I'm involved on the ten-thousand-foot level, and then I have a marketing company that has different departments—there are publicity people who deal with publicity, and touring people who deal with touring; you know, a lot of different people have dealt with Vince and the band. I deal with the big picture. Where people are going. What they're trying to accomplish. What we think we can help them accomplish.

Lately, I've been saying to Vince, "Look. All artists have a hundred ideas, but you gotta concentrate on the first three and get them done before you try to do number ninety-nine." The problem for Vince is that in the past, he wasn't willing to let anyone manage that. So the way I manage that is I've got a big company. I'm focusing on the three things that I think are the most important for Vince Neil. And he signed off on it. He has the book, the record, and the tequila and the tattoo shops. The tequila has distribution in thirty-three states. He also has Feelgoods in Florida and Vegas; that feeds off everything else of course. And the tattoo shop right now is in Vegas in two locations. If I can help him focus in on the priorities, I think we can do all right by him.

In some ways you can see the upside already beginning to show. Like he just made the video for the title song on the album, he's done the song, he stayed within budget. You gotta keep your record within a budget because the record's just really gasoline—the tour and the merch and the tequila and the book are how you're going to make money. You know records aren't selling today. But you have to have new stuff. Getting him to do that and keeping him in line hasn't been easy. But you know, lately it has been a lot easier. This record isn't being made for a million dollars or half a million dollars, or even a quarter-million dollars. Here we have a guy adhering to a budget and working with the people that we're putting around him. That's an extremely good sign in terms of what Vince's future will look like.

My hope is that Vince turns the corner in this real-time situation. I've been able to do it for a lot of artists; I don't know if I'm going to be able to do it for him. I'm gonna try. But a big part of the equation, a big part of being able to get this done, is him deciding that he's willing to do things. Sometimes he's sort of one foot in, one foot out. You're not exactly sure what he's thinking, you know? I can only hope he wants the best for himself and his family.

And that's really your story. Being able to sort of reveal to him in real time the things he needs to do. Being able to say, "Hey, Vince, what are you going to do? Are you going to slip down the slippery slope, or are you going to finally climb the mountain?"

Because he can, I'm telling you. He has a lot of opportunity; he's gotta focus on the few things that are going to succeed and not the hundred things that all his friends are throwing at him all the time. And then he's gotta surround himself with professionals and be willing to take guidance and hear the word "no."

And then?

You wait and see.

One thing you learn in my business—never be surprised by anything.

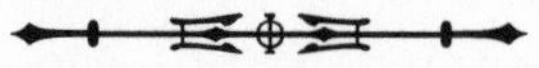

My capitulation didn't occur overnight; a meeting was eventually set up with the rest of the guys at the Continental Hyatt Hotel. Things were far from harmonious—Nikki showed up wearing a

T-shirt with the word "John" written on it, in memory of his beloved Corabi. What a joke. A table full of rock stars and their high-priced lawyers. It took them a couple of hours, but by the end I gotta give the shysters credit for making us see the bottom line: the name-calling, suing, and countersuing were costing us all a fortune. My legal bills alone added up something like $350,000; they would at least double if I continued with the lawsuit. By the end of the meeting, it was agreed. There was only one rational plan of action.

I couldn't believe I was hearing myself say it, but I did. I told my lawyers, "Let's do it. Let's get this thing back together again."

A week or so later, as I listened to some of the instrumental tracks for the next album, *Generation Swine*, I was not so sure I'd done the right thing. *Fuck!* I knew it. I'd made a big fucking mistake! The bastards talked me into it and now here I was. It was money talking. And greed. Theirs and mine, too.

The setting was Nikki's house; the moment I'd walked in, I couldn't help myself—all the old feelings surfaced; my skin crawled. I hated everybody from the jump. And I hated all the songs. The songs sucked. Period.

On top of that, from the first minute of the first day back, me and Tommy were at each other's throats. It was sort of like even though they decided they were going to get back together, nobody was going to make it easy on anyone else. If I was being honest, I'd say they didn't want it any more than I wanted it. I don't think they wanted me back even a little bit. Clearly they'd been talked into it, too. It was a forced relationship, like staying together for the sake of the kids. Tommy, especially, was acting like a fucking diva. Since he'd married Pam Anderson his ego was all over the place. Suddenly *he* wanted to be a singer. We're in there the first day and *he's* telling *me* how to sing the songs! He was like, "Sing it like this; sing it like that." And I'm like, *Why don't you fucking sing it then?* I mean, the guy can't fucking sing for shit. What does he know about singing? The only reason he and the others do backups is so they can get the AFTRA money. That's the American Federation of Television and Radio Artists. That's the union. If your name is on a record as a singer, you can claim their insurance—health and dental and stuff like that. If you don't sing on the record, you don't get those benefits. That's the only reason Tommy ever sang backup. Not because he's fuckin' Pavarotti.

After about an hour, I'd had it. I was done.

I was like, *Fuck all of you.* I didn't need their shit. I got in my car and drove home.

Day one of my reunion with Mötley Crüe.

Great idea, right?

That night, somebody called me and apologized. Fuck no. It wasn't Tommy. Are you crazy? I think it was Burt. Or it was Kovac. I can't remember. Probably it was both of them calling on a fucking conference call together. That's the only thing those fuckin' guys know how to do. "Wait a minute; let me conference you in."

Of course they talked me into giving it another shot. Heidi was in agreement. I had no money. I gave it another shot. We made it work. We made the album.

I never heard the record they did with Corabi, but I did get together with him at some point and we had some drinks. John told me that he'd actually gone at one point to the guys—this is when he was with the band—and told them, "You gotta get Vince back. You know this is not working." And I think that's when the whole thing to get me back really mushroomed. I think it was initiated by John. It's true, I guess. We are all for one or we are nothing. I hate like hell to say it, but it's true. I know it. And they know it. I wish it could be a little less like having to eat a bitter pill.

"Generation Swine," the single, came out in January '97, the day after a reunited Mötley performed live at the American Music Awards in Los Angeles. Later, the album peaked at #4, with sales of 80,500 copies. Truthfully, the song sucked. The whole album sucked. The sales were totally out of loyalty from our fans. I think the only fun time I had that entire time we were doing that album was this one afternoon when I landed a helicopter in Nikki's backyard.

When we weren't in the studio I was taking flying lessons. I was up with an instructor putting in some hours. Just about the time we got over by Westlake Village, out the 101 toward Thousand Oaks, west of Calabasas, where I used to live, my instructor and I ran out of beer. I knew Nikki lived in Westlake Village, so I called him on the cell. I was like, "Look up!" He was in his studio and he came outside, and he looked up. There was a helicopter hovering right above his house.

We landed in his backyard. We got out, went into the studio and listened to some stuff, drank a couple beers. Then we took off.

Nikki got hell from the homeowners' association; it's probably the nicest memory of him I have.

December again. The last month of 1997. If my life was a movie, the soundtrack would change up right about here. Something was ready to go down. It didn't take long to find out what.

Mötley was on a small tour. Like with *Feelgood*, somebody had decided it would be best if we all stayed sober. If you were caught fucked up, it was explained, there would be a twenty-five-thousand-dollar fine. I don't know how that was established. I never voted on it. I mean, we're not just talking, like, staying away from heroin or cocaine. They were saying you could not have a glass of wine or a cocktail. Nothing. Nada. It was fuckin' ridiculous. I was nearly thirty-seven years old. You're gonna tell me what I can and cannot do? You gonna fuckin' tuck me in at night, too?

The next stop was San Francisco. A buddy of mine had volunteered to fly us in his private plane from LA to SF and then on to our next stop, in Boise, Idaho. The guy's name was Neil McNeice. He had a sweet Gulfstream jet. His father basically owned the whole state of Wyoming—he had the uranium rights, anyway. I guess the story was Neil's father and mother had been antelope hunting in the Gas Hills; for some reason Mr. McNeice brought along a Geiger counter; they discovered uranium in the hills. Later Mr. McNeice went on to found this huge uranium-mining company. The family was worth like a billion dollars.

The son, I'm pretty sure his name was also Neil, was just this cool dude I met somewhere. We started hanging out together and we got along well. He'd be like, "Here, take the jet. Do whatever you want, man." I mean I have a little bit of money, but this guy had real "fuck you" money. He could do whatever the fuck he wanted, basically. He wasn't beholden to anybody. We'd take the jet to Hawaii and go hang out at his house in Maui. When we got tired of Maui, it would be like, "Hey, let's go to Japan. Let's go get some sushi." That's how you rolled when you were partying with him.

So using my connection, the band flew in McNeice's jet to San Francisco. After the show, I went to a strip club, had a drink, and then took a taxi home. I didn't get that fucked up or anything. We'd been touring for a while. I'd been straight. I just needed a goddamn drink and some pussy, you know? Somehow, later, Nikki ended up taking the exact same cab as I'd taken. The driver of course got all excited and told Nikki he'd had me in the car—plus he told Nikki I'd been *drinking*.

The next morning, Nikki called my room and demanded a check for twenty-five thousand dollars. I was like, *Fuck*, you know? I didn't really want to be in the band, anyway; I was tired of the rules and the bullshit. I remember the tour manager, Mike Amato, came to my hotel room door with a pee bottle—I think it was him. He wanted a urine sample from me. He declined to be interviewed for this book.

There was an altercation in the hallway. I was pissed off. I was like, "You know what? I don't need this shit. Fuck all of you."

I packed my shit and went downstairs. I was actually calm, but I was mad. Really fuckin' mad. We were all supposed to meet in the lobby at 4:00 P.M. for our ride to the airport to take the jet to Boise. The guys were down there, as were Nikki's grandfather and Nikki's wife, the former *Baywatch* hottie Donna D'Errico. I looked at Nikki and I said, "I quit. I can't fuckin' do this anymore."

Nikki's like, "What are you talking about?"

"I've had it," I told him. "I quit. I'm going home."

Nikki just exploded. To my surprise, he fucking took a swing at me—nailed me right in the jaw with an uppercut. Then he jumped on me like a man possessed, grabbed me by the neck, and dug his fingernails in, screaming that he was going to rip out my vocal cords.

We wrestled on the floor for a few seconds. I've always been stronger and in better shape than Nikki. I punched him in the face and threw him off of me. Finally everybody held us back. I was like, "Fuck you, I'm out."

I went and grabbed McNeice and we went to the airport. When we got there, the whole band was in the waiting area. It was a private field, not a regular airport. So all they had was this tiny waiting area by the runway. Me and McNeice and the pilot walked into the facility and walked right past the band. "Wait here a minute," I told them over my shoulder as we filed out onto the tarmac and got on the plane.

And started it up.

And rolled out onto the strip and took off.

I can still see their faces as we were pulling away—they were all staring out the windows of the waiting room, like those fuckin' cats that stick up against the back windows of cars? Garfield. They were all looking out the window like Garfield the cat, the plane pulling away without them.

I remember Nikki calling me on my cell. He's like, "You can't do this! You can't just leave us here. We have a sold-out show in Boise."

And I was like, "The hell I can't, motherfucker." I was *done.*

Again.

We flew back to LA and went directly to the bar at the Peninsula Hotel. Heidi joined us there. And thus began another epic night... I guess. I can't really remember.

I found out later that since it was a private airport, there of course weren't any regular flights. The band had to stay there like eight or nine hours waiting for a flight. They ended up canceling the show in Boise and flying home.

A few days later, Nikki called and we made up again.

We went to Boise and fulfilled our obligation.

I think something broke that time. Maybe it was Nikki finally being man enough to take a swing at me and connect. We'd come a long way. We were grown men now. We were getting too old for this bullshit. We knew our bread was buttered by Mötley Crüe. We knew what had to be done, whether we liked every single thing about it or not. I don't really hold a grudge that long. It's like let's get it on, let's just do it. But I just don't trust Nikki. I don't trust him. I don't trust any of the guys in the band. Because they're not trustworthy. They always have ulterior motives. And that's why I have to always think ahead when I get a phone call from one of them. I'm always trying to figure out, *Okay, what's in it for them? What are they really angling for?* I do get along better with Nikki than I guess anybody.

And so it would go for the next thirteen years to the present. We don't really like each other anymore, maybe, but we've stayed together for the benefit of the kids. And I prefer to think that despite everything, deep down, each of us *loves* the others. For the benefit of the whole, we each sacrifice a bit of ourselves. Like it or not, we are the four musketeers, all for one and one for all, placed on this earth to do what we do. Over the course of time, we have pumped out a number of albums, some better than others. There was *Greatest Hits: Supersonic and Demonic Relics*; *Live: Entertainment or Death*; *New Tattoo*; *Red, White & Crüe*; and *Carnival of Sins*. Who would ever have predicted that 2008's *Saints of Los Angeles*, with all new material chronicling our life together as a band, would debut at #4 on the *Billboard* chart after selling 99,000 copies in the United States during its first week of release. It was the biggest sales week for Mötley since Christmas of 1991, when *Decade of Decadence* sold 121,000 copies. Once again, despite our own efforts to self-destruct, Mötley Crüe was back and being relevant. And so we remain today.

I finally married Heidi on May 28, 2000, at L'Orangerie. We'd already been together for like six years. I don't remember what the final straw was that moved us to tie the knot. I think I was probably in the doghouse big-time and was trying to make things right. "Mercurial" is the best word to describe my relationship with Heidi.

It was just a small wedding, like thirty people. We were married to the tune of Van Morrison's "Crazy Love," which explained us exactly. The bridesmaids were mainly *Playboy* Playmates; Nikki stood as my best man—don't ask me how that happened. Like I said earlier, he was at all four of my weddings. It's a love/hate thing between him and me. Some things are best left unexplained.

All in all, life was good. At least I *thought* it was good. While I was on tour—almost a year to the day after our wedding—Heidi calls me and tells me she found somebody else, some fuckin' plastic surgeon.

Obviously, she'd been fucking him the whole time. After she told me she was leaving me she moved in with the guy within a couple of days—so obviously it wasn't like she'd just met the guy. This had been going on for a while. I don't know how long it was going on, but it was, it was going on.

After that it got ugly. The June 4, 2002, edition of the *National Enquirer* featured this huge story: "Playboy Playmate Tells All. My 10 Years of Abuse at Hands of Mötley Crüe Rocker." In the story, Heidi alleged that I first started abusing her three months into our relationship and that I continued to pull her hair, slap her, and punch her at times over the course of our relationship, including one time when I supposedly hit her so hard that I broke her breast implant. She also alleged that I once kicked her karate-style in the stomach in the middle of a Beverly Hills restaurant and that I cheated on her at Skylar's funeral. I stayed out of the fray, preferring to have my lawyer respond. He told the press that the allegations were "outrageous and defamatory" and added that Heidi was the abusive one with the bad temper who frequently threw things at me during our years together.

The truth is we fought just like every other married couple fights. I think maybe at times we both drank too much. There was a lot of, there was definitely verbal abuse, from both sides. She could give as good as she got. But we had something special together, you can believe that.

I know you will hear some juice from Heidi, so I'll just let her have her say. She's still a beautiful woman. I will always cherish the good times we had.

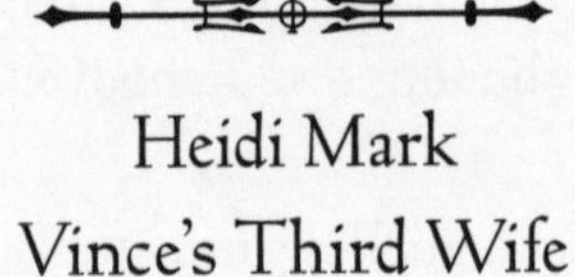

Heidi Mark
Vince's Third Wife

He definitely knew that alcohol was his problem. And he readily admitted it to me. I remember sitting on our couch and him being on the floor with his arms on my legs crying. And I could tell it was bullshit. This was a broken person. This was a scene that played over and over.

One time I'm thinking of, he's like, "I can't stop drinking, Heidi. I can't stop it. Once it starts going and that light switch goes off, I don't know what I'm doing anymore." And of course he's like, "Please, I'll do anything. I'll do anything you want."

That was one of the times Promises picked him up. They pick him up that day, and that night I was getting a phone call: "We need thirty grand." I gave them fifteen thousand, I called our friend Roger King, who has since passed away, he gave me another fifteen thousand, and I had it in their bank account the next day. It was like they were going to bring him back home if I didn't give them the money. And I go, "Do *not* bring him home. Do *not* bring him home, please."

What would happen is he'd start off with good intentions. He'd be like, "Okay, I'm going to have three drinks, and that's it, Heidi. Three drinks. That's *it*." And then the third drink would be finished. And he looks at me. And he's like, "Okay, I'm going to have one more." You get to a point...you know you try to enforce the rules? And you get to a point where you're just a nagging bitch and it's just not worth it. So, I just wouldn't even fight the fight. You know what I mean? Nobody wants to be that person.

I put him through I think it was five rehabs. Vince knew exactly what to say to get out of each rehab, so he may remember a lot more than he wants you to think he remembers. He can play that game. He knows exactly what to say. He's dumb as a fox. Granted, he has definitely lost a lot of time to blackouts. There's no doubt about that. He's a blackout drunk. He functions without functioning.

I know for a fact that if I wouldn't have left, we'd still be together. Because Vince is a lover. He would never leave anybody, you know? He would cheat on you like a dog, but he would never break up with someone. He would never leave. He can't be alone. He would wake up somewhere with a girl and literally he would come home crying, "I didn't know, I'm sorry, I don't know, I'm sorry, I'm sorry. I'll go into rehab; I'll do anything, I'm sorry." And he'd go into rehab; he'd do what he needed to do. He'd talk the talk and walk the walk and all the people in there would fall in love with him. Vince is a charming, charming guy. So that's how it would go. There would be some big thing—like when I found him in a hotel with two hookers, you know? Then he'd go into rehab.

One of the nice things about Vince was that when he was home he would drive me to my auditions or to my meetings so I didn't have to drive. Then he'd wait for me or pick me up after, when I called. It was great because on the way to an audition, say, I could look over my sides and get ready. He did so many lovely gestures that weren't about money. Though he also did things I didn't like. I think in the gesture department he had a couple of go-to moves, like I'd get a couple dozen red roses. But roses meant nothing to me. It took no thought. He probably had his manager's assistant call it in—the card would always be very generic. Like one card was: "To Heidi, I love you, your husband Vince." Like when would he ever tell someone to sign a card that way? How about a personal note? Thought, not money. It never even occurred to him that I hated red roses. That is a whole book in itself, but suffice it to say, red roses were not the way to my heart or anything else. In fact, I had a favorite rose—he could've found out. It isn't hard. I like ambrosias. They're kind of an orangey color with like dark red.

I remember he had this pink shirt. He loved to wear it all the time. He had gotten in a fight in it; it still had the bloodstains no matter how many times he washed it. I think it meant something to him. I think he won the fight. And he had these shorts that he loved that had a hole in them. I remember one time after we'd been fighting and he was wearing this outfit. And he just says to me, "Heidi, I think our problem is that we don't kiss enough. If we started kissing enough, I think that we'd get back on track." And it was like, the look in his eyes, he was totally serious. He meant every single word of it, no bullshit. That was him at his best, you know? When there was nobody around, when there was no bullshit or ceremony. It was just Vince being Vince and me being myself. Vince and Heidi. That part was great.

Sharise and I are similar in many ways. We just went out a couple weeks ago. Thankfully we got along well when Skylar got sick—it would've been horrible if she hated me. Of course, I had nothing to do with their breaking up; she had no reason to hate me. She didn't exactly welcome me at first with open arms, but what ex-wife would? But we all had to work together for the sake of Skylar. She was a wonderful little girl. She used to stay with us all the time. I was the stepmom. I have a tattoo of Sklyar. What a wonderful little girl, so full of life. We used to play dress up and all kinds of girl stuff—another reason why it was good that Sharise and I got along. I guess the thing is, all of Vince's wives or ex-wives, what have you, all of us like to believe that we were the greatest love of his life. My thing is that I went through the hard times with him. When he was not with Mötley Crüe, when he was really adrift. Sharise was lucky. She was there during the excess and the great times and the helicopters and all that. Beth got the pure times, in the early days. But things were really crazy then. Your husband kills somebody? Oh my god. I can't imagine. I was with him the longest and went through the hardest times. I don't like the new wife. I call her

Trixie, because she's a groupie like all the rest of them. I'm pretty sure he started seeing her when we were still married.

One important thing I learned in my marriage to Vince was that you can only fight with somebody who fights back with you. I know I was responsible for part of our, for half of our fights. I fought with him. So I was part of it. You know what I mean? It takes two people. But he would always take the side of denial. He would literally be like, "It wasn't me. I don't know what you're talking about. I love you. I wouldn't do that. I love you. What are you talking about? I love you more than anything. I've never loved somebody so much. I love you. Look at me." And then he'd cry, the whole nine yards. I'd be thinking, *Is he really this good of an actor?* And then I'd think. *Okay, maybe he means it.*

During Skylar's illness I would talk to Sharise. And she'd be like, "He's great at apologizing."

And I'd think to myself, *I really thought I was different. That he was going to be different with me.* I really thought I was going to be the one who saved him. It was going to be me. Come to find out I was no different. I was exactly the same as every other wife.

I actually I did leave him. I found he was cheating. He had fucked some girl. I took all my dirty clothes, put them in my suitcase—I figured everything in the hamper was what I liked the best. I called Delta, got a first-class ticket, drove to the airport, called my manager, and left a message. I said, "My car is at LAX; will you please pick it up and take it back to my house?" And I flew to Florida. And yes, there was another man. A plastic surgeon. But I didn't go to him. I went to my girlfriend's house. He didn't really mean that much to me. He was all about safety and getting away. And I had to, I had to get away. I couldn't take it anymore. I'd had enough.

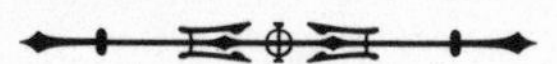

In October 2002 I moved into a house in the Hollywood Hills for ten days as part of a new Warner Bros. reality series called *The Surreal Life*. The concept for this show was really hot at the time—reality TV, who'd have thought it would have gotten so big? This was just the early days. I figured it would be fun and would also raise my profile. I went for it.

It was quite a group they assembled. There was Emmanuel Lewis from the TV show *Webster*; Corey Feldman from *The Lost Boys* and some other classic movies; Mindy Cohn from *The Facts of Life*; the *Baywatch* actress and *Playboy* model Brande Roderick; Jerri Manthey, the hot bitchy girl from *Survivor*; and the rapper MC Hammer. There were six half-hour episodes recorded in this house in the San Fernando Valley. The cameras were on us 24/7 and they filmed everything. I saw the show as a once-in-a-lifetime opportunity; I felt I just had to do it. And the great reviews and high ratings justified my doing so.

Watching the show now, of course, I see how a lot of it is bullshit. But I think it really does show the real Vince in action in parts. You can see how I'm pretty charming most of the time, and how the chicks always just naturally gravitate toward me, and how the guys and I get along great. You can also see what it's like when I get pissed off. At one point, they drive us to Las Vegas—I kind of lost it when the bus driver went the wrong way and got us stuck in endless traffic. I guess you could say I displayed a rock star moment. Then, when we finally got to the hotel and I was reunited with my then-girlfriend, Lia Gerardini, you could witness me in another mode—drunk off my ass. People have said to me it's amazing how I seem to keep going when I'm totally out on my feet. I guess it's a form of alcoholic sleepwalking. I do know it's gotten me in a lot of trouble over the years.

In January 2005, I married Lia at the Four Seasons Hotel in Las Vegas. I'd been living in Vegas pretty much full-time since a year or so after Skylar died. The officiating duties were performed by MC Hammer, my new pal from the show, who also happens to be an ordained minister. It was my fourth marriage and I was determined this one would work.

Some people would have given up on marriage by this time, but not me. I don't like being alone. My man Hammer did a great job. It was pretty cool. He's a good guy, a genuinely nice person with a great heart. When we were done he shouted, "It's Hammer time!"

Lia is an amazing person—she looked so beautiful on our wedding day. We honeymooned in Miami and I was the happiest I'd been for years. We remain together to this day. She is my partner and my rock.

Lia Neil
Vince's Fourth Wife

I grew up the ugly duckling. I was teased at school. I didn't have the boobs then. I had red hair and boys used to make fun of me. I was not the popular girl. I wasn't with the cheerleaders.

I was born in East Oakland, adopted at birth, and raised by a nice Italian family in Pleasanton, California. I've had the same phone number my whole life.

I went to a local junior college called Ohlone. Then I went to work at the front desk for the Marriott Corporation. I kind of didn't know what I wanted to do. I did a lot of temp jobs for a while. I finally found my niche in plastic surgery. I was an administrator for a plastics and reconstructive office in Northern Cal.

Ten years ago, when I was thirty-two, I met Vince and my life took me in a different direction. We met at one of his concerts. A bunch of girls and I all went. I was really into Mötley Crüe in high school. Vince was the pinup poster in my room.

I went to the concert wearing these little cropped holey jeans with butterflies on 'em. My top was black pleather and tied mid-waist. My boobs were out, my hair was big; I had my highest heels on.

We were sitting way back in the lawn section—really far from the stage. We started drinking and it was like liquid courage. Out of nowhere, I just said, "I'm going down there." My friends were like, "What?" I was always the commonsense one. I was the designated driver. I was always everybody's mom. I said, "I am going down there. I used to have the *biggest* crush on Vince Neil." I told them about the poster in my room. My friends were like, "Oh my god! You're crazy. You're going to get kicked out." And I said, "Well, if I get kicked out, I'll just meet you guys back at the car."

I started working my way past the barricades. I was living in the moment. I was really tipsy. Clearly I had gone *insane*. I was having this weird groupie moment. For one day, I had been transformed. I worked my way all the way down to the front.

I stood there a moment. All of a sudden it hit me. *What am I doing here?*

I looked around and noticed my old hairdresser. She happened to be at the show, sitting down front of course. She's a total rock chick. Her brother was in a band. She asks me, "Lia, what are you doing here?" I said, "Oh my god, Renee . . . I don't know. I just wanted to come down and see the show." And we're looking up at Vince and we're listening and she says, "He's singing to *you*." And I was like, "No, he's *soo* not singing to me." There were like *multitudes* of people there.

Next thing I know this big bouncer guy walks up to me. He says, "Vince would like to see you after the show." It was sobriety all at once; I might have been a little tipsy before, but the surge of adrenaline put me totally sober. I wondered, *How did he pick me out of the crowd?* It was the boobs, I think. I was flattered. I asked if I could bring my girlfriends with me. He said the backstage pass was just for me. I said, "Then there's no way." I don't like to put myself in predicaments.

So we went backstage—*with* my girlfriends. Vince came out. He was all sweaty. He had on a pair of shorts. He sat down and he was a normal guy—really complimentary. We exchanged a few words. He was adorable. I never asked him for his autograph, nor did I get naked. We all just had regular chitchat. Then he asked for my phone number. I thought, *He's never gonna call.* At that point I didn't know that he was married. We exchanged numbers.

He called immediately and he kept calling.

He asked if he could fly me to New York, or Dallas, wherever he was. I would just say, "No. I'm not that kind of a girl. When you want to date me, you can come here and date me." He would call from Osaka, Japan. It was kind of cool. At some point I found out he was married.

Then he said that he and his wife had split. He was taking the next flight out. He said he wanted to meet my parents.

My dad seemed okay about meeting him, but my mother thought I was off my rocker, and there was a part of me that agreed. She was born in Italy. Neither of my parents had ever heard anything about Mötley Crüe. That was probably a bonus for me. Just knowing that he was in a rock band made my mother think I had lost every marble in my head. But I was having a good time. I wanted to let this romance play out. I'd be crazy not to.

Vince met them wearing a long-sleeve shirt and his hair pulled back in a ponytail. He was very respectful. He impressed my dad. Last year my dad passed away. He was a mechanic. He owned the only garage in Pleasanton for years. Vince's dad was a mechanic, too. The minute they all met they were enamored with him. They loved him. He was just sweet and courteous and kind and they just loved him. I miss my dad. I will never be able to replace him as a person in my life who thinks so fiercely about my needs. His death has made a big hole in my life. I think everyone who knew him feels that way. I know it's tough on my mom. I do my best to be there for her.

What they didn't know is that Vince had been an alcoholic pretty much his whole life and, unlike me, he had no connection to his parents. We would travel and holidays would come and go. I'd ask him about his parents. I'd try to bring them into our lives. I'd say, "They're getting older. You're getting older. They don't know you. They don't know me." Vince would only say that his mother was a little crazy.

By the time we moved to Vegas his parents were living in Laughlin, Nevada. I thought that would be the opportunity to meet them. Vince invited them over and we met. They seemed relatively normal. I was really good to his mother, very gracious. We let them stay at our house. I knew they drank and that was okay. I mean Vince drank and they drank. Everything changed on our wedding day. His mom totally crossed the line.

On our wedding day, everybody was drinking. It was a wedding, of course. My dad was in his eighties and in ailing health. He hadn't been diagnosed with cancer yet, but for the last five years he'd been in and out of hospitals. It was a huge thing for me to have both my parents there.

After the ceremony, Vince and I went to sit at a table with my parents and some neighbors that lived across the street from them. Vince's parents came over and Vince's mother starts asking how come we're not sitting with her. We tried to tell her it's not arranged seating. A couple at the table got up so that they could sit down.

Vince's mom looks over at my dad, and she says, "Your daughter's lucky that my son is marrying her."

My dad laughed it off. He smiled and he said, "They're both lucky. They have each other."

So she says, "My son is going to make your daughter very rich."

It's been five years now and I still don't speak to her.

Chapter 10

VIVA LAS VEGAS

I finally got sober on March 4, 2007. That's the date I give. I'm not gonna subject you to the whole AA testimony... the fact is, I don't believe I'm an alcoholic, per se. I still drink on occasion. I have a little champagne now and then, sometimes a little more probably than I need. And sometimes I'll have a shot of tequila, but only Tres Rios, my own brand.

I'll tell you how I got sober. What's remarkable, I guess, is that it wasn't that remarkable at all.

I had been going through a period when I was really drinking heavily for about a month, maybe a couple months. And it all kind of came to a head. I remember I went to Guadalajara, Mexico, where they make my tequila. I was there for about a week, just drinking every day, kind of nonstop. They had this big fiesta all week with the mariachis and all this stuff—they wanted to show me a good time down there. Everybody kept calling me El Jefe, the Chief.

And then I went straight from there to South Beach, Florida, for the food and wine convention. I was staying at the Ritz-Carlton in South Beach and I was drinking a lot. We'd wake up and go to breakfast and have some Bloody Marys or whatever. And it just continued; I drank all day long. I'd pass out in the afternoon, wake up, drink again, pass out again, wake up again.... It was just a vicious, terrible cycle. It's like I had no control of myself. My bar tab was about nine thousand dollars while I was there. Maybe even more. Maybe it was like *eleven* thousand. I can't remember. It was fucking crazy.

Things just snowballed from there—I don't know how it happened, but I just started drinking and I couldn't stop. My mind-set just purely focused on drinking. It wasn't that I was actually physically dependent. I wasn't that kind of alcoholic. I wasn't sick in the morning and had to have a drink. It wasn't like a DTs kind of thing. It was just like you wake up and your friends are there. And they say, "Let's go to the bar...let's drink...let's go to the beach and drink...let's go get a drink." And that was it. It just kept building. And that ended up going on for a couple of months.

Finally, I just got tired. You see you're in a pattern. You just want to get off the merry-go-round. It came to a point where I just couldn't do it anymore.

I called Lia and I said, "Find me a place to go. I gotta get some help."

As I said earlier, I have no idea how many rehabs I've been to. I'm not sure what was different this time. I was tired, I guess. Drinking wasn't fun anymore. It wasn't any fun at all. It was *expensive*.

Plus, I didn't get anything done. I was going nowhere. I was where I was for a reason. I had bad people around me. I let it happen. I guess drinking becomes your hobby in a way. For me, I don't think it was ever about the alcohol. I think it was about the socializing that goes with drinking. It's that not-wanting-to-be-alone thing again. That's the biggest part. It's like 90 percent of it. I never drank at home by myself. I never would just go sit somewhere by myself and drink. I was not pouring myself shots at home. It was all about the socializing. Being with the crowd. Having a drink in my hand was part of it. I always had to have a drink in my hand—social lubrication, if you will. Remember, I've always been the shy one. The frontman who didn't necessarily want to be in front—in the early days people say I sang with my back to the crowd. If you watch me on *Surreal World* I *always* have a glass or plastic cup in my hand, almost every single time you see me, in every scene. I always felt more comfortable that way.

But over time I sort of realized that drinking was not working for me anymore. I realized that I'm the kind of drinker who blacks out. I try to drink and have a good time, but it never really works well for me. I get to a point where everything's... it's like a switch, you know? All of a sudden I'm gone. I don't know what happens. I don't remember anything the next day. I'm like on autopilot, I guess, where I'm not making sense—you get into that mode and then you're not fun anymore. You know what I mean? 'Cause it's weird. It's like this switch goes off. It sort of sneaks up on you. It surprises you, you know? One second you're having fun, and the next... who knows?

In the past I would try to go out with a limit in mind. A plan of attack. I would say to myself okay, I'm only going to drink three or four drinks. Or okay, I'm only going to drink white wine; I'm not going to drink, say, Jack Daniel's. And it might work a couple of times. But eventually, you're back to where you started again. You can't control it. You can switch up drinks, you can do what you want, but basically it is what it is, you know. It's all your body's chemistry.

These days, now that I'm sober, I'm way more productive. I've got the book and the album; I've got the Vince Neil Band; I've got the Mötley touring. I've got the Feelgoods franchises—coming to a town near you, I hope. I've got my lifestyle here in Las Vegas.

I really love it here—our other house in Northern Cali is more for Lia, to be close to her mom and her roots. Myself, I feel like I need a little more pulse around me. You can feel it here in Vegas. It's the strong beat of life pulsing beneath the surface.

These days, I wake up early, feeling clearheaded. I'm up in the morning, I make the coffee. I get stuff done. Would you believe I produced the entire video shoot for the title song of my new album? I won't be credited as the producer, but I was on the phone, calling people, pulling strings, making things happen the right way. This is how I roll now. I was on the phone all morning with this guy who wants to do a licensing deal with his airplanes to be part of Vince Neil Aviation. I have so much stuff going on right now. There's been *so much stuff* going on in the last couple years. It's been nonstop, you know?

When I was drinking, I never thought about what other people thought of me. To tell you the truth, I never thought of it; it never even crossed my mind. But just thinking about it now…hm.

I'm sure, in the past, a lot of opportunities came my way, but I was just too fucked up to move on them. I'm sure a lot of opportunities that came in probably never went past my management—I'm sure they were like, "This guy can't deal with this," you know? That's probably why deals didn't get passed to me. But there's no sense crying over the past. What's done is done. I have always had a talent for living in the moment. And so I continue.

Not that I don't have my dreams. I mean, I'm only forty-nine. Celebrity is a blessing and a curse. As you go along, you kind of turn into another person. I like my job. I like what I do for a living. I just don't like a lot of what comes along with it. Sometimes you *want* the attention. I *love* being able to walk into a restaurant and get a table right away: "Oh, Mr. Neil, how are you doing? Good to see you again." Blah blah blah. That kind of stuff I *love*. Who wouldn't, right?

But I don't like people coming over and asking for autographs while I'm eating. Thankfully, it doesn't usually happen.

The fame I've achieved, where things are right now, it's good for me. Basically, on an everyday basis, nobody cares if I go about my business. I wouldn't want to be like the Beatles for instance, where they couldn't leave their hotel room. Or Michael Jackson—he couldn't fucking do anything or go anywhere. That would be a terrible way to live. All the money in the world, but what can you do? You can't go anywhere; you can't enjoy your life; you're basically in prison.

I like it where I can go down the street, get my own gas, go to the grocery store if I have to, live a normal life. And when I'm on the road, or onstage and doing a concert, then yeah—you're going to have people who want autographs and stuff. That's part of the deal. I love that, too. Everything at the right time. And then you get home and you get a break from it, which is a nice level of fame. All these celebrities that bitch, "I want my privacy," I feel like sometimes I want to slap them. You're famous, you know? Get over it. You signed up for it. That's the way I look at it. It's like if I wanted to be totally left alone, I could have stayed an electrician.

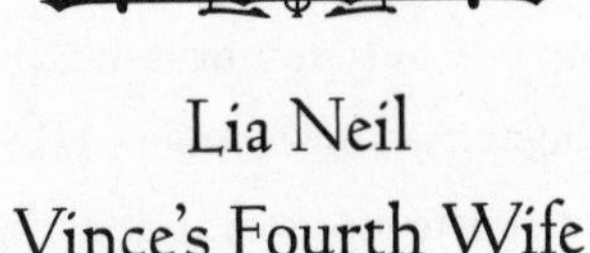

Lia Neil
Vince's Fourth Wife

When Vince and I met he didn't have a pot to piss in. He had a rental, a bed, and a car. And that's it. I mean there was no Mötley Crüe when we met. There was nothing. He had filed for bankruptcy. He had three bad marriages.

It's been three years since we did an intervention with Vince. Before that, he was a nightmare. I threatened to leave, so he went from hard alcohol to wine. But an alcoholic's an alcoholic. I kept wondering, *Why isn't anybody who cares for him trying to stop this?* I mean he was so self-destructive. He was bloated and had put on so much weight. He was either screaming at the top of his lungs or he was slurring. He wasn't eating. Nobody could find him. I didn't know if he was going to be dead. He wouldn't call. I couldn't live that way. I was out here in Vegas with the dogs by myself without my family.

Then it became booze and pills and girls . . . again. I wasn't having any part of it. I wasn't going to fly there and be his mommy. I mean after you've been with somebody for so many years, I don't want to babysit. You know this is somebody who should be responsible for himself, and me flying here and there and everywhere with him just aggravated me. I called up his manager and I said, "Look I'm just going to let you know if we don't do an intervention, if you don't step up to the plate and call somebody to help him, then I'm leaving him and you're going to have a serious problem because there's going to be another divorce."

We called Nikki. He was an inspiration. If it wasn't for Nikki I really didn't have any hope. Vince had been to Betty Ford and Promises. He's been everywhere. Yet, every few years he goes back to drinking.

Finally, he's sober now.

He does indulge in a few pills every now and then. I can hear it in his voice. It's an issue. It may be a very minor issue. It's nothing compared to the alcohol. He says he needs something to take the edge off. But you know that's just the door to the monster. I don't know what'll happen. I don't know how long he's going to be sober. You just never know. It's very difficult.

My dad was my rock. He was the most amazing man—honest and kind. He provided for his family and he never judged me. He was always there. When I went through difficult times my dad was always there. Now he's not. I don't have my rock. I love my husband but he's not my rock. He can't be. I'm his rock.

Vince seems in a good place now, with his business and everything. Ever since he hired 10th Street, the pieces have seemed to come together in a better way. The change couldn't have come too soon.

He was in the dark for a long period. One time, Vince and I were staying at the Four Seasons in Beverly Hills and we ran into Allen Kovac at the valet station. Allen asked Vince why he wasn't coming to the band meeting. And Vince was like, "What band meeting?" And Allen was like, "The one about creating a Crüe Fest tour." And then he said that if Vince wasn't going to tour with Mötley that summer, then the promoter was thinking of replacing him with the lead vocalists of the other bands already signed: Buckcherry, Papa Roach, and Sixx:A.M. Allen told Vince that he "owed it to himself" to come to the band meeting and hear the proposal. Of course, this news didn't sit too well with Vince. He screamed at Allen until the valet brought around the Ferarri. He peeled out into the street, mad as a hornet.

As usual, Vince cooled down and reconsidered after a little thought. He eventually decided to hire a new lawyer and a new accountant to represent him in the band negotiations. I think it was all a good move because with Vince on board at 10th Street, Mötley Crüe really took off again. Crüe Fest was the number one Rock Festival of 2008. You can't argue with results.

Vince lived it and he owns it. Now it's really interesting to watch him get older. I mean he still gets a lot of attention, but there are times when we'll roll up to the valet and you'll get some young girl and she'll ask him for his last name. It kills him. He's not the superstar that he was. He's aging. He's on his third face-lift and he's forty-eight years old.

Life goes on. I ground him and try to show him what a normal life is. You don't have to run with the wild dogs all the time. You can have something else. When I met Vince he didn't know how to use the ATM. He'd never been to the grocery store. He needs the excitement. He likes to be seen. He gets antsy. He can only play so much golf.

I was very nervous when I made the decision to go with him. I had the plastic surgery practice that I loved and the doctors that I worked for who I admired. I had my family and my friends. Vince said, "I want you to move down here with me." There was one side of me that thought, *This is great.* The other side thought, *This is not real.* When I resigned, the doctors I worked for told me that whatever happened, the door would always be open for me. At the time, I thought, *I can stay in this office forever, or I can take a chance and see what happens.* Not very many people get that opportunity. It is what it is.

As to the guys in the band…I don't know. It's weird because after all this time of being with these guys, there is stuff I still don't understand. Mick is still a complete mystery to me. I don't talk a lot to Mick; I don't see a lot of Mick. He shows up onstage and then he's gone. He's a great guy, but he gets a little too into certain things, like it seems like sometimes he likes to make a big deal out of a small thing just so he can act like he's contributing. I feel bad for Mick. I know he's in a lot of pain and that's shaped his life. I know sometimes he is in so much pain it's hard for him to play. What comes out of his amplifier is always amazing, though.

After all these years Nikki and me are still great friends. The press likes to blow things out of proportion, but we love each other like brothers, for better and for worse. We've been together for so long. You're going to have fights with people, it's human nature. You can't be around somebody for twenty-five or thirty years and not have an argument. That's just what happens. Nikki does a lot of things that irritate me, but I'm sure I do a lot of things that irritate him, too. It's just called life.

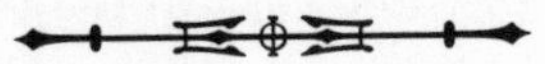

Nikki Sixx
Bassist, Songwriter, Founder of Mötley Crüe

How did I meet Vince? Tommy told us about him and we saw him play in a club band called Rockandi. This was at the Starwood in 1981. I remember thinking he reminded me of Robin Zander meets Iggy Pop and I loved that. There was a little bit of a snarl to him 'cause his voice was kind of raspy. He had a very melodic voice on top of that. It was cool and different.

To me, my vision for the band was always metal. Punk rock, pop, and heavy metal mixed together. But I think when you're kids you don't think that far in advance. You just want to be in a band. For me, from the start, it was all about crash and burn, search and destroy. It wasn't about longevity. It's never been about longevity. The fact that there is longevity is the actual joke. That's the whole pun. It's like God's cruel joke: Something that's meant to die *won't* die. It's like we're rock 'n' roll vampires. And you're in the vampire coven, forever stuck together in the same cave. That's the, that's the cruel joke. You get to live forever. But is that necessarily a blessing or a curse? That's the question. We never had any intention of lasting beyond probably the first gig—that's the whole interesting part of Mötley Crüe...

...and that's what makes those first few albums by a new band magical. It's the reckless abandon. There is no upside and there's no downside. It just is. It's a perfect, perfect place to be. And you just hang out together, you make music together, you're just in this zone. It's really cool. I love seeing bands at that juncture. It's just a fantastic thing.

Being in Mötley Crüe is not a chore for me. It has never been a chore for me. I love Mötley Crüe and Tommy, Mick, and Vince with all my heart. I am sorry to hear that Vince doesn't speak very highly of anybody in the band; I'm sorry to hear that. I give 200 percent to something that I've believed in for thirty years. So I don't just show up. I couldn't be in this band if I didn't think very highly of the guys. It must be hard for Vince to feel that way and still be in the band. . . . I feel bad for him . . .

I'm a songwriter. I love writing music. I'm in a band, and I love the band. And I think all the members of the band are really talented and really unique. I feel pretty blessed.

I've always believed Vince was our emblem. I always believed he was magical. I always believed he has a unique voice, that he's one of the greatest frontmen in rock. When we're onstage together, I'm always proud to stand next to him. I'm proud to fucking see him do what he does. And I'm proud to do what I do. I realize that I would *never* be able to do his job. It's a hard job. It's a fucking hard job. And you know—I got a job to do, too. And so does Tommy. And so does Mick. But it's the four of us *together* that makes it really magical. We all know that for a car to run it needs more than the emblem. It takes a motor, it takes a chassis, it takes the fucking paint *and* the emblem. It takes all of it to make it a finely tuned machine.

I wake up every day and I think, *I'm not a rock star, but I am in Mötley Crüe.* There's a lot of other things I want to do in my life. From being a father to being a successful songwriter, producer, photographer, radio host. There is so much out there to do and to dedicate my creativity toward. If I ever wake up thinking I am a rock star first and I'm in Mötley Crüe second, I've got it upside down.

This is what I understand: I'm in Mötley Crüe. I get to be in a band. It's the same band that started out playing in a garage. And I'm really fucking lucky. I mean, I look at Mick Mars and everything he's been through. Look at Vince and everything he's been through. Look at Tommy and everything he's been through. And then me. I've been through a lot myself. Sometimes, when we're onstage, I'll look at us playing. And I'll think to myself, *Wow, we're still here, man.* It's fucking cool. It's different, but it's the same. I live in gratitude, man, it's fucking pretty fucking cool, man.

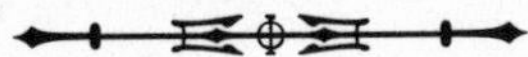

Deep down, in my heart of hearts, what I really want is this: I want to get to that next level. I want to get to the Ozzy level. I want to headline arenas with my own band.

That's why I hired Allen Kovac and 10th Street Entertainment. I don't like Kovac. I don't like him at all. We have a lot of history, most of it not that great. But this is business—this isn't friendship. I've had plenty of friends screw me over, believe me. The thing about Kovac is business, and he knows how to say "no." His motivation is helping me to make more money so that *he* gets paid more money. The way I see it, dealing with 10th Street is dealing with a company versus being managed by only one or two guys. It's like having a gang behind you, all of them strapped and down for your cause. Allen has invested in his people; he gets the best out of them. Like my man Eric Sherman, the creator and president of VH1 Classic and the former president of Fuse, who now runs 10th Street. With guys like him at the helm, I know that 10th Street can do for me what record companies can't do anymore: radio promotion, new media, press, touring, etc.

The thing about it is this: 10th Street really isn't just a management firm. It's a marketing and business development company. Look at the history: Kovac and 10th Street have done amazing things with Mötley Crüe, Buckcherry, Papa Roach, JET, the Cranberries, Blondie, Meat Loaf's *Bat Out of Hell*—the list goes on and on. He sees my potential as a solo artist on his roster. And, hey, if Kovac can do what he promised me—put out a record and a national tour, tie it in with the book, tie it in with the tequila and my tattoo shops and Feelgoods and my aviation company—then that's fucking wonderful.

I don't care how much I like him or not. The truth is, you can't do it yourself. It's like doing a deal with a devil I *know*.

My old management had me going out playing fairs and theaters. Kovac's right: You have to have a record out to tour with. And I haven't had a record out, you know? And my old management just kinda kept me touring and touring. Just touring and touring and touring and touring and touring. But all I was doing was repeating the same things over and over and over and over again: You know: Mötley Crüe stuff. Don't get me wrong. I love the songs. And as a fan, you know, if I go see David Bowie and he doesn't play his hits, I'm fucking pissed. 'Cause that's what you want to hear. I want to go hear David Bowie sing "Rebel, Rebel" and shit like that you know. So it's the same thing with me. And with Mötley. And with any band. But you still have to have new music. You still have to keep moving forward. Maybe an old rock 'n' roller is like a shark. (Shark Week on Discovery! One of my all time favorites!) You have to keep moving or you die.

Deep down, I still love it. I love the songs. I can sing them a million times, it doesn't matter. I can sing them every single day of my life and I'd be happy. I like them. Our hits are all fuckin' immortal. It's almost like as long as I can sing the songs, it makes everything else in the world not as important. Because it's the ultimate satisfaction in a way. Like I have a lot of shit going on, but I really love what I do, and that's really the center of it, and that's what's the most important. You may have crap that wants to drag you down, but if you really like what you're doing, there's always a silver lining. Here I am, I'm almost fifty or whatever, and I still have idealism. I still have things I want to achieve. So many guys my age are like getting ready to hang it up. Not me. I'm like, *Hey, I got a lot of shit to do, man.*

I think I have at least another ten years in me.

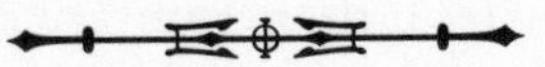

Neil Wharton
Vince's Son

Unless you're a hard-core Mötley Crüe fan you wouldn't know my dad's real name is Vince Neil Wharton. When I was born he wasn't planning on changing his name, so he gave me his middle name. Then he changed it and I got stuck with Neil Neil.

I grew up in the same area as my dad. My mom and my dad and grandparents literally grew up within a half mile of each other. I went to the same school my dad went to. I had all the same teachers.

From what I know, my mom and dad loved each other. My mom says my dad was a great father. But when you're seventeen years old and you basically get handed the keys to the world and you get to do your dream, what do you do? Do you say, "Oh, no problem, I'll get another chance to be a rock star," or do you say, "I'm going to stay and be a father"? Or do you go and do what you're meant to do? He made the right choice. I'm not bitter.

The misconception of being a rock star's child is that you get everything. I was lucky enough to have a well-grounded single mom. Right now she's a clothing manager for Harley-Davidson. She's been there sixteen years or seventeen years. She's great at what she does. I don't expect special treatment 'cause my dad's Vince Neil. My dad's just got a cool job.

When I was growing up, my grandparents, my dad's parents, took me to every Mötley Crüe show. Literally I was like a baby and a toddler and then a little kid. I used to go to the shows at the Whisky and the Roxy and the Canyon Club and Santa Monica Civic. My mom would take me, too. My greatest memory of any Mötley Crüe show when I was little was that I got to sit upstairs in the little sound booth. I remember it was just a ton of people. When you're little everything's big. Even a can of Coke is gigantic when you're little.

At the concert, they had candelabras on the stage and smoke. A guy would come out dressed up like a skeleton and he'd do this whole thing. But the one thing I remember is my dad would come out with a satchel. He had wrapped presents in it. I was two or three. I didn't know what they were; I just knew people were getting presents. But I remember as a kid I always wanted one of those things.

I didn't go back to the Whisky until I was like twenty-one or twenty-two. I walked in there and I looked around and I thought, *Did you guys close in some walls or something?* It's kind of cool to come full circle, 'cause then *my* band played there. And for me that was a big, big deal. My band is called the Rock and Roll Junkies. I'm the singer. We're a Mötley Crüe cover band. We play charity events called Crüe Fest. That's where Nikki and them got the name Crüe Fest. But we've been doing that for eleven years now. They kinda stole our name. But that's okay, 'cause I guess you could say we kind of stole all their songs.

To be honest with you, I never wanted to be in a band. I want to be the guy that goes in a plane and says, "You guys have it. I want to sign you." I want to be that guy. I didn't start doing a band until I got the charity idea. Now it's the only reason I do the band stuff. If I make money from it, great, but I'd rather make money for the charity. The money my band makes gets donated. We don't keep any of it.

Recently I moved to Las Vegas. I got laid off from my other job. It was Christmas and I texted my dad to say: "Merry Christmas and love you." I might have called him, but I always text. And besides, I didn't know where he was. And he texted me back right away and he's like: "How's everything going?" And I said: "I have a favor. Do you know anybody who's hiring? I lost my job." And I was like: "You can just give me a phone number of somebody just to call. I don't expect a job from you. I don't expect anything. I just need, you know, a lead."

I didn't hear anything back for a couple months. And my band was playing out here. Mötley Crüe was closing the joint at the Hard Rock. It was the last night and they were the last band to play. That same night, my band, the Junkies, was playing O'Sheas, where Vince's tattoo shop is—we billed it like: "If you can't see the real thing come see us." We packed the place.

Anyway, so I ended up running into my dad. Now I live here in Vegas. He got me a job running the warehouse next door to the tattoo parlor. We do all the clothing for Vince Neil Ink, Feelgoods, and Count's Kustoms. We also have our own line.

Living here is different. Last year I got to spend my birthday with my dad. That was the first time we've ever been together on my birthday. You know what we did? My band opened for his band for the first time ever at Count's Kustoms, and it just happened to be on my birthday. We couldn't play Crüe songs—they said we couldn't, something about song rights and stuff—but it was the greatest for me. It was awesome. I'll never forget it.

Elle Neil
Vince's Daughter

I never felt like a celebrity kid because nobody knew who my dad was. When I was in elementary school and middle school I learned quickly not to brag about my dad, because kids that age never heard of Mötley Crüe. They knew 'N Sync and Britney Spears. If I'd said,

"I'm Vince Neil's daughter from Mötley Crüe," they would have been like, "*Who?*" I'd look like a total poser. So, even through high school I'd just lie.

I went to a concert with a good friend a couple years ago. Somehow he found out I was Vince Neil's daughter. Apparently he was the biggest Mötley Crüe fan in the entire universe. He fell over himself talking to me. I'm like, "Calm down, calm down; it's cool. Don't shake my hand. Just talk to me."

So, on his thirtieth birthday I invited him backstage to one of my dad's concerts. You should've seen the look on his face. He had this thin veneer of cool that could've cracked in an instant. I could see in his eyes that he was jumping up and down like a little boy. It was so darling.

Now that I'm older I meet more people my age who know about Mötley Crüe. I just play it off like it's no big deal because to me it really isn't a big deal. I mean he's a musician, but I've met famous people and I see that they're real people with real problems.

I don't really have a sense that famous people are different because I know from personal experience that they're not. They just have really cool jobs.

I thought about doing music for a while. There was some talk of me going to Juilliard and studying classical singing. But instead I chose the alternate path of writing. I'm just as good as anybody else out there, and I'm extremely stubborn and vain about my abilities. At least when it comes to writing I've got my shit together.

I call him Dad; we text each other all the time. Texting is easier for us. It's hard to reach him and I know he gets really, *really* tired after a show. I don't want to bug him. I just wait for him to text me whenever he has a sec.

I saw him for Thanksgiving last year. We had a really nice time. Whenever I visit him it's at his house, a hotel, or a concert. It's very rare that I just walk down the street with him. When I do, it's weird for me because even though he's not trying to be seen, he has sunglasses on and whatnot, people literally drive by yelling his name out of car windows. Then I remember: *Oh yeah, that's right. My dad's famous.*

Did I want my dad more in my life? Sure. But I also understood that my parents were human. I understood that he had his life to live and his things to do and that he wasn't out of my life because he didn't care about me. He wasn't technically even out of my life.

One of the greatest things about having him as a dad is that I never listen to anybody telling me I can't do something. If somebody tells me something's "a one-in-a-million shot," I think, *No problem, I got it.* If Vince Neil could become a rock 'n' roll superstar, being from such a humble beginning, I can do anything I set my mind to. He played the Viper Room and the Whisky a Go Go and he got famous. He did it. He was talented, ambitious, lucky, strong, and courageous. I think I can do it, too. Whatever I put my mind to I can do. Dreams can come true. You can do anything you want.

I'm actually going to New York in March to meet my dad. I can't wait. I've never been there before.

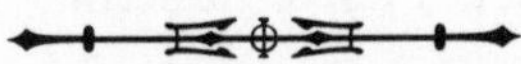

By doing this book, I hope to accomplish . . . I don't know. Nikki had a book. Tommy had one or two books. People have asked me why didn't I have a book a long time ago. This seemed to be the right time. I think my voice needed to be heard because nobody has ever heard *my* side of things—people have pretty much heard only one telling of the story. So it was just kind of my time to be heard a little bit, I think. All through the years, Nikki and Tommy were always out there talking. They have always liked to hear themselves talk. And I have never really been a blabbermouth. I'm just more laid-back, you know, just a little Heinz 57 mutt of a SoCal surfer kid. That's me.

One thing is sure. I think we'll be remembered. Mötley Crüe started something in the eighties that's still with us today. You can call it a hair band. You can call it the LA Sound. Other than KISS, before us, there was no such thing as arena rock, you know what I mean? And then all of a sudden we come out, we do it, and people emulate us. Presto: The arena-rock hair band was born. And it wasn't just the hair. There was a certain sound that came up in rock 'n' roll at a certain time and a certain place, and we were at the forefront. We were *it*. And to still be around after thirty years… that is pretty fucking amazing. Say what you want. When you look at all the other bands that came out of that LA scene, off the Strip and whatnot, *where are they today?*

Mötley Crüe still never got the respect I think we deserve. Why are we not yet in the Rock and Roll Hall of Fame? Is there some question that we belong? I don't think people look at achievements we've had. Instead they look at the other crap that we've become infamous for. The marriages, the arrests, the drugs, the bankruptcies—how we blew all our money and drank it away, how I had that accident that killed Razzle and how Nikki died of an overdose and came back. People remember every bad thing that's happened to Mötley Crüe, but they don't look at us like those guys who started this thing, who've sold this many records, who've had all these hit songs and are *still* out there doing it. People just look at the garbage that the four band members have created. And it's a fucking landfill, man.

Mötley Crüe: We started something great. But we also created a monster.

ACKNOWLEDGMENTS

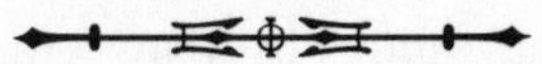

Mike Sager wishes to thank:

Vince Neil.

Chief researcher Sohrob Nikzad, who was intimately involved in every step of the research and writing process. Never was an assistant more willing or able.

Rebekah A. Sager, who provided additional writing on deadline. She is a beautiful and estimable woman by any standard.

Shirley and Odell Wharton, Valerie Saucer, Neil Wharton, Beth Neil, Elle Neil, Sharise Neil, Heidi Mark, Lia Neil.

Skylar Lynnae Neil, RIP.

Nikki Sixx, Joe Marks, Robert Stokes, James Alverson, Jack Blades, Dana Strum, Jeff Blando, Zoltan Chaney, Bret Michaels, MC Hammer, Ron Jeremy.

Allen Kovac, Doc McGhee, Alan Koenig, Dina LaPolt, Doug Mark, Doug Thaler, Gary Negherbon, Jeff Varner, Peter Pappalardo, Reisha Roopchand, Tom Coppini, Tom Werman, Jerry Buss, Michael Peters.

David Vigliano, Ben Greenberg, Shawna Morey, Alan Light, Benji Feldheim, Aminata Dia, David Granger, Peter Griffin, Tim Heffernan, Chris Nilsson, Eric Sherman, Ben Epand, Roy Bank, Ron Ward, Michael Eller, Yvonne Negron, Josh Scheinker, Harlan Levy, Steven R. Cohen, Henry Schuster.

Miles Sager, Beverly and Marvin Sager, Wendy Sager, Lawrence Alfred, Ph.D.

Special admiration and thanks to: Paul Miles, curator of Chronological Crue, recognized world-wide as the ultimate Mötley Crüe historian. Neil Strauss, author of *The Dirt*.

ABOUT MIKE SAGER

MIKE SAGER is a best-selling author and award-winning reporter. He has been called "the Beat poet of American journalism." A former *Washington Post* staffer under Bob Woodward, of Watergate fame, Sager worked closely with gonzo journalist Hunter S. Thompson during his years as a contributing editor to *Rolling Stone.* Sager is the author of three collections of nonfiction and one novel. He has served for more than a dozen years as a writer at large for *Esquire.* Many of his articles have been optioned for film. He lives with his wife and son in La Jolla, California. For more information, please see www.MikeSager.com.

VINCE VIP FAN CLUB

Get access to exclusive content, meet and greets with Vince, and a ton of other awesome privileges by signing up for the official Vince Neil Fan Club today at www.vinceneilfc.com.

VINCE MERCHANDISE

Make sure to pick up all your official Vince Neil swag at www.vinceneil.net. Exclusive shirts, playing cards, belt buckles, shot glasses, and much, much more available 24 hours a day, 7 days a week, 365 days a year.

WITHDRAWN